NEW AMERICAN DREAM

New American Dream

A Modern Take on Work in America

CHRIS RUDKOWSKI

Christopher Rudkowski

Contents

ISBN: 978-0-578-99966-1

First Printing, 2021

Cover design by nskvsky.

Prologue

At the root of who we are as individuals is our purpose in life. And our purpose in life is, or at least should be, reflected in our work. Yet so many of us don't find purpose or meaning in our work. Without meaningful work, we're missing a part of our identity. And in the United States, we have little to no agency in the way we work. Some people understand this and lash out at the powers that be, blaming others for their predicament. Some people blame themselves and live with a sense of guilt or shame. Some people inflict self-harm through one unhealthy vice or another. But most of us tend to accept the status quo of work as we know it, and by necessity live life going through the motions.

That feeling of just going through the motions isn't a life. It's an existence. This state of being is something I wanted to write about because I notice it more and more in this country, and I wanted to know why. I wanted to know why we're okay with our present culture of work, one that has proven useful in the past but no longer suits the needs of a 21st-century world that is faced with unprecedented challenges. Challenges that simply cannot be met with old thinking and outdated models of work.

Working each day without a purpose, without a sense of social or individual responsibility that we can take pride in, leaves us in the wrong state of mind. Work then becomes a means to an end and the end is just money or extrinsic reward that satisfies us only in the short term. What we need instead is a new definition of work. Work should be about the process, not simply the outcomes. I champion a lifestyle that all of us deserve, where work is an end in itself.

The American dream we've been sold is just that- a dream. It's not a real possibility for most Americans today and was never a possibility for every- even a majority of- Americans in the past. But I'm sure you already know this, as the large amount of inequality and systemic flaws within our institutions are hard to ignore. And that's not to say you can't find success and pride in making a life for yourself. It is to say that our idea of the American dream is not what we think it is and surely isn't what we deserve. We need to set aside that dream and devise a new one. An actionable dream based on our values today and the demands of the 21st century. That means rethinking our traditional nine to five jobs as if working forty hours a week Monday through Friday is the best use of our time or the most productive. It's not. Much of that time is wasted and we don't need to work forty hours a week to be productive.

We need to rethink the worth of a human being, is one hour of someone's time worth $7.25? You and I both know the answer is no when it comes to workers living paycheck to paycheck, yet we pay so many Americans minimum wage which is not enough to live off of. We can send people to the moon, but we can't pay people enough for basic housing, food, and transportation? Great.

We need to rethink our concept of a workspace. It took a pandemic to help many of us realize that half our meetings were unnecessary or too long. And it turns out we can do much of our work from home because ya know, computers and stuff.

We need to rethink how much time we spend working because there's a certain point when work becomes burnout and burnout leads to health issues. It turns out that we can work less, be more productive at work, and live healthier lives- benefiting both workers and their employers. Sounds too good to be true, but it's not!

We need to rethink the intersection of education and child-care with work and our economy. When you combine expensive and inaccessible childcare with a broken, outdated school system, and mix in a piece of paper that is valued more than any other (aka university degree), then what you have is chaos for workers everywhere.

We need to rethink the American work ethic, individualism, and success in this country. Work hard, pull yourself up by your bootstraps - *just grind until you make it* - and you can be just like Tom Brady, Jeff Bezos, or whoever your picture of success is. That mindset is deeply rooted in American history and our transition to a digital age has only pushed the message even further. Our work *ethic* isn't the problem with work today, it's our ideals around looking out for number one and an unhealthy misunderstanding of success that is the problem.

We need to rethink our guiding light of merit and meritocracy. We don't live in a complete meritocracy, but that's okay. A complete meritocracy shouldn't be the goal, as I will explain later.

We need to rethink the political and economic structures that guide us. Capitalism and the GDP. Corporate America and growth. Consumerism and "abundant" resources. These are some of the elements of our guiding structures which serve against our individual and collective interests. Rethinking our corporate and government models so that they work in unison, putting workers first, and focusing on sustainability is exactly what we need.

We also need to rethink how our concept of time intersects with work itself. So much of our time working is wasted, precious time that could be used outside of work. Time is our greatest asset, which means it should be our greatest concern regarding equality. Yet it is not treated as such, with many Americans having unequal access to time- a phenomenon rarely, if ever, talked about. Figuring out what it means to truly have a work-life balance is no easy feat, but that's because our idea of work is completely wrong.

Finally, we need to redefine work. Right now, we work to "make a living". But that saying implies that work is separate from living. Work should *be* the living- or at least a huge part of it. Work should be the reason you get up in the morning, excited to tackle the day. I know that sounds a little woo-woo and trust me I thought the same thing when I started researching for this book. But thinking that a new and better system of work is unattainable and undeserved, simply illustrates how conditioned we are to view work and personal meaning from our weary, distorted lens.

Unfortunately, any conversation about changes to our economy or politics becomes an *us* vs. *them* conversation. But our qualms shouldn't be based on capitalism vs. socialism or Democrat vs. Republican. Our qualms should be with the very culture of our country surrounding work which has sacrificed our time, our money, and our opportunities in the name of some American ideal of hard work and success. This is a waste of our time and our potential. We should be working towards long-term goals with a collective spirit in mind. We will never get rid of making personal sacrifices for the common good or individual progress, but we must get rid of sacrificing our own lives in pursuit of a life that doesn't exist or isn't guaranteed.

Changes to the way we work have happened rather quickly over the past two decades. We live in an information-based economy, in which knowledge, information, and services have taken precedence over our traditional industrial economy. If the entire way we work has changed to adapt to this new economy, doesn't it make sense that our underlying structures of work change along with it? These political, economic, and social systems have not adapted to 21st-century demands, and it is up to us as a nation to bring forth a new mindset around work and demand the structural change that will give us our time, opportunities, and lives back.

This book is part history, economics, politics, questions, answers, and everything in between. I seek to *redefine* the concept and culture of work here in the United States. Thinking about work, what it means to us, and what it should look like, is crucial to the national dialogue we need around creating a better life for everyone. My hope is that this dialogue will make it easier for leaders in government and business, U.S. citizens, and anyone else who finds this work meaningful, to develop and emplace solutions that redesign work as we know it- here in the 21st century.

I

The American Work Life

This is the real secret of life — to be completely engaged with what you are doing in the here and now. And instead of calling it work, realize it is play.

-Alan Watts

Chapter 1

Work Today

I hypothesize that our definition of what constitutes work is wrong, that we have fallen short of addressing the structural inputs and outcomes laying at the intersection of Work and American culture. Work is too narrowly defined in our country and as a result, not everyone's contributions are counted. The value that we currently attach to people and our work falls short of the true value we as human beings, our time, and our contributions to society provide. We have yet to have a conversation around this value and how it relates to compensation for all members of our economy. I would also argue that we place too much emphasis on the *individual* in our nation's culture around work, yet not nearly enough emphasis on our collective *environment* including the political, economic, and social structures that guide our work every single day. The onus of creating opportunity falls squarely on individual shoulders, and unrightfully so.

We are at a moment in history right now where we need to address major issues around the way we live. Otherwise, it'll be difficult to make progress on issues such as climate change and the environment, our political system, education, and so forth. Reform in these areas, which is likely what we need, is hard to achieve. We cannot address some of this reform individually, and quite frankly most of us are just busy working. Most of us are simply trying to get by and pay the bills. When the majority doesn't have the time, money, or energy to tackle these larger issues and be a part of the solution, is it any wonder they haven't been addressed?

We live our American lives acknowledging that our nation is certainly flawed but also thinking that at least we have a strong and powerful culture. A culture that we can take pride in because we have the American dream, hard work, a meritocracy, perseverance, power, and influence. We may have a very divisive culture between specific factions in our country right now, but at the end of the day, we all espouse American ideals based on what America was in the good ol' days, or what a fairer and more equitable America should look like in the future.

In both instances, of comparing our current situation to the America of the past, or a brighter future, we tend to get lost in arguments about what our country *should* look like. We place our politicians, CEOs, and celebrities on a pedestal, asking them or explaining to them what they should or should not be doing. What all of this equates to is noise, and this noise misses the point of what I think is really at the root cause of our nation's major problems. The root cause is that we neglect our true value as human beings and the limited time that each of us has. Our value as human beings and how we spend our time is primarily reflected in the *work* we do, every day.

Working is the one part of life we spend the most time doing. How we structure work in our society determines more than just pay and opportunity, it determines how we live our lives. Whether or not we are fulfilled in life can be tied directly to what we spend most of our waking hours doing. How we structure our work determines how we structure our lives. But instead of structuring our work based on how we live our lives, what our life's purpose is, and what we value in life, we accept it for what it is- a means to an end. Accept the *end* usually isn't meaningful. Work should be about finding purpose in the process. In other words, the work we do every day should be purposeful, not a means of which to attain some material, status, or ideal that our culture of work promises us and expects from us.

We spend almost all week focused on our job, even when we're not working. If your work is still a part of your life on the *weekend*, then technically it's not a weekend. Is there something wrong with this way of living? Of course not, if you enjoy your job because it's your life's passion or you simply enjoy what you do. Some would argue that it is fine to work your entire life in a job that you may not be passionate about, as long as you can live comfortably. Waking up and not feeling excited about the day, and then repeating that process five times a week, 261 workdays a year, isn't a life though, it is an existence. And existing can certainly be comfortable at times, but at what cost? What if you worked every day on something that truly matters to you and what if your time was maximized to provide value to both yourself and others? Most people aren't passionate or excited about their work, yet as a society, we are okay with working 5+ days a week so we can get to the other two days. *"Mondays, am I right?"*

This idea of work is wrong. As I said earlier, the problem is that we value our lives and our time less than we should. If you make it a habit of asking those around you whether or not they are fulfilled in their job and their work, there's a good chance they will say no. If you ask someone a bit older if they've worked any unfulfilling jobs over their life, it's essentially guaranteed the answer is yes. You might think well yeah, that's the price we have to pay to "make it" to the job we want- the position we want- the career we want- the lifestyle we want... But that idea is completely wrong. It's not the price we have to pay, it's just that we've been conditioned or forced to accept work as we know it as this ladder of hard work and success. I enjoy success as much as the next person, but what about purpose? Why not work hard *and* with a sense of purpose? Isn't that more important than some ideal and usually unattainable view of success (especially when the view keeps changing)?

Unfortunately, our conditioning and life circumstances have left us with little time to explore our passions and what type of work might be meaningful to us. This is in large part due to our flawed school system, which is immediately followed by a job that cares not about our "work-life balance". Even the term work-life balance itself implies that work and life are separate and that we must work before we can live. And once we're working this way, we're just going through the motions. After completing our chores and errands each day we are left with only some time to pursue our passions, our hobbies, our meaningful relationships, and so forth. We are a cog in the machine of American work-life, unable to break free from the structures, models, and pieces that keep us from finding, pursuing, and living our best life.

What happens to our country in the long term when so many of us consistently neglect ourselves to such a degree? Well, our country starts to decline, and it becomes increasingly difficult to maintain this facade of strength. We are not as strong as we would like to think. We can have the strongest military in the world, but when our internal structure of work and living is not built on a strong foundation, we decline and become vulnerable. Vulnerable to many of the challenges we find ourselves faced with in these unprecedented times. Our health in this country- even our life expectancy has gone down in recent years.[1]

Now, of course, I am not going to blame your job at so-and-so for a declining life expectancy. *But*, I will argue much of the health issues we face as a country (and even globally) are in part due to the culture of work we exist in and contribute to. We are more stressed out as a nation than we have been in the past. According to an American Psychological Association survey about stress levels and the main sources of stress for Americans, the most common source of stress was "the future of our nation" (63%), followed by money (62%) and work (61%).[2] This statistic shouldn't be surprising. We've all lived it. It is not a coincidence that the future of our country, money, and work is stressing out this country- not to mention stretching us thin. Work and money of course go hand in hand, which is why they are both at the top of people's concerns. I do not honestly believe that one singular business or government policy solution will reduce these levels of stress or our health. If work is one part of our lives that is core to these issues, then it's worth digging deeper into our wellbeing and how we exist in the world.

We have high expectations for ourselves and our career outlook when we're young, around the same time where we tend to be the happiest. This phenomenon isn't unique to the U.S., but it helps to see the larger picture so we can then see our nation's place within the global theme of work. "Research conducted by Dartmouth professor David Blanchflower on hundreds of thousands of people in 132 countries shows that people around the world experience an inverted, U-shaped 'happiness curve'."[3]

According to the happiness curve, we are happiest before 18, after which our happiness declines until around 48, and then we don't reach the same levels of 18-year-old happiness until around our mid-60s. It is unclear what the direct cause of this unhappiness is across the world, and there are likely several reasons depending on the person and the country. But the study showed that money was likely not a major factor, and even other socioeconomic factors such as employment status and education played little to no role. According to the Global Wellness Institute, global workers are also unwell. That includes serious economic insecurity, many of the global jobs are low-skilled/ manual, many are unstable, and most workers report that they're struggling with wellbeing.[4]

Blanchflower has theories about what causes the happiness curve phenomenon and this overall global decline in happiness, one of which is expectations. This idea that we have these dreams and aspirations of the world and our future in it, when most of us go through life with anywhere from a few to a good chunk of those expectations proved unrealistic and infeasible. A huge part of those expectations includes our ideal vocations, and a generally positive outlook on our careers and work life. Is it possible that many of those aspirations meet reality and fall to the wayside, causing us to slowly adapt over time until we find a path forward that makes us generally happy (when the happiness curve picks back up)? And is it possible that we simply don't have the wisdom or perspective yet to grasp our place in the world, which is required to set realistic expectations and find purposeful work? I would argue yes.

My experience in high school was that I wanted to be a professional chef. But then I realized my aspiration was more of a hobby, and that to make a good living (by my standards) as a chef, I had to work hard and often for little money. Reality kicked in and it has taken me time to fully grasp both my place in the world and which type of work would be meaningful. I'm sure most of us had at least some goals of what our "work-life" would be like, just to discover these goals don't mesh with "the real world" or who we are as a person.

Waiting until your midlife crisis to get a grip on reality and what your purpose is in life is no way to live. It certainly isn't right. We should have optimism about the future, we should develop enough of the right expectations, and have experienced enough self-exploration to navigate our way into and through a fulfilling career. The problem is that work as we know it today just isn't designed for that level of self-exploration, meaningfulness, personal growth, and the proper setting of expectations; nor are there enough of the right amount and type of opportunities that would lead us into a purpose-driven career. The status quo of work culture in the U.S. primarily revolves around money, capitalism, consumerism, and an individualistic lens of making a living that is the foundation of the American dream. I will explain later why this culture of work is wrong and what we can do to shift our mindset.

The misalignment between workers' expectations and reality certainly coincides with global worker engagement too. In 2013, only about 13% of employees were engaged at work, worldwide, according to a Gallup study on the *State of the Global Workplace*. About one in eight workers or 180 million employees in the countries that were studied, are "psychologically committed to their jobs and likely to be making positive contributions to their organizations." The remaining workers are either "not engaged" (63%) or "actively disengaged" (24%), "meaning they lack motivation and are less likely to invest discretionary effort in organizational goals or outcomes" or "are unhappy and unproductive at work and liable to spread negativity to coworkers." Regionally, Northern America (the U.S. and Canada) have the highest proportion of engaged workers at 29%, followed by Australia and New Zealand at 24%. It's great that we have the most engaged workers, right? Yes, but 29% is surely nothing to be proud of.[5]

In 2020, worker engagement was on a rollercoaster ride, as one could imagine. Gallup found that in early May, the percentage of "engaged" workers in the U.S. reached 38%. That was the highest since Gallup began tracking the metric in 2000.[6] This is an interesting stat, considering the impact of COVID on employees nationwide. Following the killing of George Floyd in late May 2020, engagement dropped to 31%. But then the percentage of engaged employees rebounded to a new high of 40%. "This [again] surpasses the measure's decade-long upward trajectory since Gallup began tracking the employee engagement in 2000."[7] So as the percentage of engaged employees has steadily gone up, the percentage of actively disengaged workers has steadily (albeit at a lesser rate) gone down and leveled out in recent years.

The fact that only 40% of workers are engaged is still unsatisfactory at best. To me, it shows something wrong with the way our work is structured. Unsurprisingly, throughout the March-April 2020 time frame, U.S. life satisfaction fell to the same level it did during the 2008 Great Recession.[8] The pandemic has caused up and down results in employee engagement and life satisfaction, and between the new highs and new lows, something is up.

How can we have new levels of employee engagement while simultaneously having life satisfaction at the lowest of lows? A couple of reasons come to mind. There is such great inequality between workers in America that many service-sector jobs, or "essential workers" as they came to be temporarily known, were essentially forced to work when others were furloughed or laid off. Many of these workers were likely engaged more at work, but not necessarily because they had a choice. Covid also allowed workers who were already doing well, working from home, and working in careers least affected by the changes to the economy, to become more engaged and committed to their jobs. Through these disparities, we can see that workers in the U.S. are struggling and what we need right now are large structural changes to the way we work.

The recent pandemic that ravaged the world and sent countries into economic recessions and periods of chaos, provided us an opportunity to sit alone and question the way we live, including our underlying political, economic, and social structures. I know the words pandemic and opportunity sound strange in a sentence together, but we were indeed forced to think about the world in its enormity and question our role within it. Not often are we forced to be alone and think about the pieces of the system that make up human connection, healthcare, economics, education, and work.

In a developed and powerful country where emergency strikes, not only were we not prepared en masse, we saw the stock market tank overnight. In a matter of days and weeks we saw investments take a hit, educational progress derailed, job prospects squashed, and our way of life upended. Almost all of us were deeply impacted by some or most of these structures-structures that intersect with the way we work. Unfortunately, workers weren't prioritized by the powers that be, and even with temporary relief through direct cash payments and un-employment benefits, workers are still suffering greatly from the effects of the pandemic plus inequities experienced be-forehand.

Countless articles, opinion pieces, and Americans every-where had been talking about necessary changes to the way we live due to Covid. Such as *will this pandemic revolutionize the way we work, will it force more students to take online courses, will we finally get a grip on healthcare reform, will we travel differently, or will we finally pass bold legislation and create structural reform.* These ideas on how we can change the system for the better are not brand new. We are just stubborn and tend to make structural reform only- and I mean *only-* in the face of dire consequences. I think what is going on here is that we are hoping some of these ideas stick this time around. I honestly do not know if any of them will or if we will learn our lessons and improve the systems we live in.

The way we work has been slowly changing or adapted over a few decades and the past century, but the type of change we need today is much greater than the industrial and technological changes we've experienced during this time. These changes are important and will be discussed later, but it's important that we understand the demands around reforming work today require *deeper* analysis and reflection of what work means from a cultural and ethical framework. In this country, we have yet to reflect upon our modern definition of work- we've simply transferred the meaning from generation to generation. It's important that we take a moment and really *define* work in more meaningful and relevant terms. Defining work according to 21st-century demands, our time, our values, and our purpose in life, is what this nation needs right now.

Redefining work will allow us to redesign the structure and culture of work to revolve around our lives, not the other way around. This redesign to how we work will create the environment we need to make progress as a country- which in turn will impact other nations and the planet.

Chapter 2

The Nine to Five

The eight-hour day... we wake up. We show up to work. We work eight hours with a lunch break in the middle. Then we go home just to do it again the very next day. This pattern repeats itself day after day, and most of us don't give this repetition too much thought. For the most part, we have accepted the nine to five mantra as the price we are willing to pay to make a decent salary. Is it acceptable for us nine to fivers (or anyone working a standard forty-hour workweek) to simply accept the status quo and work the same forty hours a week for the rest of our working lives?

I ask because it's not something we talk about often. A conversation on how many hours we should spend working and how many hours we should spend living outside of work has not occurred on a national level. By the time three or four rolls around on most workdays, we become less productive at work, instead thinking about our plans for when we get off. Or maybe we got in the office an hour or two earlier and completed eight hours' worth of tasks in half the time. Or maybe you worked late last night and already knocked out some of today's morning work. The list goes on, and the point is that eight hours is a long time to be productive and not everyone works effectively or efficiently on the same time horizon as others.

There are plenty of issues with working a continuous four-hour shift in the morning until lunchtime and then repeating the same shift after lunch. First, our brains don't operate productively in four-hour (or greater) intervals. A study done by the Draugiem Group used a computer program to track employees' working habits, seeing how much time was spent on various tasks and compared that to productivity levels. They found that the length of the workday did not matter much, it was how people structured their day that made a difference. Those who continuously took short breaks throughout their workday were much more productive than those who did not. The ideal work-to-break ratio in this study was 52 minutes of work, followed by 17 minutes of rest. From Dr. Travis Bradberry on Quartz:

> *People who maintained this schedule had a unique level of focus in their work. For roughly an hour at a time, they were 100% dedicated to the task they needed to accomplish. They didn't check Facebook "real quick" or get distracted by e-mails. When they felt fatigue (again, after about an hour), they took short breaks, during which they completely separated themselves from their work. This helped them to dive back in refreshed for another productive hour of work.[9]*

The idea here is that the brain operates in short spurts of high energy followed by spurts of low energy, roughly an hour and 15-20 minutes respectively. If we do not adhere to our brain's natural ebb and flow, it becomes easier for us to be distracted- by checking emails or our phones for a short period- which we may *think* is a break. But a real break involves completely unplugging from work for those 15-20 minutes, maybe going for a walk or sitting back and relaxing.[9]

What about if the type of work is different? There certainly is a difference between someone working the same repetitive task repeatedly (e.g., a cashier), and what many traditional 9-5 workers do now, which is knowledge and information-centered work. The type of work where you're required to think critically or be creative, often sitting behind a computer at a desk somewhere, makes up a large chunk of workers today. If you're working in a waged position and much of your job is the same repetitive task, then it's still important to have those periods of short breaks. The issue with this type of work is primarily the low pay, which I will go over in the next chapter.

Productivity guru and author of the book Deep Work, Cal Newport, talks about the importance of being focused on work for a shorter and specific period, unlike much of our traditional 9-5 work. "Deep work is the ability to focus without distraction on a cognitively demanding task. It's a skill that allows you to quickly master complicated information and produce better results in less time."[10] Deep work is vital to many jobs within the knowledge economy, and it is vital to our happiness and work satisfaction because of the many benefits of being productive with our time. This level of concentration at work is usually unsustainable for most workers towards the second half of a typical eight-hour shift.

To take advantage of this deep work, there are several principles that Cal recommends. One is to distance yourself from social media. We often fall for the "any-benefit" approach, where we think that using a network tool is justified if it has some possible benefit to its use, or we feel we will miss out by not using it. Another principle is to give yourself strict periods of time to work and complete specific tasks. Doing so can limit burnout, work creep, and all the wasted time distracted by non-work-related tasks. When we are conducting nonwork-related and often repetitive tasks such as exercising, commuting, or cleaning the house, it is helpful to use that time to work out any concepts we are trying to figure out for our work.[10]

Roughly three to four hours a day of deep work bodes well with surveys of workers when asked how much time they truly spend working. A study conducted by www.vouchercloud.com polled 1,989 UK full-time office workers on their productivity levels and online habits. Most workers admitted to not being productive the *entire* working day, which I'm sure most of us would agree on. When asked how much time they spent specifically being productive during work hours, the average answer was 2 hours and 53 minutes of actual productivity. Rounding this up to three hours, it is right around the same amount of time conducting deep work as previously mentioned. Just for fun, the UK survey had the following list of unproductive activities (or distractions) as the most common:

1. *Reading news websites--1 hour, 5 minutes*
2. *Checking social media--44 minutes*
3. *Discussing non-work-related things with co-workers--40 minutes*
4. *Searching for new jobs--26 minutes*
5. *Taking smoke breaks--23 minutes*
6. *Making calls to partners or friends--18 minutes*
7. *Making hot drinks--17 minutes*
8. *Texting or instant messaging--14 minutes*
9. *Eating snacks--8 minutes*
10. *Making food in office--7 minutes*[11]

Not only are we unproductive for almost half of the workday, but we also spend much more time completing a task than it truly requires. This is called Parkinson's Law- *work expands to fill the time available for its completion.* This statement on productivity was made by the famous British historian and author Cyril Northcote Parkinson in The Economist and was later the focus of one of his books, Parkinson's Law: The Pursuit of Progress. What this law means "is that if you give yourself a week to complete a two-hour task, then (psychologically speaking) the task will increase in complexity and become more daunting so as to fill that week." The extra time may not even be filled with more work, but stress and tension about having to do the task. "By assigning the right amount of time to a task, we gain back more time and the task will reduce in complexity to its natural state."[12]

Parkinson was primarily referring to his time working in the British Civil Service where he saw this law take place throughout the organization's bureaucracy. It doesn't just apply to bureaucracy though; this law can be seen in many if not most work environments to at least some degree. This law is an observation on work culture, and "it works because people give tasks longer than they really need, sometimes because they want some 'leg room' or buffer, but usually because they have an inflated idea of how long the task takes to complete."[12] We don't become aware of how quickly some tasks can take until we test this principle.

Many Americans and organizations still follow the unwritten rule of "work harder, not smarter" even when that mindset doesn't provide a greater return on investment. Oftentimes working smarter, not harder is unappreciated. Instead, our work culture champions "the idea that the longer something takes to complete, the better quality it must inherently be."[12] This thinking is completely wrong, yet it pervades our offices and assignments every day.

One hack in preventing Parkinson's Law from creeping into your work is to separate all your tasks for the day, give them the normal amount of time you think it will take to achieve each, and then cut that time in half. What you do next is pay very close attention to meeting the new time limit, and you will see that you overestimate the time required to complete most of your work. Another hack is to track the major time wasters throughout the day, such as that list provided earlier. If you normally spend thirty minutes a day parsing through emails, then make a specific effort to bring that down to five minutes. There are measures we can take that reduce our unnecessary and inefficient expansion of work, but to truly squash these mindsets and habits, we must change our work culture around productivity.

Think about how much time is spent at work and how much time is spent at home (or at home not doing work if you work from home). Our work-life balance, as we call it, is out of whack and hardly counts as any form of *balance*. I would argue that balance is when we get to spend much of our time living life in a fulfilling manner. For me this is being at home, cooking meals, and being with those I love. Or maybe even partaking in an hour or so of my hobby. What happens to most workers is all the things we wanted to do throughout the week (chores, appointments, grocery shopping, yard work, etc.) we are having to do on the weekend in a short two-day period. What this means is less time spent *living* and more time spent *working*. Sure, this additional work is just a part of life, but it also prevents us from spending time doing the things we enjoy.

After an exhausting day at work, after we are done commuting, doing chores, and running errands, what little time we have left in the day is spent unwinding because we are physically and mentally drained. I feel that the nine to five and standard work schedule simply gets in the way of more living and that it's not fair for us to spend the first half of our life working down to our bones and working overtime in hopes of a nice retirement. For many people, forty hours a week might be no problem at all, but just because you're physically able to do it, does that mean there aren't other ways you would like to spend your time? What if you got back one extra hour a day? What about two hours? What if you had Friday or Monday off, leaving you with a four-day workweek? More about these ideas later, but you can start to see what *actual* work-life balance looks like.

Where did the forty-hour workweek even come from? The nine-to-five gig was not always around, nor was there always a law that limited the number of hours we could work in a given week. In the past, working sunrise to sunset or after-dark was a lot more common. After the American Civil War, we started to see more favorable labor laws, but it was a slow process. A Welsh textile mill owner and social reformer named Robert Owen is credited as the first person to articulate the idea of an eight-hour workday. He called for "eight hours labor, eight hours recreation, and eight hours rest" for workers in the early 19th century. This was much better than the 12 or 14-hour days that most factory workers -including children- were expected to put in at the time. Over the next century, you finally started to see a push towards labor laws between labor unions in specific industries, major businesses, and the government. Illinois and certain classes of federal government workers received protection with limited eight-hour day laws in 1867 and 1868 respectively, but they were hardly enforced. Working ten to twelve hours was still very common at the time. *Fortunately*, there was a labor movement on its way. *Unfortunately*, it took roughly sixty years for it to be implemented into federal laws that were mandated by the government.[13,14]

In 1884, the Federation of Organized Trades and Labor Unions demanded that workers have eight-hour days by 1886. When this deadline was not met, the organization called for demonstrations, one of which was in Haymarket Square in Chicago, 1886. Peaceful protests there turned into violence, and an explosion killed seven police officers and four workers. As you can imagine, the eight-hour workday turned into a national issue after that- yet progress was still slow.[14] If demonstrations don't achieve the desired result, maybe market solutions such as competition will help? That is essentially what happened in 1914 when Ford Motor Co. enacted eight-hour shifts- albeit sometimes six days a week- and increased wages by double to $5.00 an hour.

This was at a time when most employees still lacked the guarantee of an eight-hour day. Of course, the five-dollar wage only happened at the time if Ford's Sociological department went to the workers' home, inspected it, and determined they *deserved* the money. Not to mention, the increase in wages and eight-hour shifts were not legally binding, meaning the company could change and revoke the conditions at any point. Ford Motor Co. eventually moved to the traditional five-day, 40-hour week in 1926. A few years earlier, Edsel Ford, Henry Ford's son, and the company's President explained to the New York Times that:

> *Every man needs more than one day a week for rest and recreation....The Ford Company always has sought to promote [an] ideal home life for its employees. We believe that to live properly every man should have more time to spend with his family.*[15]

Henry Ford said of the decision: "It is high time to rid ourselves of the notion that leisure for workmen is either 'lost time' or a class privilege", but he also admitted that the decision would increase productivity.[15] Ford understood that working less could actually *increase* productivity and that no matter your class, time away from work for leisure should be experienced by everyone. I couldn't agree more.

Further action around that time was when the government guaranteed eight-hour days and overtime pay for railroad workers in 1916. In 1919, roughly a fifth of the entire work-force went on strike- 4 million American workers- demanding a five-day workweek. Finally, guaranteed limits on working hours were achieved in 1938 with President Franklin D. Roosevelt's passing of the Fair Labor Standards Act. Initially starting at 44 hours a week, reduced to 40 hours by 1940. Most experts on labor history would agree that it was the labor unions that deserve much if not most of the credit for labor reform.[14] Today, for better or for worse, we have less union membership among wage and salary workers compared to a few decades ago. The union membership rate- percent of wage and salary workers belonging to a union- was only 10.3 percent in 2019, a slight decline from the year prior.[16]

We have kept the forty-hour workweek until today in large part because of our work ethic. But even then, we still end up working more than the forty hours allotted to us, which just shows how pervasive this mindset around work truly is. "According to the Bureau of Labor Statistics, the average American works 44 hours per week, or 8.8 hours per day. A 2014 national Gallup poll put the average number at 47 hours per week, or 9.4 hours per day, with many saying they work 50 hours per week."[17] Craig Storti, author of "Communicating Across Cultures," said Europeans consider the typical American workload an ineffective use of time.[18] The American work ethic with its long hours doesn't make us more productive just because we put in more hours. What matters is how we spend our time, not how much time we spend.

Nonetheless, that is where the nine to five came from- the forty hours and five-day workweek were fought tooth and nail for over sixty or so years, with some help from industry who also had productivity and profits in mind with the change. The concept of nine to five made sense when we could rely on a job for our entire working lives, saving up for retirement, and then simply retire with enough savings in the bank. But guaranteed lifetime employment is no longer the norm today, with younger generations of workers realizing that long-term security cannot always be relied upon through one stable job. Work is now interspersed with periods of home activities, leisure, and other responsibilities.

This new norm may require a different model of work, such as more flexible work schedules. Changes to our traditional work schedule may be a slap in the face to those who enjoy structure- myself included- but that is the reality we increasingly find ourselves in. We are seeing 21st-century changes to the way we work, with more work being done online and from home. Increasingly for many workers, 21st-century work schedules mean not receiving structure externally from our employers, with the structure instead deriving from agreed-upon times and methods of work between employers and employees. 21st-century work also means more of the responsibility for setting up and adhering to a work schedule falls on the actual workers themselves. Of course, this depends on the type of employment, the specific industry, position, and so forth, but these changes are occurring, and we must change to keep up. Less structure may be beneficial or harmful depending on personal preference, but regardless there still needs to be measurable work that is getting done, with progress being made.

The fact is that many of our jobs are simply not what they used to be. They are not all industrial factory jobs where you can measure the amount of work being done, by the number of cars that roll off the factory floor. Instead, we are sitting at home, hounding on our keyboards until we have completed our work. And not only is this work not the same as what it used to be; our skills aren't the same either. We don't teach coding in school en masse, but given the change in our technology, should we? What skills are worth teaching or even worth having? Building a car is certainly a great skill to have if you're in that line of business or simply interested in mechanics, but that skill alone does little for everyone else's work prospects. We are now at a point where you can give two people the same task and the person who takes the longest to complete it may end up doing a worse job than the person who finished in half the time. Yet we still cling to this whole 9 to 5 concept, concerned less about the work you do and more about meeting that eight hour-mark so we can have our work considered *full time*.

This is the point at which I'd like to explore *work-life balance* in more detail. I know you have heard of this elusive phrase, probably wondering if you have achieved it now- and if not when you might achieve it. We would all enjoy a work-life balance, as it means spending more time living and less time listening to an unnecessary or overly long meeting. Large organizations and leaders have been discussing this need for work-life balance for some time now, yet we still see the same job descriptions posted with the same full-time hours and pay as before. As long as workers are completing the work, does it matter how many hours they take to do it (within reason)? It depends on the job. But what if we paid individuals for the *work they do*, not the *time spent doing it*? We can't expect these changes overnight... or can we? Is it that hard to make changes to the way we work? Let's look into it.

Some companies and organizations have been on top of this new way of work for some time, and they have promising solutions. One of which is flexible scheduling, another is reduced work hours altogether. Personally, I like to spend the first half of the week putting in extra hours. That way, I can relax by the time Thursday and Friday come around, only working half the time. Allowing your employees to work a flexible schedule will lead to a better work-life balance for your employees, all with the same quantity and quality of work. Another concept is that of summer hours. There are many European countries where large chunks of the population take summer months off. This is allowed because some European countries tend to have a greater amount of paid leave and paid vacation. "The average French worker can expect 30 days a year of paid vacation, compared with 28 days for workers in the UK and 25 for most workers in Denmark and Sweden."[19]

When you have this amount of paid time off, of course, you would save your days off for the most relaxing time of the year- summer. Summer is also the time for graduations, family vacations, weddings, and just relaxation. So why *not* save your time off for that time of the year? Will workers be less productive throughout the year or less hard-working if offered this extra paid time off? Not at all. Much of Europe even reduced business hours in the summer to close early so that both employees and employers can enjoy the summer months by themselves or with family and friends.

There are countless benefits to this amount and culture of work. One example is how workers in France and other OECD countries work fewer hours than workers in Greece, yet "in terms of productivity, the output of Greek workers generates far less value than these other countries" and "shorter hours worked are even associated with greater output."[19] Another potential form of change at work could be an increase in team-building days. I am not talking about the type of team building you might have seen from an episode of The Office, but more so just one day a month or quarter dedicated to employee engagement and cohesion. Forming these relationships and building on them will lead to a more exciting and fulfilling work environment.

What about getting rid of Fridays or Mondays altogether? Otherwise known as a compressed workweek, it leaves workers with an extended weekend where they can truly focus on living for one extra day. Is there something wrong with reducing hours altogether? A compressed workweek may do just that, possibly having total workweek hours estimated around 32. Do fewer hours of work directly lead to less productivity? In most circumstances, it does not.

It seems counterintuitive that working less will lead to the same or increased productivity, but that is why I go back to my last point of paying employees for the work they do, not the time they take to do it. If we are paying people for time, and that time does not equate to guaranteed equitable productivity, then why not reduce the amount of time worked? Would more time spent living outside of traditional work not prepare you more for work itself- leaving you feeling well-rested, satisfied, and motivated to put in the work when it's time to do so? Or it may leave you rested enough to work on other, more meaningful, activities which we might consider work (starting a business, writing that book, etc.). Intuitively that makes sense, but more on that later.

Aristotle stated that a virtuous life is not one devoted to work. In *Politics*, he stated the following:

> ...*in the most nobly constituted state, and the one that possesses men that are absolutely just, not merely just relatively to the principle that is the basis of the constitution, the citizens must not live a mechanic or a mercantile life (for such a life is ignoble and inimical to virtue), nor yet must those who are to be citizens in the best state be tillers of the soil (for leisure is needed both for the development of virtue and for active participation in politics).*[20]

I wouldn't go as far as Aristotle in saying that citizens should hardly work and should not be "tillers of the soil", but I do agree that if we find ourselves too busy working, we will not develop a mature sense of morals, nor will we be able to perform our civic duty. Do we not already see this happening in the U.S.? Many workers are unable to vote because election day falls on a day they have work (most likely during voting hours), not to mention the many other impediments to performing one's civic duty. Are we willing to sacrifice our civic duty for the sake of more work? Should we not make it as easy as possible to perform our civic duties? And think about the connection between Aristotle's two arguments here- if we do not develop sophisticated morals in life, are we not then more likely to make political and civic decisions with a lack of ethical understanding? In ancient Athens, citizens who played no part in politics were seen as useless, not one who simply *minds their own business* or *doesn't care about politics* as we have no problem describing ourselves today. Citizens from all classes were even paid for serving the state in this manner so that they were compensated for the time spent away from their traditional work.[21] My larger point here is that working too much isn't just bad for our work-life balance, it's detrimental to our civic duty, and in turn our relationship with politics.

To provide some context, there is a historical reason why we are so focused on work. London School of Economics anthropologist David Graeber, in his book *Bullshit Jobs*, talks a lot about how we ended up with our current attitude of work and the system we have today. He illustrates that Judeo-Christian religion is much to blame. "The Judeo-Christian God created the universe out of nothing," writes Graeber. "His latter-day worshippers, and their descendants, have come to think of themselves as cursed to imitate God in this regard." Work is divine, in other words. "In the feudal societies of medieval Europe, the function of paid work was explicitly founded on these theological ideas."[20]

You had children from as young an age as seven, from all classes, working in other people's households or taking on apprenticeships- designed to give these children self-discipline and manners, which supposedly made them better people. Is that not a similar mindset for children today? Taking out the trash and completing chores can build discipline, as can working that first not-fun job working at a cash register or doing busy work. The difference is, these apprentices would learn specific skills from their work and eventually become masters of a trade, allowing them to set up their own personal businesses (if in a privileged enough position or living in the right area).

We have gone from that system of work to one where we are okay with everyone working jobs, at least at some point, that are painstakingly unfulfilling or miserable. Monotonous jobs such as flipping burgers, to name one. To name another, think about whatever it was you did for your very first paid job. There is a good chance it wasn't your dream job or that it did not lead to the development of some useful skill- at least not career-oriented. The reason we ended up with this system is because of capital. "When the means of production moved out of the hands of the producers themselves and into the control of an ownership class, apprentices increasingly lost opportunities to grow into self-governing masters."[20]

At some point near the 16th century, the path from apprenticeship to a better life as your own boss, became less likely. The value of work for its own sake started to be emphasized by English, middle-class workers at this time. Graeber writes "Work was self-mortification and as such had value in itself, even beyond the wealth it produced."[20] These ideas were perpetuated even more during the industrial revolution. 19th Century philosopher Thomas Carlyle's theories on the "Gospel of Work" revered a religious theme for work; "All work, even cotton-spinning, is noble; work alone is noble, be that here said and asserted once more... Oh brother, if this is not 'worship,' then I say, the more the duty for worship; for this is the noblest thing yet discovered under God's sky. Who art thou that complaints of thy life of toil? Complain not."[22] Personally, I cannot imagine spending almost every waking hour of everyday cotton-spinning and considering that noble work.

Graeber writes that "suffering has become a badge of economic citizenship."[20] Self-sacrifice is meant to build character, an assumption that remains today, even without a religious context. We have come to define ourselves by our work. Something that still happens today, albeit not as much as it was for our parents, grandparents, and recent ancestors. There used to be a more common conversation starter of "what do you do for a living?" as if the answer to that phrase would tell you most of what you need to know about that individual. As if our *life* could be summed up by one job. Yes, the work I do alludes slightly to the person I am, and the life I live, but it does not allude to my entire whole- especially not today when so many of us don't even know what our purpose in life is or aren't conducting fulfilling work.

In a country where so many of us are unfulfilled in our daily work, it can be hard to see what we do, being defined as *a living*. I think we could certainly have a culture of work where our jobs illuminated much about who we are, but that would require many changes to the way we work and more importantly, what we consider *work* in the first place. All of us can creatively express ourselves and provide value to those around us- doing work that may not seem like traditional work but has the potential to become just that.

Aristotle illustrates that a virtuous and meaningful life involves leisure and not toiling your life away. I couldn't agree more, and I am sure you agree with that to at least an extent. There is something wrong with us describing to our friends and family how overworked we are, while simultaneously feeling a sense of pride that we sacrificed much of our limited time away for economic growth- growth for growth's sake. Everything stops growing at some point, and that includes humans. Thus, it only makes sense that we focus on growing our personal lives and life itself, as opposed to some outdated view of a growing economy equating to a successful nation (and the people therein). A complete capitalist society would have us working until we are physically, mentally, and spiritually unable, at which point we are discarded in the wind for we are no longer of value to the economic-growth machine.

The nine to five, Monday through Friday, forty hours a week model is quite common in the United States, with most of us wishing to have one of these jobs because it usually means some form of financial stability. If someone makes $50,000 a year in after-tax, take-home money, and you divide that by the number of workdays in a year (261), you will see that that person made roughly $24.00 per hour. And with a typical salary position, the money comes with other benefits as well such as a 401k, healthcare, etc. Now, what happens if we take away that person's benefits, offer them only $7.25 an hour, and cut their hours from 40 hours a week to 20, because the employer doesn't want to risk overtime pay, and can hire younger workers, who are new to the job market, at the same minimum wage, $7.25 pay rate?

The employer cuts down on costs, receives the same amount of revenue, and now has a greater profit. Except, now these workers can barely afford to pay rent, are just getting by on bills, are having to cut down on costs associated with shopping or hobbies (which means less spending in the economy), and are now a part of an ever-growing system of income/wealth inequality in this country. Part-time and wage jobs are fine... if they pay a *living* wage. That is what our next chapter is about.

Chapter 3

A Living Wage?

Working minimum wage, even part-time in the past was a nice way to make some money in the summer between classes, build your savings, pay for extra expenses, and build experience in a certain career field. What most low-wage, even full-time jobs are now though, are underpaying positions that allow us to afford gas, groceries, and maybe a few bills. That's it. When we talk about the value of work that is being done by wage workers, the work varies quite a lot. Everything from service-sector jobs, where most Americans are employed, to government, and manufacturing.[23]

There are certain numbers and economic indicators we should look at when determining if wages today are what they once were, or more importantly, what they *should be* for someone to afford to live. One important number is purchasing power. "Purchasing power is the value of a currency expressed in terms of the amount of goods or services that one unit of money can buy. Purchasing power is important because, all else being equal, inflation decreases the amount of goods or services you would be able to purchase."[24] Why is today's purchasing power, or how much you can buy with a dollar today, important? It is important because inflation causes prices to rise and if we don't receive an increase or growth in our wages and salaries, then we receive a decrease in purchasing power. In other words, if our wages and salary do not rise over time to match inflation, then we can afford less today than we once could.

Unfortunately, today's average wage is no longer a living wage, with many workers still making minimum wage or close enough to it, where they can only afford the bare necessities-if that. Only in certain industries and in many salary positions (especially in the knowledge economy) are individuals paid an amount of money that is enough to afford living and then some. But is someone making minimum wage or someone working in a financially stable salary position being paid the amount of cash that is most reflective of the value they provide to our country? For the most part, we are paying people based on perceived value to one company, and not paying based on what their true value is to the economy and society.

Stay-at-home parents whose work involves watching their kids most of the day as opposed to physically working elsewhere are of value to society. We need parents to be able to provide for their families so that those kids can grow up and contribute to the world. Yet we don't pay nearly enough paid leave, paid time off, or maternal/paternal leave to American workers. My point here is that there is a constant pattern of not valuing and not respecting our workers, regardless of the type of work involved. If we do value them, then we should be fighting for their rights (and our own). Individually, we see the value of a single mother who is struggling to pay for childcare and a teacher who is paid little but still shows up for the kids, and we value those working in the service industry who make our lives that much easier. But all too often we ignore them, their time spent working, their wellbeing, and their *real* value to our communities.

Before we examine the current state of making a living wage in the U.S., we must review the costs associated with living today. Cost of living is important because "if inflation causes purchasing power to decrease significantly, and the cost of living goes up, that will lead to more cash-strapped consumers."[25] Looking at wage alone is only half the picture, as the whole point of that wage is to purchase primarily what we need and secondarily what we desire. So first we look at what our major costs are in this country- what do Americans spend their money on? And how has it changed over time?

The top three expenditures for American households, on average, are *housing, transportation,* and *food.* As of 2018, these three expenditures made up almost two-thirds of average annual household expenses. Let's look at each of these costs in a little more detail.[26]

First, let's look at housing. Owning a home in American cities can be very expensive today and out of reach for many. Patrick Sisson (Curbed) ran the numbers on this for a teacher in San Francisco seeking his or her first house:

> *Educators in the City by the Bay earn a median salary of $72,340. But, according to a new Trulia report, they can afford less than one percent of the homes currently on the market. Despite making roughly $18,000 more than their peers in other states, many California teachers—like legions of other public servants, middle-class workers, and medical staff—need to resign themselves to finding roommates or enduring lengthy commutes.*[27]

When you look at the math behind homeownership in the U.S., you see that over the past 70 years, household median income has not increased nearly fast enough as the median home value and median rent costs have, to keep up. Rising rents and stagnant wages make finding enough money for a down payment even more difficult.[28] Not to mention the difficulty of younger generations in qualifying for loans in a difficult regulatory environment. Millennials made up only 32% of

the home buying market in 2016, which is the lowest percentage of young adults to achieve said milestone since 1987.[27]

> *Nearly two-thirds of renters say they can't afford a
> home. Even worse, the market is only getting more chal-
> lenging: The S&P CoreLogic Case-Shiller National Home
> Price Index rose 6.3 percent last year, according to an ar-
> ticle in the Wall Street Journal. This is almost twice the
> rate of income growth and three times the rate of infla-
> tion. Realtor.com found that the supply of starter homes
> shrinks 17 percent every year.*[27]

These harrowing stats are not solely due to stagnant wages
unable to keep up with the cost of owning a home or affording
rent over time. Much of it has to do with the post-war boom in
the 50s. "Widespread government intervention that tipped the
scales for single-family homes, more open land for development and starter-home construction, and racist housing laws
and discriminatory practices that damaged neighborhoods and
perpetuated poverty—have led to many of our current housing
issues."[27]

Out of the cities with the largest black populations, not one
of them has anywhere close to an equal homeownership rate
between black and white people. Cities in the North and Mid-
west fare the worst with the widest gaps, including a staggering
50% in Minneapolis, Minnesota. And the gap still exists even
in cities where black households are the majority, such as Al-
bany, Georgia.[29]

There is a large wealth gap in American housing today,
largely due to Americans being locked out of suburban development. Americans a few generations ago who were denied access to the mortgage market and homeownership were forced
to rent instead of owning property and gaining value over time
for themselves and their family. The average homeowner to-

day has a net worth of $195,400, 36 times that of the average renter's net worth of $5,400. In many regions, we have reached the limits of suburbanization due to buyers and commuters unwilling to make super-commutes. Add to this the idea of NIMBYism [Not In My Back Yard] and local zoning battles, which have become the norm when developers try to add much-needed housing density to expensive urban areas, plus other factors, and you have a situation where homes have become increasingly expensive. It's a great time to own a home, but if you're in the market for one, the outlook is often grim.[27]

Most workers who are struggling in this economy are faced with high rent prices. Rent is so expensive in many if not most areas that it becomes difficult for anyone making minimum wage to afford it, even if they're full-time. A minimum-wage worker would need to work well over two full-time jobs to be able to afford a two-bedroom rental anywhere in the U.S. according to the National Low-Income Housing Coalition's "Out of Reach" report published in 2020. According to the report, the states with the largest shortfall between average renter wage and Two-bedroom housing are Hawaii at -$21.59, Maryland, California, New Jersey, Vermont, Massachusetts, Washington, and Connecticut at -$8.55.[30]

When you look at income distribution and all wage and salary workers, you can see for nearly every worker in the bottom half of the wage distribution, even modest rental housing is out of reach. For more than 40% of wage earners, an ordinary one-bedroom home is unaffordable. Add to all of this that twelve of the twenty largest occupations in the U.S. pay less than the housing wage, and it becomes difficult *not* to see the issue with housing for millions of low-income Americans. I mean working even minimum wage forty hours a week used to be enough money to help afford college or a new car. Now it can barely get millions of Americans by on rent- if that. These types of inequities are not only troublesome during a growing and strong economy, such as what we saw pre-Covid, but it is also worrisome in a time when renters are relying on assistance such as unemployment funds and stimulus checks to survive through a crisis.[30]

The next largest expenditure for Americans is transportation. Americans pay quite a bit for transportation, especially when compared to other developed nations. Americans spend somewhere around 13% of their household expenditure on transportation costs, owning on average 2.28 cars. Within transportation expenditures, almost 90% belong to personal vehicles. And unfortunately, as one would expect, the total costs for transportation are not shared equally among different income groups. "Lower-income households generally pay a larger portion of their expenditure on transportation and as people move up in income brackets, they pay a smaller portion on transportation- [meaning] the lowest income is burdened with the largest portion of expenditure."[31]

This of course makes sense. Personal vehicles are not cheap and unlike some public transportation, are not subsidized. American cities fail to provide alternative transportation options, forcing people to travel by personal vehicle. This leaves low-income Americans with few options. A lack of public transportation of course has damaging effects on our environment (e.g., more personal vehicles, more CO_2), yet equity is also a major transportation issue. "People are forced to make burdensome financial decisions and are left in a cycle of poverty that becomes harder to escape."[31] Many workers are forced to travel from communities where the cost of living is cheaper than their actual workplaces, which is not only burdensome financially, but also awful for commuting and the associated negative consequences. How much money on travel would be saved if workers were simply paid a living wage in their own community?

The idea of purchasing a working vehicle for those who are trying to break the cycle of poverty is essentially a pipe dream. They often remain stuck in place, without adequate public transit options. Many countries throughout Europe have already addressed the issue of transportation and its impact on equity through policy measures. Policies in much of Europe make driving an expensive endeavor, discouraging citizens from using personal vehicles to get around. "Petrol is taxed, parking is expensive, and toll roads are abundant."[31]

These policies create more opportunities for public transit, which then becomes more accessible for a large share of a city's population. Furthermore, the costs of these policies do not cost more for individuals over any given year, they pay less for transportation overall compared to Americans.[31] We have a prominent culture of individualism in America, and we take pride in our fast cars, big trucks, and abundance of bumper stickers. I have a few bumper stickers myself, but I would gladly dispose of my personal vehicle if mass public transit was easily accessible and reliable. At the end of the day, transportation is expensive. Expensive to our health through the fumes we breathe, expensive for our infrastructure as roads deteriorate over time, and expensive for residents trying to reach job opportunities away from home. Thus, the U.S. needs to create similar policies which discourage driving and create a more equitable system of transportation. You can place your bumper stickers on your backpack or satchel if that's what it takes to move you into a public transportation mindset. Either way, it's the more equitable and sustainable solution.

According to the Institute for Transportation & Development Policy (ITDP), a path forward does exist:

> *Should Americans move to live closer to work? In a perfect world, yes but unfortunately, that option is not very easy. How space is designed in the United States is*

a major contributor to this problem. Single zoning laws force residential neighborhoods to be separated from commercial districts. Roads and suburbs are designed to be car dependent limiting options for public transit. Over 75% of commuting car trips in the United States are made by one person in one vehicle – a reality that is inefficient in both time and space. Additionally, most car trips in the United States are relatively short, between 1 – 8 kilometers, a distance that could arguably be made through other means if the option existed. By focusing on Transit Oriented Development, cities can create spaces that support use of public transportation.

As seen in the Indicators for Sustainable Mobility, very few Americans take public transit, walk, or cycle to work and that's not for lack of interest – it's for lack of options. The design of American cities and regions forces millions of Americans to pay for something that perhaps they wouldn't choose to if they actually had an option. This lack of option is why Americans are shelling out more and more money for a depreciating asset. Public Transportation is not a lost cause in the United States. Looking towards other countries, Americans can learn how to create and support spaces that are less car reliant. Not only will this create better cities for the environment and the consumer, but this will greatly reduce the financial burden inflicted on America's poorest. By helping those with the fewest resources, America can create public transit that benefits all.[31]

In an ideal world, access to quality public transportation would be a public good, available for everyone. But not every community can support large, robust public transportation for every citizen. For those communities who can, I think they should do everything in their power to provide accessible public transpiration, and for those who can't- the state and federal government should step up and provide assistance.

Work is intertwined with food, the third-largest expenditure within your average American Household. We eat, go to work, eat again, come home from work, and then we eat some more. "Back in 1900, families spent about 40% of their income on food, [and] by 1950, it was just under 30%."[32] As of 2017, we spend around 13% of our average annual expenditure on food. Spending less of our budget on food year after year is a testament to our grocery and restaurant supply chain and other parts of the food process. In a culture where work is so important to our everyday life and takes up a large chunk of our days, that often means it is less likely for us to cook wholesome meals at home. And cooking meals at home is usually a means of coming together as a family or group of loved ones, but that act of *coming together* has increasingly lost its prominence over the years. Over the past century, each new generation, on average, has spent a larger percentage of their total food expenditure on food away from home as opposed to eating at home.[33]

Unfortunately, an increased quantity of food consumed and decreased quantity of money spent does not equate to quality of the same. Much of this food away from home is unhealthy and convenient such as fast-food restaurants, which heavily concentrate in predominantly black neighborhoods.[34] What this means for many Americans, is an increase in negative health outcomes. Negative health outcomes such as obesity and heart disease- the number one cause of death in the U.S.- end up costing much more in terms of medical bills than what it would cost someone to make food at home or choose more expensive (short-term & monetarily), healthier, food options. Unfortunately, our system of work is not set up to prioritize Americans' health prospects.

It is very costly to our economy for Americans to be so negatively affected by poor food options and poor healthcare. It's just that saving on short-term costs and immediate financial gains take priority in our present system, which places long-term wellbeing and economic sustainability on the back burner. The potential cost savings associated with having a healthier workforce (e.g., less expensive employer health insurance premiums or less time away from work due to health issues) could be quite large. When convenience is the driving force in our food system, it is detrimental to our health and our wallets.

Furthermore, many workers live in food deserts. A food desert is an area in which people living nearby do not have access to a food source, such as a supermarket. Food deserts vary by geography too.

> In urban areas, the U.S Department of Agriculture considers a food desert an area with no ready access to a store with fresh and nutritious food options within one mile. In rural America, a food desert is defined as 10 miles or more from the nearest market.[35]

Unfortunately, food deserts are fairly common in the U.S., and "it's estimated there are more than 23 million people, more than half of them low-income, live in food deserts."[35] Food deserts also exist where there is no access to local food pantries. Food pantries are often sparse in rural communities because many of the government funds that they rely on are based on population density. Food insecurity does not impact every worker, but it certainly impacts a lot- especially impoverished communities. As you can imagine, it is very difficult to focus on work, nonetheless anything else, if you're living day to day food insecure.

The three major costs of housing, transportation, and food cost a lot for your average household, and oftentimes take up a larger percentage of income, the lower the household income. What I would like to see instead is for households and Americans in general, not to be forced to spend too much of their total income on these three expenditures alone.

Now that we have reviewed the major costs for American households today, we can see how important workers' wages truly are. It is not enough to simply pay an employee; they deserve to be paid a wage with which they can support themselves.

According to the Pew Research Center, for most U.S. workers, real wages had barely moved in decades as of August 2018. That was at a time when unemployment was very low, and private sector companies added more jobs for 101 months straight. The issue is that "despite the strong labor market, wage growth has lagged economists' expectations... [and] real average wage (that is, the wage after accounting for inflation) has about the same purchasing power it did 40 years ago."[36] Covid wreaked havoc on the labor market, so you can imagine how stagnant wages have impacted your average American. An increase in the Federal minimum wage has been discussed as of late and it would certainly help Americans making low wages, but more on that later.

On average, Americans' paychecks were larger than they were 40 years ago but purchasing power hasn't moved at all. I wouldn't exactly call that progress. Putting it differently, when you look at a similar measure of "usual weekly earnings" of employed, full-time wage, and salary workers, the median usual weekly earnings- in real and inflation-adjusted terms- barely moved at all as well.[36] To add to this lack of growth over time, it seems what little gains had occurred, mostly did so for the highest earners. Between 2000 and 2018, usual weekly wages rose 3% in real terms for workers in the lowest tenth of the earnings distribution, compared to 15.7% for earners in the top tenth of the distribution.[36] Of course, workers are compensated in other ways besides wages (retirement accounts, health insurance, etc.), but wages and salaries do make up most compensation workers receive. There has been much economic analysis on wage stagnation, but some of the potential reasons for it may consist of any combination of the following:

> *One theory is that rising benefit costs – particularly employer-provided health insurance – may be constraining employers' ability or willingness to raise cash wages... Other factors that have been suggested include the continuing decline of labor unions; lagging educational attainment relative to other countries; noncompete clauses and other restrictions on job-switching; a large pool of potential workers who are outside the formally defined labor force, neither employed nor seeking work; and broad employment declines in manufacturing and production sectors and a consequent shift toward job growth in low-wage industries.*[36]

Slow and uneven wage growth certainly isn't helping most workers, especially those in the middle or lower class who often rely on wage growth year after year to keep up with rising costs of products and services, as well as the impact of inflation. To make a *living* wage, we must address the potential causes of wage stagnation above, with policy decisions.

Increasing wages isn't just about giving workers enough money to pay for basic costs of living either. It's also one way of lifting Americans out of poverty and into the middle class. A strong and large middle class is extremely beneficial for everyone involved. It's good for workers, businesses, communities, and the overall economy.

From the Atlantic:

Societies with a strong middle-class experience higher levels of social trust but also better educational outcomes, lower crime incidence, better health outcomes, and higher life satisfaction," a 2019 report from the Organization for Economic Cooperation and Development concluded, citing several studies. "The middle-class champions political stability and good governance. It prevents political polarization and promotes greater compromise within government." The report warned that members of the middle class increasingly say the economy is unfair because they see so much income and wealth flowing to the rich, while their own lifestyles—their middle-class security blanket of a home, education, retirement savings—have become more expensive.[37]

A strong middle class should be a large goal of ours and paying workers their actual worth as members of society, is one step towards realizing that goal.

The argument about increasing the federal minimum wage often gets into the weeds about costs for businesses and whether most businesses can handle it, but we're missing the point when we start talking about the issue by itself. We end up skipping the whole point behind the wage increase, and that is to pay workers a living wage so they can continue to contribute to society and become more likely to make it into a vibrant middle class. We must talk about a living wage in the context of what a human life is worth. We must create policies to reflect the importance of healthcare, childcare, communal relationships, and so forth if we wish to improve our way of life.

If everyone's wages increase from minimum wage to a living wage, some argue that will end up hurting entire sectors of the economy, many businesses will suffer, and many employees will be out of jobs. But the reality is if you pay wage-employees more, and enough to live at a minimum, guess what they will do with their money? They will spend it. On goods and services, plus all the purchases one usually makes in our capitalist society. Some studies demonstrate the high costs to businesses who increase their employees' minimum wages, forgetting that any study which does this would have to study an entire state or large area to incur valid results.

If only business X or neighborhood Y sees an increase in the minimum wage for their workers, then we mustn't neglect the fact that other businesses and neighborhoods that do not see an increase in their wages will be unable to increase their number of purchases. A real study on the impact of minimum wage on a large population should study an entire state who raises their minimum wage, both before and after the raise. When we talk about the federal minimum wage, we tend to talk about some numbers such as $15 an hour that could and should be applied to all states. The problem is that not every state or every city has the same cost of living.

That is why I think it would be useful to find the average cost of living between all fifty states and then use that number to determine the federal minimum wage rate. As the cost-of-living changes year after year, the government could go back to the calculator and slowly increase the minimum wage every year or two, to match the most recent average cost of living. And for individual states, if the cost of living is higher than the federal minimum wage- which is bound to occur in states where the cost of living is much higher- then those states could simply increase their minimum wage to reflect their average. MIT created a living wage calculator on their website *https://livingwage.mit.edu/* which I highly recommend checking out. The living wage calculator "estimates the cost of living in your community or region based on typical expenses", and acts as a tool to help "individuals, communities, and employers determine a local wage rate that allows residents to meet minimum standards of living."[38]

You can see by looking at the minimum wage in your state or community that your *living wage* is likely higher than the minimum wage. And that is the case for even 1 adult with no children, the outlook is much worse for adults with multiple children. *"The living wage shown is the hourly rate that an **individual** in a household must earn to support his or herself and their family. The assumption is the sole provider is working full-time (2080 hours per year)."*[38] In my previous state of North Carolina, the minimum wage is $7.25 which is closer to the *poverty wage* than it is to the living wage for one adult and no children: $11.98.

The saying goes, a rising tide lifts all boats, so it only makes sense that any tide at all will lift all boats off the ground- not just a few. This will of course take a lot of work between the government and business, but we can certainly achieve these goals when we start asking ourselves and our leaders what the value of a human- and their work- truly is.

So, what we need to do in addressing wage concerns is to address the reasons why wages have stagnated, while simultaneously increasing wages. Increasing wages without tackling the issue from the business' perspective likely won't get us far though. That isn't to say there aren't companies out there who could simply afford to increase wages but choose not to. In those instances, that is exactly what should happen.

Chances are the answers will have to be some combination of increasing the federal minimum wage (plus specific states depending on their cost of living), providing a government-sponsored health insurance plan to take pressure off employers, increasing labor unions and worker rights, education reform, tossing out noncompete clauses, reforming our formally defined labor force, and investing in high wage jobs such as manufacturing and production services. A combination of targeted policies that make it easier for employers to pay living wages and mandating state or country-wide increases in minimum wages is necessary.

When you look at the increasingly large costs of major life expenditures next to stagnant wage growth, which is not feasible for most Americans, we can see that something must give. When we look at the shrinking middle class, we know something must change in the way we compensate American workers who are *all* essential. We must address wage issues in this country and pay Americans a living wage, and not just during crises either.

We have seen during Covid that many workers such as those working in grocery stores were paid "hero wages" to compensate them for being "essential workers" during the pandemic. For the most part, these wage bonuses were soon rescinded, even though those temporary wages were closer to, if not exactly, a living wage for the employees. These workers have and always are essential because last time I checked most grocery stores don't operate themselves and we still must buy food and water, pandemic or not. Hopefully, I have painted a large and detailed enough picture of our current wage practices in the U.S. And I hope if nothing else, you take away the importance of *every* worker and the reason everyone needs a living wage is because we value them and understand their true worth to not just our economy, but our communities.

Chapter 4

Where and How We Work

The Physical Space

The open office set-up vs. cubicles. Designated desks vs. roaming workstations. Space designed for group work or an individual set-up. These are some of the questions we ask ourselves when designing a *productive* workplace. There are tons of articles out there that prescribe each variant of the workplace, deeming one specific set-up as *the most productive one*. I would have to disagree with most of those articles, as there likely isn't one *perfect* set-up that leads to productivity. The modern office and the modern workplace vary by industry and position in the organization, but there stands to be improvement across the board. The environment and process with which work is conducted make up the workplace, and both aspects are essential to understand when defining and analyzing the workplace. 21st-century jobs require a new approach to physical workplace design.

First and foremost, many if not most of our work is done away from the outside world, and in environments that go against human nature. It is human nature to be surrounded by our natural environment, work with our hands, and be active. It is not, however, human nature to sit at a desk in an uncomfortable chair for eight hours a day without much natural movement and connection to the outside world. Some advances to the physical workspace are welcomed because they are easier on our work, our brain, or our physical body. No one would prefer to rely on cattle for plowing land when we have tractors, nor would we wish to rely on physical letters when we have email. Most advances were made to make our work easier, both physically and mentally. Unfortunately, we still haven't been creative enough with where and how we work.

Some organizations were unsure of how moving to virtual work would impact overall productivity during the pandemic, which is understandable as working from home is a completely different environment. We may naturally think that workers being physically distanced from supervisors and coworkers will impede their ability to accomplish work, but for the most part, these concerns are overblown. What we need is an environment that naturally coincides with human's physical and mental requirements, allowing more flexibility in how and where work can be done. Doing so will allow workers to accomplish their job in an appropriate setting- since some of us might be more productive in a coffee shop, at the library, or simply at home. Flexibility is important to the degree to which it is feasible for the work involved.

Whatever the solution to our physical workspace is, it is likely not a one size fits all model. There are countless options we can provide workers in a shared office space or at home, where they can choose to work in a conference room, single-occupant office, on a treadmill desk, outside near a green space, and so forth. The workplace as we know it is quite uncreative, just these giant slabs of concrete we commute to every day, which just happen to be as far from a natural setting as can be. In response to Covid, cities, and businesses have had opportunities (forced or not) to get creative with solutions in where and how we work, plus how we interact with one another. It is important now more than ever to provide equitable, healthy, and sustainable spaces for working as we recover and start to head back to work.

One example of where the disconnect between the value of work and the actual workplace comes into play is during *meetings*. The often-dreaded meeting provides some mix between a social gathering and business. Meetings are important, but they often become a social gathering because workers want a break from work and naturally want to socialize. Some leaders and employees enjoy others' company or have nothing better to do so they let the meeting drag on when in reality, social gatherings and events should be kept separate. There's nothing wrong with socializing, but it is important that socializing does not interfere with the mission and goals. The better way to view a meeting is as a defined period, relatively short, where you can discuss work matters until they are done, and the planning/work has been accomplished.

A more effective meeting has a set time, start-to-finish. It also has a defined purpose that is stated at the beginning of the meeting, along with an agenda that is followed together so that it is harder to fall off track. Social gatherings should certainly happen as well with coworkers, but these social gatherings must be seen solely for what they are, not mistaken for work meetings. This allows the organization or the team to conduct necessary work during productive meetings while also getting in that bit of social cohesion which makes work an exciting and fulfilling environment. Harvard Business Review recommends asking ourselves the following questions before setting up a meeting, that way we maximize time spent and do not waste the most precious resource- our time.[39]

SHOULD I HOLD A MEETING?

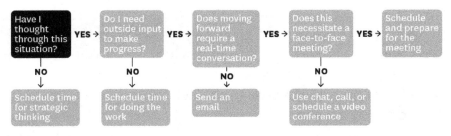

SOURCE REAL LIFE E TIME COACHING & TRAINING   HBR.ORG

Source: Saunders, 2015. https://hbr.org/2015/03/do-you-really-need-to-hold-that-meeting

You can ask yourself several questions to determine if a meeting is required for your group, team, office, or organization. And as you can see, there are alternatives to holding a meeting if it is not necessary at the current moment. If you are not the one in charge of scheduling meetings, then it does not hurt to simply recommend one of the other options and emphasize the importance of separating in-person communication around work and those discussions best left for email, video conference, or social events.

If you have determined that a meeting is necessary, you could hold a different type of event or activity that accomplishes the same goals. This allows you to switch things up and it provides everyone a break from the natural grind of work. One idea is to create a visual presentation, where you can show the steps of completing a task that is best done during your coworker's or employee's free time. Not to mention, it would be a resource they could reference later if they need to revisit the material. Going off that idea, you could also develop some reference sheets in document or video form that provides FAQs you would normally receive during a potential meeting. Instant messaging is another alternative, which is something already being done in platforms like Slack and Microsoft Teams. Of course, the issue here is like text messaging, you can end up taking work with you anywhere. It can be difficult to not check for instant message updates from your team even when out of the office, simply because it works a lot like social media. If you use instant messaging, make sure you set up appropriate channels and a time where you are specifically working or not working. Many messages you would provide in a meeting, you can also provide by starting an email thread. No need to get everyone together in person or online for a few points that could be relayed via email.[40]

Something I am accustomed to in the military is the conducting of status reports. These go a long way in getting messages across to those who need it most. If your conversations don't involve every group member, then why have everyone together for an hour or two- just so you can provide updates to select personnel? Give status updates and reports to those who need them instead of getting the whole team together. Brainstorming is also a great alternative, as many of the discussions you would have in a meeting are tailored to those who have something to say now, not necessarily what information is most important or valuable. Having a brainstorming space for everyone to use at any point during the day allows for greater collaboration since we all come up with ideas and valuable points at different points of the day. This can be as simple as having a whiteboard in the middle of an office space that everyone can use or a virtual space in which the same work can be conducted.

Meetings can also be avoided by providing an open-door policy or space for more casual conversations. By providing time for new employees or team members to come by and casually talk about any happenings, you are saving time during actual meetings because you're not having to talk about those other points as much. Having a space for projects and group work to be shared and collaborated on, can also save time during meetings, or prevent meetings altogether. There's no need to bring everyone together for work that can be achieved on an individual level in a collaborative space. Setting up smaller, more focused meetings at the beginning or end of the day is also useful, as it provides a space to inform others of important information, which in turn creates consistency of work, progress, and deadlines.[40]

Another alternative, as we have seen more with the recent pandemic, is video conferencing or virtual meetings. These can be very helpful, especially when doing remote work or when unable to meet in person. But just like a regular meeting, you should make sure that it stays work-focused with set guidelines on an agenda or make it a social meeting. Finally, when it comes to meetings you do not always have to have them with your usual or traditional setup. You can conduct meetings outside or set up walking meetings, where you and coworkers walk and talk for a short period. This could be in person or via audio-only. I enjoy having audio-only conference calls, where we all go for a walk and talk about work. I use a comfortable pair of headphones when I do this, ones that block outside noise and allow me to really enjoy the conversation as well as the time spent walking outside in the nice weather. Nothing like stretching the old legs while being productive.[40]

When it comes to creating a work environment catered to a healthy, comfortable, and worker-centric workplace, there are plenty of options available. It is important to keep in mind that a great workplace that is productive can and should also be one where workers have options in how and where they do their work. Flexibility is so crucial that many employees are willing to take a pay cut for their work if it means being able to work remotely. Not to mention, providing flexibility can be cost-saving for both employers and employees. Having flexible arrangements available for your team and organization is essential to making sure that workers feel valued and thrive in their respective roles.

As opposed to being hindered by uncomfortable, stagnant, poorly built, and inflexible workplace arrangements. I also can't stress enough the importance of developing and maintaining trust in the workplace. Redefining the workplace means creating solutions within your organization's environment and throughout your workflow. Both environmental and workflow factors need to be considered when maximizing organizational effectiveness and productivity.

The Remote Space

During the recent pandemic, we had almost every organization scrambling to adjust to the new reality where work either wasn't happening or had to be done differently. What we saw a lot of was remote work, where employees were forced to work from home (WFH). This was in conjunction with schools being closed, the constant health risk of infection, and many workers who are usually overlooked being considered essential. Hopefully, a shift towards remote work and WFH will empower workers to work for the company they want, the position they want, and in the field they want. Remote work is advantageous for many reasons. It provides more opportunities for workers as they can avoid having to move for a potential job.

The future of work could be more equitable and sustainable for workers across the nation. And the great part is that not all the work has to be remote. A company could slowly transition their usual in-person work with remote work, giving more flexibility to employees in how and where they conduct it. There are plenty of meetings that could be achieved through conference calls for example. There are plenty of tasks, depending on industry and position, that can be accomplished just as well from the comfort of someone's home, their local coffee shop, or on their way to pick their kids up from daycare. If only some hours of the day or days of the week are remotely done, that in itself has great upside for employers and employees.

There are incentives for businesses, governments, and communities to embrace remote work. Emily Courtney from Flexjobs.com goes into great detail about the benefits of remote work. I will go into detail about those benefits here. First and foremost, there is greater flexibility for employees to start and end their work on their own schedule. This makes time management much easier than our current rigid set of hours. Between school schedules, errands, medical appointments, and exercise, just to name a few, we deserve to have more say in how we spend our working hours. If we get the work done, does it really matter where we do it?[41]

A large problem with traditional work is the commute. The average one-way commuting time in the U.S. is 27.1 minutes. To and from work, that's almost an entire hour altogether that could be spent doing something else. Not only do "commuters spend about 100 hours commuting and 41 hours stuck in traffic each year", "more than 30 minutes of daily one-way commuting is associated with increased levels of stress and anxiety" and can lead to health issues like higher cholesterol, elevated blood sugar, and increased risk of depression.[41] Working shouldn't mean risking our health, or the health of our communities as increased commuting and traffic only creates more air pollution which in the long term is not good for our health either.

If we value our workers as much as we say we do, we need to make work commutes easier. That means lower-paid workers not driving or taking public transit two hours out of their day just to get there on time. There are countless solutions here, but the key is to provide greater access and affordability to public transit. As well as new forms of micro-mobility (e-bikes), and possibly automatic, self-driving vehicles that are capable of carpooling or commuting short distances. There are many creative opportunities for transportation infrastructure and commuting, but luckily remote work avoids all of that.

Many job seekers in small towns or rural communities have little employment opportunities so remote work can provide location independence, reducing the need to move closer to work or make strenuous commutes. Many people prefer to travel with their work- digital nomads as they are called, just as there are individuals who must travel (or constantly move) a lot such as military spouses. Remote work helps them tremendously. I mentioned earlier the high costs of living we experience today and how they can prove to be a large barrier to economic equality, but remote work allows us to avoid high rents and high mortgages by living and working somewhere more affordable.[41]

Furthermore, employers are less restricted by socioeconomic or geographic backgrounds when hiring remote workers, meaning it is easier to achieve greater diversity and inclusion in your organization. Not to mention that often, stay-at-home parents or caregivers are restricted in how they can work if they can work at all outside of their normal daily routine. In the U.S. we tend not to recognize the true value that parents and stay-at-home parents play in our economy and more importantly, our lives. Raising children to be the important members of society that they are, is a foundational building block of our communities and should be valued as such. Remote work makes it easier for parents working from home to still have a career, continue their career, or start working. This type of work would be especially valuable to single parents who are faced with the high costs of daycare or commuting long distances to work.[41]

There are great cost savings that can be achieved with remote work, even if it's only part of the time. Not only can workers save a few thousand dollars a year on items such as gas, car maintenance, transportation (including public transit), and meals bought out, employers can save even more. "According to Global Workplace Analytics, a typical company can save around $11,000 per year for every employee who works from home at least some of the time."[41] If you think about the overhead and real estate costs just to name a few, you can see how increased remote work leads to increased savings for businesses. I wouldn't be surprised if more businesses realized this during the pandemic and decide to keep some or most of the WFH.

As you may know, the environment is in rough shape right now. Well with the number of workers working from home today, we are seeing a decrease in our environmental impact by taking the equivalent of roughly 600,000 cars off the road for one entire year.[41] With even more workers working from home during COVID-19, we saw an even larger decrease in air pollution. Some countries are even able to see nature within skylines that were originally hidden by poor air quality. Many direct and indirect costs to the environment are avoided with this style of work. On a similar topic, remote work supports many sustainability efforts. These include economic growth, a reduction in inequality, sustainable cities, and climate change. Reducing our footprint on the environment and living more sustainably is in everyone's best interest.

Taking a step back from the large and structural benefits of remote work, we can also enjoy the simple perk of customizable office space. Many of us in our traditional work environments are unable to enjoy a comfortable and ergonomic office setup. This may seem like a minor point but if you're spending most of your waking hours in an uncomfortable, poorly set-up, and energy-draining office environment, then your work and energy levels are likely to suffer as a result.[41]

A huge benefit to remote work is increased productivity and performance. Not only do most professionals think they would be more productive working in a remote environment compared to a traditional office, roughly half already do much of their difficult work at home anyways. When workers are at home they tend to be interrupted less, have more efficient meetings, and are more productive by not wasting time and energy on commuting. Measuring performance can be measured with greater accuracy with remote work because you can measure and review specific work and tasks being accomplished as opposed to relying on potential false positives like showing up to work early or leaving late. When I say measure and review work tasks, I mean that in a general sense, not in a big brother sense.

Unfortunately, many employers have used the recent crisis' shift to remote work to start installing more work laptops with monitoring software that tracks keystrokes, video, and screens.[42] There are obvious intrusion flaws with this approach, but the greater dynamic here is a lack of trust in your employees. If anything, this degradation in trust will make your employees think more negatively about management, the organization, and not be as productive at work with this setup. Many organizations have figured this out, understanding the importance of trusting their employees to get their work done without directly tracking their every move.

A shift towards virtual work (or distributed work as it's often called) and creative workplace solutions mean organizations will have to think about these deep issues of trust between employers and employees. Trust in the workplace is essential as we think about changing where and how work is done. I think the key here is that it's important to differentiate between working for *time* or working for *tasks*. If you're working a low-skilled job for eight hours a day and are paid hourly wages, it makes sense to clock in and clock out with direct supervision (which isn't direct because it's not as if your supervisor is *always* watching you). You're being paid for your time in many of those jobs.

But many salary jobs and jobs of the knowledge economy are less about time and more about the actual tasks, assignments, and creative work being accomplished. In these instances, it may take one worker to complete the very same task half a day and another worker two days. These employees could be paid for the specific work they are doing and not for time. The disconnect in whether workers are being paid for time or actual work is what is leading to much of this distrust and breaks within the employer-employee psychological contract. Trust should be a driving mindset within this contract, and it is in the best interest of every employer to see this.

A final and most important benefit to remote work is a happier healthier work-life for workers. "Remote, flexible workers tend to be happier and more loyal employees, in part because working from home has been shown to lower stress, provide more time for hobbies and interests, and improve personal relationships, among other things." Most employers report that employee retention increases with remote work, with a major factor being better relationships between coworkers and managers. I would argue that increased work-life balance associated with distributed work leads to greater well-being among workers, which in turn enhances relationships with coworkers and managers.[41]

Health is an often underlooked facet of our work-life, but they are intricately linked. As one might imagine, it becomes easier for employees to make time for physical activity and healthy eating on a remote schedule, since you're not burdened by typical time or office constraints (e.g., commuting, office environment, lack of healthy eating options). Also, healing from injuries and decreased exposure to illnesses are other benefits as well.

The main takeaway with remote work is that it's beneficial, more equitable, and cost-friendly for many (not all) employers and employees. I would advise any organization interested in making this switch to remote work to test out a pilot first if possible or move to partial-remote work and see if it leads to some or most of the benefits mentioned in this chapter. This can be anything from making two or three days of the week virtual workdays to making every day virtual except for weekly physical check-ins between coworkers and managers. There are countless ways in which to design your distributed work, and flexibility is crucial. Increased distributed work can also provide a competitive advantage in many industries where working remotely is a possibility.

Of course, there are still drawbacks to distributed work. We mustn't completely transition to distributed work without understanding the toll it takes on us as people, spending less time connecting with others. Physical connection with others is essential to living a healthy life. Being alone is a feeling someone can feel even when surrounded by others but removing all forms of close physical contact has the potential to make us even more lonely or left with a feeling of disconnect. That is why employers and employees need to come up with creative ways to communicate and still have that connection. Zoom calls are nice because you can connect on a basic level, but they're just not enough long-term. If that means you get together once a week or once a month for some meeting or night out for brainstorming sessions or social events, the benefits of that connection will transcend through your work and your business. Social contact is a biological need. Yes, even for us introverts.

The recent pandemic has streamlined the movement towards more remote work throughout the country. According to Gallup, by April of 2020 "Sixty-two percent of employed Americans [said] they have worked from home during the crisis, a number that has doubled since mid-March." This is alongside results that found that three in five U.S. workers who worked from home during the pandemic would prefer to continue their remote work as much as possible once restrictions were lifted. "In contrast, 41% would prefer to return to their workplace or office to work, as they did before the crisis."[43] Sure, not every job can be done remotely, and not every worker wants to conduct remote work- at least not full-time. But the number of workers who do want to increase the amount of remote work is astonishing and should be taken into consideration as employers start to alter their work policies over the next few years.

In a culture where we respect everyone's time and the value they bring to our organizations and communities; we should strive to provide more flexibility in where and how work is done. It is important now more than ever to evenly spread human capital and talent across every community- urban, suburban, rural- because talents and skills should be just as distributed in work as they naturally form in our communities.

Floating work

Another type of work that provides flexibility for workers on their own terms is that of gig work. Gig work is part of the gig economy which is an economic system where many people work flexible, part-time, and often temporary jobs, which is unlike traditional long-term employment relationships. In this economy, many workers provide services that are contracted out by companies as independent contractors or freelancers. So, is anyone conducting gig work, a gig worker? It depends. The short answer is yes, but some people define gig work in one of three ways: the work arrangement, legal classification, or nature of work. The work arrangement just refers to the contract and relationship between workers and the person or organization who pays them. Legal classification or tax status refers to whether they are provided a W2 or 1099.

If provided a W2, they are a normal employee with benefits, tax deductions, and are covered by minimum-wage and anti-discrimination laws. If provided a 1099, they are independent contractors who provide services to a company without being a direct employee, pay no payroll taxes, and both parties are not covered by the usual laws and regulations normal employ-ees are. Some contracted work is still regular W2 employment, but it is usually provided by a contracting company as opposed to the actual place of work. Lastly, the nature of work refers to what someone does day-to-day. It is important to distin-guish between these types of gig work to better understand how many workers are truly involved in the gig economy, in what capacity, and which workers are not afforded the benefits and legal rights they deserve.[44]

What are the downsides of the gig economy? Well first, gig work is often technologically centered and concentrated in cities. Cities are entrenched in the gig economy, which pro-vides a great opportunity for job seekers in the urban jungle but less so in rural communities. You are unlikely to see many Uber drivers in low population towns across the country. WFH is also less prevalent in rural communities compared to their suburban and urban counterparts. Demand for gig work soared during the pandemic due to the amount of unemployment in the economy. What this high demand means is workers receiv-ing fewer shifts and being unable to make as much money as they normally would. If you have 5 Uber cars operating in one city, that's low supply and likely high demand. But if a large chunk of newly unemployed workers joins Uber, then you may end up with 50 cars in one city- where supply is greater than demand. It's hard to make a living as one of those 50 drivers.

Many gig workers are taken advantage of by their employers, who often provide little to no employment benefits due to being hired as *independent contractors*- what I mentioned earlier. One example of this would be adjunct or part-time professors, who are provided less stability and benefits than their tenured and tenure-track counterparts. Another example is ride-hailing drivers who are considered independent contractors by the company, with opinions and rulings by the Department of Labor, federal judges, and (mostly state) legislators in the past few years trying to work out this classification.

California has become a testbed for what will likely happen in the rest of the U.S. on issues of gig workers, their classification, and what benefits they are entitled to. California had passed Assembly Bill 5, which states that California workers can only be independent contractors if the work they do is *outside* the usual course of a company's business. Conversely, workers must be employees instead of contractors if a company exerts control over how they perform their tasks, or if their work is part of a company's regular business.[45]

In September 2020, California passed Assembly Bill 2257 which went into effect immediately and rewrote many requirements from AB5. You had gig economy companies such as Uber, Lyft, DoorDash, Instacart, and Postmates put millions of dollars supporting Proposition 22 in California towards the end of 2020, which passed, and now exempts firms such as those aforementioned from having to classify their gig workers in the state as employees rather than independent contractors. This battle over gig worker classification will continue to play out across the country, so we have yet to see where this issue will eventually land in the end.

The above problems with this style of working and the economy are that you are essentially trading off job security and stability for freedom. But the costs of freedom are too high, which is why I would address those issues in what I will call a *Just* Gig Economy. A Just Gig Economy is one where workers do not have to sacrifice security for freedom. That

means workers can work flexible, part-time, and even temporary jobs while maintaining broader legal representation, minimum wage, and benefits such as healthcare and retirement. I
would argue that a just gig economy can only be achieved by
passing legislation on a state and federal level. States can increase the number of and/or types of benefits that gig workers
receive, and enough state action can act as a driving force in
convincing other states to follow suit. Or the state laws could
be looked at by the court system as well, potentially changing the outcome for all states. Congress and the White House
should certainly investigate worker rights for gig workers.

Remote work, the gig economy, and freelancing can all be
done at the beginning or end of someone's career, can act as
a supplement to one's primary income, and allows for greater
flexibility during crises or transition periods in someone's career. Also, gig work can be and often is aligned with remote
work. So, as you can see, we must move towards a system of
work where we, the workers, are not always restricted by geography and types of income. Opportunity is thus spread out
across the entire country and world even, with plenty of in-
come-generating opportunities. Equal opportunity for everyone, at any point in someone's career (or their entire career), is
the type of system we should be moving towards for work in
the future.

Gig work isn't perfect, and neither are many of the new jobs
of today. The internet and social media have created new and
nontraditional jobs that make it easier to be self-employed,
kind of like gig work. This includes everything from gaining a
following as a social media influencer to entertaining as a video
game streamer (both of which can provide income- though it's
not lucrative for most). We should embrace new types of work,
keeping in mind that new jobs and being self-employed in general, have their set of difficulties concerning health care, retirement, and other traditional benefits. The next and last chapter

sets out to address some of these concerns, because as fun as it would be to travel around the country as a digital nomad and write books, we still need access to healthcare and other benefits.

Chapter 5

Burnout and Worker Health

Our work culture in the U.S. is not only one that is fine with employees making less than a living wage but also one of working until you reach burnout. Since we view work as something separate from living, we are okay with working so much that we end up not having the energy or time to *live* outside of work. It's difficult for us to shift away from this idea of working until we reach burnout when work and life are inseparable, or your work isn't meaningful. Burnout is everywhere these days. Our medical professionals have burnout, which leads to an increase in medical errors. Burnout is sabotaging workplace retention due to heavy workloads. Employees who work longer hours are often rewarded whereas workers without an extra workload are often replaced.

Psychologist Sheryl Ziegler published the book *Mommy Burnout*, where she explains how mothers are often feeling burnout by running themselves into the ground trying to be super moms. Ziegler defines burnout as "chronic stress gone awry" and this chronic stress can even lead to health problems.[46] The WHO defines burnout as "a syndrome conceptualized as resulting from chronic workplace stress that has not been successfully managed."[47] Symptoms of burnout include three large issues of emotional exhaustion, cynicism,

63

and feeling ineffective. Other issues include frequent colds, insomnia, and increased likeliness of relieving stress through unhealthy habits such as heavy drinking or online shopping. Unfortunately, the U.S. does not define burnout as a medical illness, unlike other countries such as much of Europe, including France. Remember thirty days a year of paid vacation for French workers? It seems apparent they understand the true cost of working too much and the effects of burnout in their culture. Either that or they really enjoy vacation.

We focus a lot on addressing the *stressors* in our life when we should be focusing on *chronic stress*. The former are external events such as to-do lists and financial problems whereas stress is "the neurological and physiological shift that happens in your body when you encounter [stressors]."[48] We need to address stress itself by paying attention to our stress response cycle instead of trying to reduce our stressors by being on top of things and always checking off our to-do lists. Some tools to mitigate burnout include sleep, physical exercise, and positive social connection, all of which are easier to achieve if you're not working forty-plus hours a week to get by or because those are the expectations.

Now one might point out that stress in itself isn't inherently bad. It certainly has its advantages. We as human beings *naturally* feel stress. And we talk about stress as if it's purely negative and detrimental to our health. Too much stress and too much of the wrong stress is certainly not ideal and can have health consequences as mentioned above, but there are good and necessary reasons for stress, evolutionarily speaking. Stress is advantageous in that it prepares our bodies during fight or flight situations where we are faced with possible damage or a loss of resources. Increased stress also provides us quicker reaction times and cognitive benefits.

Preparing us for action is certainly a benefit of our stress response, but there is a mismatch between the environments of our ancestors and our modern environment. We aren't conducting the same actions, experiencing the same dangers, or addressing the same demands as our ancestors did. Our modern work environment is stressful in *different ways*, but life is not more stressful now than it was for our ancestors. our ancestors almost certainly experienced more stress, with everything from no police and food reserves to a lack of laws and prevalent predators with danger possible at any moment. From Nesse and Young on the *Evolutionary Origins and Functions of the Stress Response*:

> *Perhaps in that environment, where stressors were more often physical, the stress response was more useful than it is now. Today, we mainly face social and mental threats, so [our bodies main stress system] may yield net costs. This is plausible and supports the many efforts to reduce stress and to find drugs that block the stress response.*[49]

If our body's physical stress response, which can cause too much damage to our physical and mental health, was more useful in the past than it is now, do we not owe it to our workers to make sure they are not so burdened with stress that their health and wellbeing suffers? To say as an employer that you care about your employee's wellbeing, those words must be backed up with action. That means making sure burnout isn't all that common, that too many hours aren't worked in each day or week, that work isn't providing unnecessary stress, and that workers are provided *time* to mitigate high levels of stress that come naturally within the modern workplace.

If we as a culture shift how we view work concerning time spent working and overall workloads, we can address this problem of burnout. It won't be easy to get our entire work culture to shift but one thing we can do as individuals is set boundaries with work, blocking off specific time for only work and nothing else. As mentioned earlier, eight hours per workday isn't some magical number that we must obey in every work-place, it's simply the status quo. I will explain in a future chap-ter how much time *should* be spent working, but for now, it's safe to say it's less than eight.

Also, setting boundaries between time spent working and time spent outside work is crucial. When you're off the clock you should be off the clock, but unfortunately, we have social media and communication outlets where we are sucked back into work or into an activity (such as scrolling through Twitter) that eats up time that could be spent collecting ourselves, re-focusing, and mitigating stress. Try limiting the time you spend working or going through social media, whether you write it down somewhere or use an app on your phone to track time spent online, or even just putting your phone and work emails away after your shift is over until the very next workday.

It turns out that gender also plays a role in burnout, with women reporting higher levels of burnout.[50] Addressing women's rights in recent years has been an important move-ment, but concerning work, we essentially have a system where women are expected to do it all, being both the best at home and at work. Women are more likely to have to sacri-fice career prospects and work in general, for family matters, which certainly can't be good for stress over long periods. So, work and family conflicts can lead to more stress, but other studies show that burnout among genders can happen for dif-ferent reasons. One study showed that female physicians were more likely to suffer from burnout related to emotional ex-haustion, whereas male physicians experienced burnout most likely from cynicism.[51]

There are plenty of tools and solutions to fixing burnout in our work culture, but I think we need to take it upon our-selves to do what we can on an individual level, while entire industries enact new policies and a workplace culture that prioritizes workers health and wellbeing over hours worked, caseloads, and organization goals. Because, how effective are workers if they show up to work every day burnt out and unable to adequately perform their job, possibly even missing work due to health concerns? We're not machines, as much as we like to pride ourselves on working hard.

When we take burnout to its conclusion, we see that employees' health is what suffers. Whereas our work culture is okay with accepting- even rewarding- burnout under the guise of "hard work", we are just as okay with accepting negative health consequences for our employees as well. This could include slaughterhouse workers packed like sardines, shoulder to shoulder with each other, operating heavy and dangerous equipment during a pandemic. Or it may include sitting at a desk, behind the wheel, or in front of a screen for eight continuous hours in a very unnatural setup that at first is uncomfortable but over time may cause health problems. Research suggests a link between sitting for long periods with health issues such as obesity, increased blood pressure, high blood sugar, excess body fat around the waist, and abnormal cholesterol levels, not to mention an increased risk of death from cardiovascular disease and cancer. "An analysis of 13 studies of sitting time and activity levels found that those who sat for more than eight hours a day with no physical activity had a risk of dying similar to the risks of dying posed by obesity and smoking."[52]

Studies also show that you can counter these risks with daily exercise and to be fair, the jury is still out on sitting's definitive health consequences. Nonetheless, our health should be taken more seriously in our work environment. I would also like to mention the benefit of taking a break from work every hour or so to recuperate. Going for a walk, stretching, and natural movement go a long way in rejuvenation and positive health. If you think about what work must have been for our ancestors, you can imagine their work didn't consist of prolonged sitting for a third of a day, every day. We shouldn't be surprised that doing so is bad for our health.

Sure, the history of health conditions in the workplace used to be much worse than just described but we have much more progress to make in embedding all aspects of a healthy lifestyle into our work. Some might ask why we even concern ourselves with health in relation to work because some jobs just naturally have poor working conditions and are a necessary price to pay for working our way up the career ladder. Others might say that our health should only concern us on a personal level and is irrelevant to our work environment. Even though we often think of health falling outside the purview of our company's concerns, it is not. Setting up a healthy work environment with necessary breaks and a natural structure is the least a business can do for its employees. This goes into the idea that our workers are more than just numbers on a spreadsheet, and our work is more than just a paycheck.

Comparatively, we spend most of our waking hours at work, which means it has a disproportionate impact on the rest of our lifestyle and life outcomes. Also, unhealthy workers are bad for business, bad for our communities, and expensive for everyone involved. Expensive for our healthcare system which we all at least partially pay into, expensive for our businesses who pay high insurance premiums in their employee health insurance coverage, and expensive for employee turnover due to sick leave and the like.

What can employers do about health in the workplace and the health of their employees? Quite a lot. At a bare minimum, workers should be afforded the time to take a break from continuous work, understanding that we're not robots meant to conduct the same task or sit in the same chair for eight continuous hours. A thirty-minute lunch break during an entire 9-5 shift is not even close to enough time to rejuvenate the body and keep it going. Affording workers more freedom in how they spend their time would allow them to take intermittent, necessary breaks or take time to prepare and consume quality food instead of the likely close-by and convenient fast-food restaurants.

Remote work affords many workers this very freedom and it just so happens that employees are still getting the same amount of work done they were getting done before when they had to show up at the office. So, if workers are just as productive or even more productive given the freedom to spend time as they see fit, then we should also think about the resulting positive health effects from that style of work. Now of course some low-skilled work may have a naturally demanding work environment. But if so, then it should be the employer's obligation to pay a living wage to those employees so that they can move on to a job or career which is less damaging to the body and mind over time or at least properly compensate them for their hardship.

There are also interesting and fun solutions to embedding health in the workplace. Many employers are providing free gym memberships to their employees as part of compensation, either at a gym located in their office building or at any local gym. Some office spaces have standing desks or health-conscious restaurants inside or around the workspace. Some offices have green spaces and gardens a short distance from working space, for which workers are free to visit, relax, and unwind throughout the workday. There are countless opportunities for employers to build healthy living into the work structure. Not only would taking care of our workers' health demonstrate that we value them and see their importance, but it would also be beneficial to all stakeholders.

The benefits of a healthy employee populace are tenfold. Healthy workers are good for an employer's bottom line and workers' productivity and engagement. For employers looking to create these sorts of conditions and take care of their employees' health, it is quite easy to do so. Incentives go a long way in creating action, and there are many ways in which employers can incentivize workers to take care of their health. Not to mention, leadership can ask employees which health policies they desire or would appreciate the most. This is important because health policies tend to look different for truck drivers, as one example, than a traditional 9-5 desk job.

The priority of course is to eliminate unhealthy workplace conditions and practices. If workers are spending eight hours in an environment that goes against our physical nature, then we're not making much progress. After addressing the workplace conditions, we can look at various health policies. One is to provide free transit passes so employees are inclined to take public transit, which means they are likely to walk more than had they driven into work via other means. The same principle applies to providing bike racks and space which encourages workers to ride into work. If you include an office fitness center with showers or discounted gym memberships through local gyms, then you are also encouraging more exercise for your employees which is not only great for reducing stress but is simply important for a healthy lifestyle.

Providing assistance and resources for employees who may be experiencing some form of substance addiction or mental health concerns may also provide that first step that employees need to take care of themselves. At certain points in life, we all need someone to talk to or receive help from, so providing addiction or mental health coverage (e.g., therapy) as part of the employer-provided health insurance plan, could go a long way. Some businesses provide workplace wellness programs. Weight Watchers for example provides *Health Solutions*, which assists employers looking to "increase engagement, reduce absenteeism, address rising healthcare costs and challenges, create a positive workplace environment, and attract and retain- talent."[53] I bring this up because there are countless health and wellness programs out there that will work with employers in their health-related workplace goals. Employees can also talk to their supervisors or Human Resources and ask for these types of programs as well because like I said, they benefit everyone.

The CDC and World Health Organization also provide resources and tips for workplace health strategies, frameworks, and models. Some of these health-related policies and practices may very well be innovative or new to an organization or industry, but we shouldn't let that stop us.[54,55] One such innovation that has been increasingly used and discussed during Covid, is telehealth or telemedicine. There are more and more telehealth options available out there that allow people to seek basic medical advice or assistance from the comfort of their homes. Employers could get involved here as well offering some form of financial assistance for employees utilizing telehealth services. It is in the best interest for employees to have medical checkups at least every year and encouraging this type of healthcare could prove beneficial to all parties involved. Maybe a worker will finally receive the healthcare they need, which would then lead to a healthier workforce and all the associated benefits.

There is a role for the government here as well. If the federal government provides universal health care or some form of accessible, affordable, and quality health insurance, more employees in the workforce would move over to the government insurance plan- possibly out of necessity such as with gig work or self-employed Americans. A government-provided health care plan would also benefit businesses whose employees find the government option more affordable or just better in the care provided. It benefits employers because employer-provided health insurance is a large and increasing expense for them every year. "According to BLS-generated compensation cost indices, total benefit costs for all civilian workers have risen an inflation-adjusted 22.5% since 2001 (when the data series began), versus 5.3% for wage and salary costs."[56]

By the government playing a role in reducing health insurance costs for businesses, the money saved could then be used to pay employees a living wage and higher salaries. All of which would generally increase worker satisfaction and wellbeing. Having a greater number of employers partake in this targeted approach to health-related policies, conditions, and practices would increase overall national health which has even more positive outcomes for workers and communities across the country.

Addressing burnout and health concerns in the workplace is in the best interest of every organization and every worker. One way to provide time away from work is by providing more paid time off to employees. Without time off, what value are your employees providing when they're burnt out, unhealthy, and unable to perform their best?

Avoiding burnout and having a healthy workforce, with workers staying engaged in work long-term can be accomplished by giving back an employee's time which is often wasted (as described earlier). Regardless of if you're a waged employee or making a salary, regular time off and paid time off (PTO) is advantageous, but if you are struggling to get by and rely on low wages, then PTO is almost necessary to take time off. Otherwise, there is a good chance you must work nonstop because you can't afford not to. A worker working their bones raw is something you as an employee or employer should be concerned with.

There are federal laws such as the Fair Labor Standards Act which "establishes minimum wage, overtime pay, recordkeeping, and child labor standards affecting full-time and part-time workers in the private sector and Federal, State, and local governments."[57] The FLSA does *not*, however, require "vacation, holiday, severance, or sick pay, meal or rest periods, holidays off, or vacations, premium pay for weekend or holiday work, pay raises or fringe benefits, or a discharge notice, reason for discharge, or immediate payment of final wages to terminated employees."[57]

Paid time off is not federally mandated yet a good chunk of employers do provide it as a way of reducing burnout and being competitive against other employers. Right now, many workers are provided unpaid time off, but it might be of interest for more employers to increase paid time off or for the government to mandate more paid time off for employees up to a certain amount so that workers who can't afford to miss a day of work are taken care of.

The U.S. is behind other countries around the world, where vacation time can total four to six weeks a year or more. Workers' time should be valued and part of respecting an employee and their true value to an organization means providing more time off. Even if workers truly enjoy their job and would rather spend their time doing that work over any other activity, we all still have other things we must get done, and we deserve the time to care for our personal health. Not to mention the value we as a society place on time spent with those closest to us- loved ones, family, and friends. Building and maintaining new and close relationships is essential, so we must make more time for it.

The government could step in and increase requirements for paid or unpaid time off whether those are vacation days off or sick days off. Employers could also step in and increase paid or unpaid time off (preferably PTO), leading to a work culture where employees have their time valued and can create more balance in their lives. This would also have the added benefit of being a competitive advantage in that workers would prefer to work for an organization that respects and values their time.

Our first reaction is to think that if employers allow workers more time off, they will either be unproductive during the time they spend on the job, the business will suffer a loss in revenue, or the business will have greater expenses due to having another employee fill the time missed by an employee on leave. In the short term, there certainly is a possibility that money will be lost, but in the long term, most of these concerns hold little to no water as an argument. The reason Ford Motor Co. moved to a six-day workweek and eventually five days was to actually *increase* productivity, with the company's bottom line a major priority.

And since that time about a century ago, much about the way we work has changed- yet we still have this mindset that five days a week and/or forty hours a week is the most productive amount of time for our businesses. And in doing so we've also accepted that any extra time off, whether paid or unpaid, is just a *perk* of that job and the current hours worked are truly optimal. As explained earlier, it is very unlikely the status quo of hours worked is either optimal or sustainable for workers in the end. More hours worked does not directly translate to greater productivity across the board.

There are many inequalities here as well, depending on the job you work. The most important one is that "more than half of all [health] insurance coverage is employer-provided."[58] This means that many American workers rely on their employer for their health needs, making it less likely they can leave if work conditions are bad or if there is a crisis (personal or otherwise). Another area of concern is sick leave. As of 2019, "Seventy-three percent of private industry workers had paid sick leave benefits available from their employers."[59] The divide though is between industries. "Ninety-four percent of workers in management, business, and financial occupations had sick leave benefits, [whereas only] 58 percent of workers in service occupations and 56 percent of workers in construction, extraction, farming, fishing, and forestry occupations [do]."[59]

When only 25% of private-sector workers have at least 10 days of paid sick time a year, even after 20 years in a job, then many workers who *can* take time off may not have enough leave to weather some emergency, like 14 days off for quarantine during a pandemic.[60] There are plenty of other emergencies that come up too, in which sick leave is crucial, and employees shouldn't have to choose between health or well-being and a paycheck. Giving workers more of their time back and increasing leave would help even the playing field between industries and allow workers to better weather personal health issues or an economic crisis such as a pandemic.

Some U.S. cities have taken it upon themselves to force the hand of employers and require them to offer more leave because they understand that leave is something that impacts the entire community over time. Of the 40 largest U.S. cities, 23 require employers to offer at least some paid leave according to CityHealth, an initiative of the de Beaumont Foundation and Kaiser Permanente. "Only five cities — Austin, Dallas, San Antonio, Los Angeles, and San Diego — met the organization's "gold standard" for requiring a minimum amount of earned sick time and covering the smallest businesses under sick leave laws."[60] At the same time though, many states have stepped in and prevented these types of requirements from being enforced. Nearly two dozen states have passed laws preventing municipalities from adopting their own paid sick leave laws.

We shouldn't have a situation, especially during a crisis such as an economic downturn or pandemic, where cities and states are trying to hash out specific and local leave laws because employers aren't willing to increase the number of sick leave and because the federal government isn't willing to mandate anymore. As mentioned earlier, the idea of not providing enough leave for employees is bad for most businesses long term. As more employees take more time off (to a point), they will reduce burnout, can better manage short-term medical issues that bring them back to work even sooner, and their overall well-being is likely to increase. Also, if companies small and large start offering enhanced leave policies, competitors very well may follow suit to stay competitive with employee benefits.[60]

An extension of paid time off is that of family and medical leave. In the U.S. the Family and Medical Leave Act (FMLA) requires employers to provide... "certain employees with up to 12 weeks of unpaid, job-protected leave per year", with a requirement that their group health benefits be maintained during the leave.[61] More on FMLA:

> *FMLA applies to all public agencies, all public and private elementary and secondary schools, and companies with 50 or more employees. These employers must provide an eligible employee with up to 12 weeks of unpaid leave each year for any of the following reasons: For the birth and care of the newborn child of an employee, for placement with the employee of a child for adoption or foster care, to care for an immediate family member (i.e., spouse, child, or parent) with a serious health condition, or to take medical leave when the employee is unable to work because of a serious health condition. Employees are eligible for leave if they have worked for their employer at least 12 months, at least 1,250 hours over the past 12 months, and work at a location where the company employs 50 or more employees within 75 miles.*[61]

Employers are not obligated to pay employees during their family leave, even though it may be difficult for that employee to maintain their finances. If the person on family leave is a single parent, that leaves them with little options in making money. Many single parents would be unable to stay away from work for 12 weeks of unpaid leave, and if there are two parents, chances are one of them will still have to work to bring money in. This second parent working means that parent is less likely to use their 12 weeks of unpaid time off and more likely to go right back to work even though most parents would prefer to spend time at home with their family during this important and crucial moment in their family. Workers should not have to choose between spending time with their family after childbirth and paying the bills, especially with all the time and energy that workers put into their jobs. And as we know, many workers are just barely getting by, so 12 weeks of unpaid time off is useful, but a large chunk of workers can't afford to even take off a slim part of the 12 weeks.

Many employers know this too, they know that many low-income workers are less likely to use up a ton of leave during a major life event such as childbirth. With little to no extra PTO to use during important life events, there are few to no options left for many employees. I understand why FMLA has specific requirements for workers to be eligible for leave, so that the policy isn't taken advantage of, but right now workers are the ones being taken advantage of, so it's about time we make necessary changes to the law- or add to it.

Both government and business can step in here, mandating or allowing increased weeks of leave, preferably PTO for low-wage workers. Until we increase minimum wages to be living wages, many Americans will continue to have to work, even if provided unpaid time off. As we know, more time off and the means of which to accept it would be beneficial to workers, providing them more time to destress, relax, and live outside of work. We all benefit as a society when we value individual workers, their families, and our communities in this regard. We know the true value of our time and our lives, so it's past time we treat our workers with the respect and dignity they deserve.

Chapter 6

School, Childcare, and a Piece of Paper

Something potentially even more stressful than burnout or a lack of paid leave is trying to manage school and work. That is what this next chapter is about- school and its intersection with work. We grow up going to school so we can have the necessary knowledge and skills for work, but it should also prepare students for life itself, something our school system largely falls short of. For some of us, we head straight to work and don't go to college, and for others, we go to college to attain more knowledge and skills in a specific field, with the idea that it will prepare us for a career in that very field. And then later in life, we're reintroduced to school when we send our kids there while we work, or so we can work. School is directly intertwined with work in more ways than one. Unfortunately, the way school is structured in this country is not in alignment to best suit the needs of a balanced work life.

Let's start with the structure of American education. How we educate students and structure their learning in K-12 is outdated. This old model of education operates more like a factory floor, generally geared toward producing a fairly uniform product, than a cohesive learning environment built for personalized learning. Some say the reason for this is because a factory model of school was the initial set-up since public education became widespread in America starting in the mid-nineteenth century. Also, that this model has changed little over the years. Whereas that is true to a degree, much of the setup in schools was designed to meet the needs of the time.

Schools that were traditionally designed as analog and modeled like a factory were the most sensible way to rapidly scale schools throughout the country. This meant that American classrooms and the schools they made up weren't designed for personalization.[62] The history of education is a little more complex than that, but the way instruction is organized and delivered today, is not cohesive to learning. It's not that every aspect of K-12 public school was designed around a factory model, it's just that enough parts of it are factory-like. We teach students material as if they are uniform products within a manufacturing plant who all learn at the same rate and are all skilled in the same ways, which we know isn't true. Some students are naturally inclined to understand certain material growing up and some students learn faster or slower with specific subjects, skills, and learning styles.

Addressing education reform is certainly an interesting issue because there are societal implications for the workforce and timing as well. Any changes to our school system in how learning and instruction are provided are less likely to occur if it means students are learning in a more personalized way on their *own* time horizon as opposed to a time horizon that aligns with our work hours. When we talk about education reform, we're not just talking about the new tools we implement in modern education, nor the specific organization and delivery of instruction, nor the specific models we find most cohesive to personalized learning. We're also talking about how it directly coincides with our model of work in the United States. More specifically, the timing of it all.

As a parent or as an employer we expect that students will follow the traditional learning path, according to the traditional time frame, but that's not how learning occurs. Learning doesn't adhere to a specific time frame- you might become an expert at college-level math by the time you're sixteen if you're truly skilled and/or interested in it. Or maybe you're naturally gifted in athletics and school is just a mode of transportation for your athletic skills and goals. The economic and social expectations we place on learning combined with the preparation of students for college and a career are just as likely to be impediments to individual students' personal growth as they are useful. We live in an information economy and many changes to the way we work, and our work culture is likely to affect how we set up our schools. And in return, how we set up our schools will change the way we structure work, as well as its culture.

All in all, our current system of education is out of touch with 21st-century demands. As mentioned, our current design of K-12 education is not cohesive to individual learning, but it also kills creativity. You might be familiar with this concept as the most viewed Ted talk ever is one by the late education scholar Ken Robinson titled "Do schools kill creativity?". Ken brings up the story of Gillian Lynne — multimillionaire choreographer of "Cats" and "Phantom of the Opera"- and how her teachers thought she had a learning disorder. Her mom brought her to a doctor and the doctor's diagnosis was that Gillian wasn't sick, she was a dancer. She should be taken to dance school. Ken says that Gillian's outcome could just as well have been to put her on medication and tell her to calm down. Gillian was placed into an environment that matched her skill set and stoked her passion. This environment is the exact opposite of an American education.[63]

Instead of organizing around individual flourishing, schools today organize around standardized testing. Schools kill creativity because they're industrialized (e.g., standardized tests and learning instruction), they create a hierarchy of subjects, and classes are rigidly timed. What Ken prescribes is a shift from standardization to personalization, do away with this notion that specific subjects are innately more important than others (i.e., math over fine art), and class timing should vary depending on individual students needs in each moment around a given subject because that's where true problem solving occurs.[63]

Students should be spending more time in a school environment that matches their individual skill sets and fuels their passions. Because chances are one or both of those areas are what a student will make a life out of or contribute to in some way, shape, or form once out of school. A multidisciplinary approach where students are forced to regurgitate information (not always learn), goes against our creativity. As a result, you have students who come out of high school with little to no specialized skills, passions, or an understanding of their interests in life. None of which is good for an innovative, successful, and specialized economy. Our economy and the social fabric of our culture suffer because of poor education. We often talk about changes to education or the economy as if they are separate entities- but they are not. They are directly related. If we want this greater, more equitable, and innovative economy, we must consider education's role in creativity.

We don't care that our kids are the very best mathematical genius or musician they can be, we care that they are allowed to pursue the skills and knowledge they care about most and are then able to be contributing members of the economy and society as we know it. Many of us may disagree on what the *minimum* amount of learning should be provided on specific subjects within each grade level because we don't all place the same value on specific subjects. With this being the case, I still think that we would be okay with our students naturally pursuing a mostly personalized education where they learn about topics, they are truly interested in but are also exposed to different subject areas to be more susceptible to more topics and skills than they otherwise would be. I think finding the balance between exposure, a basic level understanding of specific subjects, and a personalized approach to learning is the necessary path to reshaping our school system.

Striking this balance will certainly require new models of delivering education in the classroom. "New classroom delivery models allow us to re-imagine new combinations of educator expertise, time, instructional materials, research, physical space, parental support, and (yes) technology in ways that achieve optimal outcomes for students."[62] But this reimagination requires us to not start with the current model, but instead thinking about "what it is we want students to be able to do, the measures of success, the resources we have to work with, and our own sense of possibility."[62] Different schools will likely have different approaches in their educational philosophies ad available resources, so understanding what investments are required for each individual school will go a long way.

Regardless of the chosen model, it is still important to have shared accountability for the outcome of each student- not in a way that encourages uniformity among students but rather teaching for the sake of individual knowledge and skills. These are the goals of education, not uniformly providing information that doesn't always translate to actual knowledge long term. How we choose to educate students will directly impact our workforce, its ability to innovate, and how purpose-driven workers are when they start their career journey.

Unfortunately, there are still many barriers to educational attainment and opportunity for Americans across the country. Internet and computer access are not provided to many Americans- both children and adults who need it. This prevents them from succeeding in school and their work lives. From a 2018 report by the National Center for Education Statistics on *Stu-*

dent Access to Digital Learning Resources Outside of the Classroom:

> *Results revealed that 94 percent of children ages 3 to 18 had a computer at home and 61 percent of children ages 3 to 18 had internet access at home in 2015. The percentages of children with computer and internet access at home in 2015 were higher for children who were older, those whose parents had higher levels of educational attainment, and those whose families had higher incomes. Also, higher percentages of children who were White (66 percent), Asian (63 percent), and of Two or more races (64 percent) had home internet access in 2015 than did Black (53 percent), Hispanic (52 percent), and American Indian/Alaska Native children (49 percent).*[64]

There is a divide in computer and internet access by state too. "For example, in 2015 the percentage of households with computer access ranged from 79 percent in Mississippi to 93 percent in Utah, and the percentage of households with internet access ranged from 62 percent in Mississippi to 85 percent each in New Hampshire and Washington."[64] Student access to digital learning resources outside the classroom also has its barriers. "In 2015, the two main reasons children ages 3 to 18 lacked access to the Internet at home were that access was too expensive and that their family did not need it or was not interested in having it" and "internet access being too expensive was more commonly the main barrier for children from low-income families and for children whose parents had low levels of educational attainment than for other children."[64] There is a large gap in the percentage of adults who use the internet, similar to the same divides presented above concerning income, race, and educational attainment. According to Pew Research, "racial minorities, older adults, rural residents, and those with lower levels of education and income are less likely to have broadband service at home."[65]

Inequality of internet access can also be seen geographically, with an urban-rural divide. Internet Service Providers (ISPs) tend to invest less in building infrastructure for rural communities due to it costing them more than it would benefit them. But unfortunately, local governments have little to no ability to create that infrastructure in their place, which leaves many Americans without accessible, affordable, and efficient options.

These inequalities as students and as adults persist throughout these individuals' lives once they enter the workforce. A lack of internet access, which is essentially required these days to be successful or accomplish education and work, has broad implications for future career success. Thus, I view internet access as a public good, which means it should be treated as such and made both affordable and accessible. We must ask ourselves what our businesses and government's obligations are to provide us the means by which to educate ourselves and conduct our work.

Moving on to post-high school learning, we can see the importance of college learning to our career prospects. Students growing up in American public schools, especially in high school, are told *you must go to college* or it's better to get a job in this field *if you want to make money.* Now, of course, these phrases aren't always stated directly, but they are often indirectly said or implied. In recent years, college has become less about obtaining additional knowledge or skills to prepare students for a career or propel them forward in their current one. It has become more about obtaining a piece of paper, which originally meant you had a one-up in the workplace, but now is less so when many other job applicants have degrees now. When over a third of the workforce has a college degree, it no longer holds the same weight in the job market.

There are many ways to structure a college education, and many other countries have their own models. Some countries provide free college, some provide few to no barriers to access, and some provide bachelor's degrees in three years instead of four. I won't go into detail here about which model is most effective or which should be applied in the American university system. But I will describe some underlying problems which directly impact our work life.

First is the role that increasing amounts of student debt (or debt in general) have on someone entering the workforce. Right now, "About 43 million adult Americans—roughly one-sixth of the U.S. population older than age 18—currently carry a federal student loan and owe $1.5 trillion in federal student loan debt, plus an estimated $119 billion in student loans from private sources that are not backed by the government." With an estimated one-third of adults ages 25 to 34 having a student loan, that means college debt is most concentrated among young people.[66] Young people who in generations past would normally start "adulting" in their twenties are now having to wait until they pay off their debt and are more financially sound before making large life decisions- getting married, having kids, etc.

This amount of debt is bound to have a large, negative effect on the economy. Many student borrowers are forced to pay unfairly high-interest rates which forces them to pay loans much longer than one normally would any other type of loan. This makes it more difficult financially for these borrowers, making them less able to afford other products and services in the economy. And of course, this debt doesn't land on American borrowers equally. Black or African American students who earned a bachelor's degree are more likely to default than their similarly situated white peers, at nearly four times the default rate. "Students who are veterans, parents, first-generation college students, or are low income are also likely to face higher risk of default."[66] These inequalities in education lead to an even greater divide in economic opportunity disproportionately based on race, income, and gender, to name a few.

There were many pieces of legislation, lobbying from higher ed institutions, and consequential actions by politicians on both sides of the aisle which are responsible for creating the conditions that lead to such a large amount of student loan debt. But just to give you a time frame of what we're looking at, the figure below shows the Average Education Costs of college from 1971 – 2019.[67] If were to compare consumer student loan debt compared to other non-housing debt such as credit cards and auto loans, we would see that student loan debt is the largest source, having gained over the past few decades.[68]

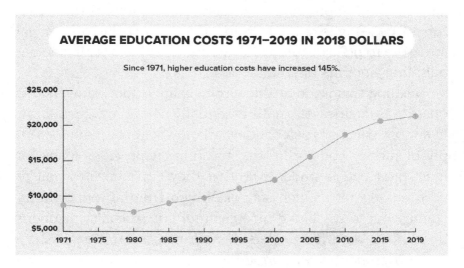

AVERAGE EDUCATION COSTS 1971–2019 IN 2018 DOLLARS

Since 1971, higher education costs have increased 145%.

Source: Issa, N. 2019. "U.S. Average Student Loan Debt Statistics in 2019." Retrieved from https://www.credit.com/personal-finance/average-student-loan-debt/

So how do we address the loan situation, which is holding back Americans in contributing to the economy, preventing them from progressing in their careers, and acts as a barrier to life goals? The Center for American Progress made a report on federal student loans, which is the largest single source of college debt (92% outstanding student loan balances). The report outlines six options for tackling student loan debt: "Forgive all student loans, forgive up to a set dollar amount for all borrowers, forgive debt held by former Pell recipients, reform repayment options to tackle excessive interest growth and provide quicker paths to forgiveness, change repayment options to provide more regular forgiveness, and allow student loan refinancing."[66]

There are certainly reasons and validity behind implementing each of these options- plus many others out there, but unfortunately, it would still mostly address the symptoms as opposed to tackling debt at its source. Of course, we need to address the symptoms, but we also need to reform the structure of post-high-school learning and the associated financial structure to prevent future college students from taking on debilitating amounts of student debt.

Tackling this issue at the source is important. Universities operate as businesses, that's essentially what they are. But unlike most parts of the economy where there is a limited supply of money coming in, the government provides loans for most prospective students so that they don't have to wait to go to college after high school. Which from an opportunity standpoint seems like a nice gesture, but in reality, it opens up a flood gate for universities to increase tuition costs. *I mean if students can borrow however much they need, then why not charge them more* is the line of business thinking here. It should be a major policy priority to tackle the student loan crisis if we want more opportunities and greater economic prospects for American workers.

Another college issue is the common requirement of non-major related courses, the general education courses. When you review the general education requirements for colleges across the country you can see that it is common practice to make them last a year or more of a four-year curriculum. I see these gen-ed courses as only being important if it applies to your specific major or is required to understand specific coursework later in the curriculum. There are always a few gen-ed courses that students could go without in their degree, which I would argue are not worth thousands of dollars for. If I wanted to spend thousands of dollars on a course, then I would sign up for that individual course or learn about it in my free time- it shouldn't be mandatory for a degree that is in an entirely different subject.

The reason I bring up gen-ed courses is that if you think about the amount of time that is wasted on useless courses for your average college student, you can see that we have a lot of wasted time. Once you take out the unnecessary gen-ed courses, your bachelor's degree would likely only take three years to complete- but that's only three years of tuition that the school receives, so you can see why changes here would be difficult to achieve.

Now of course a university will claim that these courses are essential to a well-balanced basic understanding of core concepts. Some might claim that these courses, even if unrelated to your degree, will provide useful in your coursework or career. "Recent studies show that many incoming college freshmen are actually not ready for the rigor of college classwork, underprepared by their high school courses in core subjects like science and math."[69] What does that say about our approach to high school education and American public schools in general? If students are unprepared for the "rigor" of college classwork, then wouldn't it make more sense to *make* them ready instead of piling on unnecessary student debt? Some people claim that skills learned in one class can be applied to an entirely different subject or become useful in their career down the road, but then again that is why we have books. We shouldn't be mandating students take an interdisciplinary approach to learning when they're paying thousands of dollars to receive a degree on a *specific* topic.

All the power to the students who decide on their own to take courses which have nothing to do with their major and don't mind paying for those courses. But that should be separate from the degree track. I personally enjoy this type of learning, but I do not see this mindset or approach to learning as worth the associated monetary or time costs. The university has an incentive to keep students in school as long as possible as that leads to more profits. "The longer a student takes to decide on a path of study, the likelier it is they'll extend their study... [which] means more credit hours before graduating, and more tuition dollars in the school's pocket."[70]

With college being so expensive today, it may not only be a waste of time to take these courses, but it can also be unnecessarily expensive. Moving towards a degree system of learning specific skills or gaining specific knowledge that can be applied to one's desired career would be more time-efficient and effective in reaching career goals.

For some career paths, it is becoming more common for workers to gain these necessary, specific skills and knowledge via online courses in the form of micro-certifications and boot camps. Micro-certifications are essentially a quick-paced course, usually provided online, where you learn a specific skill or set of knowledge. Aka an 'a la carte' version of a standard degree to learn the specific skills desired for your career path or just for fun. It is a skill-broadening, target-focused path to learning, that could even be stacked on top of other microcerts as a prospective employee.

An article from BBC Worklife:

Simon Nelson, CEO of FutureLearn, a UK-based learning platform that partners with universities to provide massive open online courses (MOOCs), believes that mi-

*cro-credentials arose out of three global 'macro trends.
One is the rapidly growing demand for high-quality ter-
tiary education in developing societies, while the second
is the digital transformation that has taken place in many
industries. This change is "exacerbating the traditional
skills gap", says Nelson, and universities aren't providing
the training for the "range of new skills that are in high
demand". The third factor is the digitization of the higher
education sector, he adds. It's no longer enough to obtain
a degree; having a career now requires people to upskill
continuously, yet "people can't take the time out of their
lives to attend physical establishments".*[71]

According to Sean Gallagher, the founder and executive director of Northeastern University's Center for the Future of
Higher Education and Talent Strategy, the global economic expansion in the technology fields has "really highlighted the
fact that there is a gap between the supply of people in the
workforce coming out of university with skills and credentials
to fill the gaps employers are looking for." Gallagher goes on to
say how micro-credentials often act as a supplement to their
core qualification, sort of like a master's degree but shorter.[71]

Right now, there also needs to be more industry involve-
ment. It is standard practice for universities to provide courses
and information on specific subject areas in how they relate to
current industry standards, practices, and skills. Thus, micro-
certification providers would benefit from working alongside
industries in their development of these courses and certifications. One can imagine the benefit of quickly learning in-
dustry-specific skills in pursuit of greater career prospects,
something that could become fairly common if micro-cert
providers continue to communicate with the industry.

Microcerts will have a role to play in the future, and maybe
only in specific industries such as tech for the time being but

that will change over time. Some experts think that microcerts could eventually replace degree requirements in some industries, but in others only act as a supplement to a university degree. The addition of microcerts to the marketplace means changing dynamics in how we seek employment and jockey for promotions. Certainly, something to keep an eye on.

Childcare, Work, and Inequality

We know that the American school system from K-College has much to long for in the way of change, but so does our culture around childcare. For many parents, if it weren't for school, they would be unable to work at all due to the lack of quality and affordable childcare in this country.

Not only is there a childcare crisis in this country, but it also disproportionately impacts women. Women are kept out of the workforce due to issues surrounding childcare. A group of mothers working for Amazon- known as Momazonians- organized a campaign around information-gathering and advocacy in March 2019, urging the company to provide a backup childcare benefit. "The group of nearly 2,000 Amazon employees with young children argued that a lack of affordable childcare has prevented talented women from progressing in their careers." These mothers were tired of seeing their colleagues quit due to a lack of available childcare.[72] The group called on Amazon to provide a backup childcare option for when their primary arrangements fell through, similar to benefits provided by peer companies such as Microsoft, Apple, and Google. There is a clear connection between access to quality childcare at an affordable price and labor force participation- especially for mothers. Even still, more needs to be done on the part of government, as employers cannot address the nation's childcare crisis alone.[72] According to the Center for American Progress (CAP), "many families with young children [today] must make a choice between spending a significant portion of their income on childcare, finding a cheaper, but potentially lower-quality care option, or leaving the workforce altogether to become a full-time caregiver." More parents are being driven out of the workforce at an alarming rate because of limited childcare availability, high costs, or inconvenient program hours. An estimated 2 million parents were forced to make career sacrifices due to problems with childcare in 2016 alone.[72]

Furthermore, in 2018, a CAP survey found that "mothers were 40 percent more likely than fathers to report that they had personally felt the negative impact of childcare issues on their careers." The costs of childcare don't only affect parents. they also impact the employers themselves, with American businesses losing an estimated $12.7 billion annually because of their employees' childcare challenges. "Nationally, the cost of lost earnings, productivity, and revenue due to the childcare crisis totals an estimated $57 billion each year." With half of U.S. families reporting difficulty finding childcare, our continuous neglect of the childcare issue is only increasing inequities experienced between families who can find childcare and those who cannot. But the burden lays primarily with mothers, as fathers are much less likely to have their employment impacted by childcare issues. In another CAP survey, "mothers said that if they had access to more affordable and reliable childcare, they would increase their earnings and progress in their careers by finding a higher-paying job, applying for a promotion, seeking more hours at work, or finding a job in the first place."[72]

What we need to solve these problems is a combination of workplace policies for employees that value parents and their childcare needs, plus government action such as more financial support and childcare regulation. Sending your kids to school for most of the day should not be the only solution to childcare. When children become of school-age, the childcare situation may become less burdensome as the children are likely to be at school for most of the workday, but for some reason, we tend to forget that children going through school still need care. The care is no longer just a place where children and teenagers go while the parents work, it is a learning institution- arguably the greatest care we can provide to our children is preparing them with the knowledge and skills they need to succeed in society and in life.

Unfortunately, we still don't treat American K-12 education as more than a means to an end for those who need to work. One great example of this is how little we pay public school teachers. Watching, teaching, and molding children to become prepared, competent, and successful members of society takes a lot of work, yet we don't pay teachers nearly enough to take on these responsibilities.

If the mantra *what you put in, is what you get out* holds any truth, then our return on investment for creating well-balanced, creative, and skilled people (future workers) is very dismal at the moment. Not to mention that teachers and educators are an essential piece of our workforce. Without them, we would be worse off in more ways than one. The average teacher salary in the U.S. right now is around $60,000, with starting salaries often below $40,000. Of course, average pay greatly fluctuates by state but generally speaking, many teachers are not paid enough to the point where they have to strike to demand better conditions. In 2018, 35,000 West Virginia teachers and school employees went on strike for the first time since 1990, resulting in nearly all 680 schools across the state closing.[73]

I don't have to tell you about the negative implications on workers and families and the local economy when teachers go on strike- it is surely not a fun situation to find yourself without a school to send your kid(s) to. Some politicians are concerned about teacher pay enough to propose legislation around it. At the time, then Senator, now Vice President Kamala Harris, proposed the government spend over $315 billion to raise teacher salaries over the coming decade.[73] The disparities in the average teacher salary by state is very large. Between 2002 and 2017, the average change in teacher salary was $27,688 for Alaska, but only $6,904 for Indiana. When compared internationally, the U.S. ranks only seventh in average teacher pay but pays less than half of what the number one country pays its teachers.[73] Furthermore, U.S. teacher salaries have actually decreased over the past decade. The National Education Association (NEA) found that the average teacher salary decreased by 4.5%, after adjusting for inflation. That says a lot about how we value teachers' role in our communities and our economy.[74]

Many teachers, especially younger ones, are likely to hold a second job during the summer or throughout the entire year as well. "According to NEA Today, around 16% of teachers hold a second job over the summer, and 20% of them hold a second job year-round."[74] The percentage is even higher if you include second jobs within the school system such as coaching and evening classes. Studies have shown that teachers pay a few hundred dollars on average of their own money on school supplies as well. This is ridiculous considering that if there's one place to overinvest resources, it's certainly with education. The interesting part about addressing teacher pay too is that a majority of Americans believe that teachers *should* be paid more. As a country, we are failing to execute on our shared understanding of the importance that teachers play in our students' lives but also the important role they play in our communities and economy.[74]

Addressing issues of American education, the faulty model of post-high school learning, and the reliance on school or childcare for workers will have to be done via policies from both employers and the government. The intersection of work and education is an important one and I hope we can find ways to bridge the divide and solve the many inequities of this broken system. Students, educators, and parents are all trying to move forward towards greater knowledge, skills, and opportunity. The whole point of school is to provide knowledge and skills that will set our children and adults up with the capabilities they need to succeed and prosper in this country. And the whole point of childcare is to increase participation in the economy for everyone and us to all be afforded the opportunity for success, regardless of gender or race. Hopefully, we can redesign our structures around school and childcare to build our communities up and make work-life what it should be.

II

The Structures
That Guide Us

Your corn is ripe today; mine will be so tomorrow. 'Tis profitable for us both, that I should labour with you today, and that you should aid me tomorrow. I have no kindness for you and know you have as little for me. I will not, therefore, take any pains upon your account; and should I labour with you upon my own account, in expectation of a return, I know I should be disappointed, and that I should in vain depend upon your gratitude. Here then I leave you to labour alone; You treat me in the same manner. The seasons change; and both of us lose our harvests for want of mutual confidence and security.

-David Hume

Chapter 7

The American Work Ethic, Individualism, and Success

American Work Ethic

By many in ancient Greece, "work was considered both virtuous and necessary, that idleness was condemned, and that the craftsman was held in high-esteem."[21] The type of work that was seen as virtuous likely changed depending on which class you belonged to, but the importance of work was not lost on the people of the time. Aristotle for example believed that work was not an end in itself. That the point of work is to be temporary, so one can then experience leisure and happiness.

Regardless of who did or did not value work as virtuous or necessary, success was generally valued, glorified even, in ancient times. We find this in ancient myth, such as through Homer's *Iliad*... Achilles must decide whether to fight in the Trojan War, which meant deciding between almost certain physical death alongside a glorious legacy or to return home and live a long, happy life but die in obscurity. He describes his choice thusly:

> *That two fates bear me on to the day of death.*
> *If I hold out here and I lay siege to Troy,*

my journey home is gone, but my glory never dies.
If I voyage back to the fatherland I love,
my pride, my glory dies ...[75]

As the story goes, success addict Achilles chooses death.

Up into and even during medieval times it can be hard to determine an individual's viewpoint on work and work ethic. But generally speaking, how a culture viewed work ethic was largely based on cultural norms and religious beliefs. What we do know is during the 1500s a shift occurred in attitude. This was due to the Protestant Reformation. "The Protestant Reformation was the 16th-century religious, political, intellectual and cultural upheaval that splintered Catholic Europe, setting in place the structures and beliefs that would define the continent in the modern era."[76] This reformation led to many of the conditions that made it okay to choose an occupation. The idea of working hard was encouraged more and more. Religious belief systems at the time made it so that people wanted to work hard to become one of the elects (aka. God has chosen you to go to heaven). Giving evidence that you deserved to be one of the elect meant you had to show you've been successful in life. The crux was the work ethic of the protestant ethic.[76]

Moving onto the American work ethic, through the pre-industrial revolution much of this protestant ethic was alive and well, with hard work seen as essential to our way of life. "The story of individual hard work is embedded into the very founding of our country, from the supposedly self-made, entrepreneurial Founding Fathers to the pioneers who plotted the United States' western expansion." At the same time, we often forget to "acknowledge that the riches of this country were built on the backs of African slaves."[77]

German sociologist, philosopher, jurist, and political economist, Max Weber would have said that if you have a hard-working society, you would have tended to do better. He compared countries that were generally protestant to the countries that were not predominantly protestant and found that economic wellbeing and productivity were greater in the former. He called it the protestant ethic. Even though those protestant roots are there, over time we secularized our work ethic from a religious one to just a hard-working one by itself. This has occurred over time, even during the industrial revolution.

Some people will say that we work less or harder today than we did in the industrial revolution, but the fact is that the nature of the work has simply changed. It's hard to compare when work in the 21st century is vastly different. Shifting from a primarily factory environment where hard, physical labor was the key to success, to a knowledge economy where brain often beats bronze, we have a shift in how we might measure work difficulty. Today, our work ethic is in many parts one based on individualism and our collective- and misaligned- notion of success.

American Individualism

Individualism or an individualistic culture is a culture that stresses the importance of the individual, sometimes at the behest of the needs of the group as a whole. This is the type of culture that prides itself on independence and autonomy.

The story of America is a story filled with the aforementioned ethic of hard work, a requirement and ability to pioneer our personal path towards progress, build our political and economic structures from scratch and revolution, and strive for progress according to a "better life" or an "American dream". We are a nation made up of immigrants who were looking to build a better life for themselves, and building a better life meant taking risks, putting in the work, and realizing opportunity all on our own. Of course, this isn't all of our history, as many of those before us relied on slaves and immoral acts to "make a living", for profit, exploitation, and so forth. Nonetheless, our nation is a story filled with individualistic movements, with movements within movements. To some degree, we all partake in this individualistic culture where we subtly embrace the undertones of a path forged like no other- for good or for worse.

To get an idea of what American individualism is historically, it can be useful to look from the perspective of someone who was born and lived within the midst of major human progress and inequality resulting from the two-sided coin of this cultural phenomenon. One such person was former President Herbert Hoover. He wrote a book about American Individualism, published in 1922.

Here are a few paragraphs from his book that describe his thesis:

> Individualism has been the primary force of American civilization for three centuries. It is our sort of individualism that has supplied the motivation of America's political, economic, and spiritual institutions in all these years. It has proved its ability to develop its institutions with the changing scene. Our very form of government is the product of the individualism of our people, the demand for an equal opportunity, for a fair chance.
>
> The American pioneer is the epic expression of that individualism, and the pioneer spirit is the response to the challenge of opportunity, to the challenge of nature, to the challenge of life, to the call of the frontier. That spirit need never die for lack of something for it to achieve. There will always be a frontier to conquer or to hold as long as men think, plan, and dare. Our American individualism has received much of its character from our contacts with the forces of nature on a new continent.

It evolved government without official emissaries to show the way; it plowed and sowed two score of great states; it built roads, bridges, railways, cities; it carried forward every attribute of high civilization over a continent. The days of the pioneer are not over. There are continents of human welfare of which we have penetrated only the coastal plain. The great continent of science is as yet explored only on its borders, and it is only the pioneer who will penetrate the frontier in the quest for new worlds to conquer. The very genius of our institutions has been given to them by the pioneer spirit. Our individualism is rooted in our very nature. It is based on conviction born of experience. Equal opportunity, the demand for a fair chance, became the formula of American individualism because it is the method of American achievement.[78]

Hoover claimed that American individualism is responsible for so much of the progress made in the country and that without it, it wouldn't have been possible. He also understands that American individualism is not perfect and that we have to find solutions for the problems it creates. To also have the will to work together towards solutions to the economic and social problems that ail us. He believed this progress could not be accomplished through infighting or destructive criticism. He argued that it must be accomplished through the lens of individualism. And that the U.S. will continue to see progress as long as it preserves individualism, preserves and stimulates the initiative of its people, builds up our insistence and safeguards to equality of opportunity, and glorifies service as part of our national character.[78]

But this can only be accomplished if *each individual* is given the opportunity for which the spirit of America stands. "We can make a social system as perfect as our generation merits and one that will be received in gratitude by our children."[78]

What's interesting here is that it's not just progress that is being talked about for the reason to support individualism, but also economic and social wellbeing and opportunity. If applying Hoover's words today, much of his arguments and advice could be viewed in reference to our current political, economic, and social reality.

Our sense of individuality has its benefits such as innovation and human progress as seen through our nation's development of human institutions and science and industry. Hoover is quick to point out the benefits of this progress but is just as quick to illustrate social forces which can destroy it. He argued that we should be concerned with equal dangers of *reaction* and *radicalism*.

> *An even greater danger is the destructive criticism of minds too weak or too partisan to harbor constructive ideas. For such, criticism is based upon the distortion of perspective or cunning misrepresentation. There is never danger from the radical himself until the structure and confidence of society has been undermined by the enthronement of destructive criticism. Destructive criticism can certainly lead to revolution unless there are those willing to withstand the malice that flows in return from refutation.*[78]

Lastly, he mentioned the social force of those individuals who believe the future should be a repetition of the past, that ideas are dangerous, and that ideals are freaks.[78]

The progress that American individualism sows also leaves us with negative political, social, and economic consequences which must be addressed. If left unaddressed and we "rest at ease in the comfortable assumption that right ideas always prevail by some virtue of their own", we find ourselves in what Hoover describes as "periods of centuries when the world slumped back toward darkness merely because great masses of men became impregnated with wrong ideas and wrong social philosophies."[78]

There are some great ironies in Hoover's personal story, with his book being written several years before he took office as the 31st president of the United States. One is that he came into office (1929-1933) right before the Great Depression. The stock market crashed soon after he took office. So many of those inequalities that he mentioned, resulting from the progress which comes with American individualism and its dominant economic/political/social systems, occurred on a grand scale as soon as he took office. Of course, the underlying themes here and possible lessons can be directly seen almost a century later today with our present crisis of a pandemic and large amounts of economic and social inequality.

Our preparation for, and immediate response to the pandemic was fairly poor, to say the least, and we saw many of those inequalities- racial, income, etc.- illustrated with sheer force. Just like the immediate response to the Great Depression became the central issue of Hoover's presidency, there is no denying that the initial response to Covid-19 will soon become the central issue to President Trump's legacy in office. And of course, President Biden's response to Covid upon taking office isn't the same as FDR's response to The Great Depression, but there are similarities in their effective responses. Hoover pursued a variety of policies in an attempt to lift the economy, with a focus on strengthening businesses such as banks and railroads. But he opposed directly involving the federal government in relief efforts, arguing that local and state governments plus private giving should address the needs of individuals. Democratic President Franklin D. Roosevelt decisively defeated Hoover after one term, right amid the economic crisis.[79]

I find it interesting that just years before the great depression, Hoover talked in his book about American Individualism, the need to address the social and economic inequalities that naturally arise from our culture of individualism. He was directly responsible for making sure the country could find its way out of the great depression yet opposed directly involving the federal government in relief efforts. Relief efforts were needed more than ever at the time. It's as if he talked the talk but wasn't willing to walk the walk. This is why it should be no surprise that he was defeated by FDR in the 1932 presidential election. Americans wished to take a chance on a President who may improve their lives.

Most humans are generally risk-averse, but if you have experienced a large degree of suffering already, you can see the appeal of a candidate who makes promises about lifting you out of despair... After leaving office, Hoover became increasingly conservative, strongly criticized Roosevelt's foreign policy and domestic agenda such as the New Deal. Not dissimilar from our last President's words about President Biden and his agenda. Hoover served in a couple more administrations and was able to rehabilitate some of his legacy, but in the end, most polls rank him an inadequate president and ranked somewhere in the bottom third overall.

We have already discussed many of the economic figures and statistics which show high levels of inequality between people and how an overall lack of respect for American workers' time has led to negative economic consequences. But American individualism also impacts our opportunity within and away from our communities. Chasing opportunity goes hand in hand with the amount of mobility that American workers have, also impacting family ties and geographic location. We tend to think many Americans, if not most, live far away from their family because as young adults we move away from home for career opportunities, yet in reality, many Americans aren't living that far from home or at least far from their family.

The typical adult today lives only 18 miles from his or her mother, according to a recent analysis. "Over the last few decades, Americans have become less mobile, and most adults – especially those with less education or lower incomes — do not venture far from their hometowns."[80] The explanation for these distances is in part cultural (Western families have historically been the least rooted), part geographical (rural communities, families tend to live farther apart), part career implications, part increase in households with two income-earners, and part overall levels of income. It is great for many Americans to have a safety net that includes their family, but with baby boomers aging, women making up a larger share of the workforce, and couples having fewer children, the safety net will become increasingly strained.[79]

Our concept of individualism often gives us the impression that we should be willing to leave home or our family to be closer to opportunity and follow our career path, and that may or may not be the right decision depending on the individual. It's important to keep in mind the implications of increased mobility for individual workers. Mobility creates the opportunity for many individuals, but sometimes at the expense of our families and communities- with workers being forced to leave their communities and their roots for opportunities and jobs which tend to be concentrated in cities. If we provide more opportunity close to home and spread opportunity throughout as many communities as possible, then workers will feel less inclined to leave their home for a better life- which isn't inherently bad, just something to think about. Distance isn't the only factor. Most Americans still live in the town or city they grew up in.

"The U.S. Census Bureau reported that the percentage of Americans moving over a one-year period fell to a new low in 2016; only 11.2% of the population had moved compared to the previous year."[81] A large percentage of Americans elect to stay close to where they grew up, despite that many move multiple times over the course of their life. The primary reasons for staying in the same city or area are to remain close to family (50%), familiarity and comfort (24%), low cost of living (13%), their job or career (9%), and the climate and environment (3%).[81] It's good to know that our level of individualism isn't such a driving force that it would cause most of us to live away from the places we grew up and our family; but at the same time, if more opportunities were provided and enable everyone to move where they wanted, these figures could change.

We can also look at the number of extended family households in the U.S., which have been on the rise in recent years. "About 16 percent of the U.S. population now live in multi-generational households, up from 12.1 percent in 1980, according to the Pew Research Center's Social and Demographic Trends project." Two adult generations or a grandparent and at least one other generation make up a multi-generational household. The trend towards more extended family households is actually a reversal of American living after WWII. After the war, the extended family largely fell out of favor with the American public. A quarter of the population lived this way in 1940, whereas only 12 percent did by 1980. After bottoming out in 1980, the multi-generational household rebounded to a record 49 million Americans in 2008 due to several economic and social factors. "Between 2007 and 2008, the most recent year for which data is available, the number of Americans living with their extended family grew by 2.6 million."[82]

This is much in part due to high unemployment and rising foreclosures, which is also something we have seen an increase in with Covid- so I would expect to see a spike in multigenerational households these next few years as well. American individualism isn't the sole cultural phenomenon responsible for living arrangements, but it does play a large role in our response to a lack of opportunity for many Americans. Instead of having a culture of work where it is perfectly acceptable for someone to move across the country away from their family, we can actually spread the opportunity for work, life, and well-being across the country more deliberately. Doing so could lead to a situation where mobility was less of a necessity and more of a choice for American workers (and their families).

How does American individualism stack up against other countries and their cultures? Measured by cross-cultural psychologists are the differences and similarities between individualistic cultures and collectivist cultures. Individualistic cultures similar to that of the U.S. include generalized geographic cultures found in Anglo countries, Germanic Europe, and Nordic Europe. Of course, these nations have a different history and reason behind their cultural norms, but in general, they tend to maintain the importance of the individual and individual achievement.[83]

A collectivist culture on the other hand stresses the importance of the group and social cooperation. This type of culture is often seen in generalized geographic cultures found in Arab countries, Latin America, Confucian Asia, Southern Asia, and Sub-Saharan Africa. You would think that where our individualistic nature fails, the collectivist culture succeeds and vice versa. That may be true to an extent, but it's not as simple as that. Both types of cultures provide advantages and disadvantages depending on context. The point here is that we have the culture we have, and if we wish to make inroads in the way we work, we should take the appropriate lessons from both individualistic and collectivist cultures to heart.[83]

It's of utmost importance that we make these changes to our culture soon too because much of the strife we find ourselves in today is because of this prioritization of the individual at the expense of the collective purpose and well-being of our nation. Anthropologist and author Wade Davis talks in great detail about this issue, in light of the recent pandemic.

> *The American cult of the individual denies not just community but the very idea of society. No one owes anything to anyone. All must be prepared to fight for everything: education, shelter, food, medical care. What every prosperous and successful democracy deems to be fundamental rights — universal health care, equal access to quality public education, a social safety net for the weak, elderly, and infirmed — America dismisses as socialist indulgences, as if so many signs of weakness. How can the rest of the world expect America to lead on global threats — climate change, the extinction crisis, pandemics — when the country no longer has a sense of benign purpose, or collective well-being, even within its own national community?*[84]

Davis also talks about how we got here, including our history of globalization and over-emphasis on international endeavors. Globalization provided purpose for American workers for quite some time during WWII and post-war years. But that purpose has faded now with more demands here at home that need addressing. Instead, we prioritize our footprint in distant countries than we do our own people. Prioritizing our domestic needs like other countries would provide us with similar outcomes. Take Denmark for example, where the average worker is treated more respectfully, paid better, and rewarded with pension plans, life insurance, maternity leave, and six weeks of paid vacation a year. "All of these benefits only inspire Danes to work harder, with fully 80 percent of men and women aged 16 to 64 engaged in the labor force, a figure far higher than that of the United States."[84]

One final note that Davis states is a point about wealth and purpose that I heavily agree with. "The measure of wealth in a civilized nation is not the currency accumulated by the lucky few, but rather the strength and resonance of social relations and the bonds of reciprocity that connect all people in common purpose."[84] This common purpose is greatly missing in American culture- we continuously give into political ideology and the tribalism it propagates. We must replace this enemizing mindset with one of a focus on improving our collective quality of life. Our *individual* quality of life improves when we address the collective issues that presently degrade our common purpose.

Our nation's prioritization of the individual, which has in many ways led us to the difficulties and inequalities we found during Covid, should force us to look into which facets of American work culture play a role in this individualistic mindset. One of those facets is our country's relationship with and idealization of *success*. I am of the mind that our current relationship with success and working to be successful in America is in large part due to this sense of individuality and the American dream, which prescribes an ethic of working hard to achieve success- or at least what we perceive as success. I find this relationship with success in American culture and work-life as mostly unhealthy and worth highlighting.

Our Relationship with Success

In today's world of social media and the internet, we are constantly bombarded with advertisements, posts from friends and family, and exciting success stories. About what it means to make it. About who has made it and how they got there. What it takes to be *the best*. Success surrounds us everywhere. But unfortunately, our relationship with success in the U.S. is not an entirely healthy one. Social media has led to a massive amount of social comparison unlike any level before in history. Yet the research is clear that measuring our success in this way strips us of life satisfaction.[85]

With social media and the increased availability of this social comparison, there is a much greater tendency for many of us to experience the Fear Of Missing Out or FOMO. FOMO "refers to the feeling or perception that others are having more fun, living better lives, or experiencing better things than you are."[86] FOMO naturally involves a deep sense of envy, thus affecting self-esteem. Not only is FOMO increasingly common, but it can also increase stress in your life if left unaddressed. Social comparison can be useful, but when you're constantly comparing your own life to other people's highlights, that's not healthy. Don't let your sense of normal be skewed and if you feel this way, it may be worth it to give social media a break.

Success has pervaded our way of life to the point where many of us are willing to sacrifice our personal health in exchange for some goal or a specific outcome that we and likely society views as *successful*. "In the 1980s, the physician Robert Goldman famously found that more than half of aspiring athletes would be willing to take a drug that would kill them in five years in exchange for winning every competition they entered today, 'from the Olympic decathlon to the Mr. Universe.'" To make it worse, later research found that up to 14 percent of elite performers were willing to accept a fatal cardiovascular condition in exchange for an Olympic gold medal.[75]

Unfortunately, success is something that can never truly be satisfied. Most of us never feel "successful enough." Success provides a short-term high that lasts a day or two, and then we move on to our next goal. After achieving success, the satisfaction almost immediately wears off and we must move on to the next reward to avoid feeling behind in our goals. Psychologists refer to this phenomenon as the *hedonic treadmill*. This treadmill is "why so many studies show that successful people are almost invariably jealous of people who are *more* successful."[75]

An unfortunate result of this success drive and its insatiable feeling is that it can lead many elite athletes to depression and anxiety after their careers end. Olympic athletes are known to suffer from *post-Olympic blues*. HBO recently aired a documentary "The Weight of Gold," which shines a light on the lack of holistic and mental support Olympic athletes receive during their time competing. It also exposes the notion that the success which comes from being the best of the best and a high performer- isn't without its costs. Every year there are more suicides from former Olympians which is awful and very troubling. From Director Brett Rapkin: "The metaphor I like to use is when it comes to the spectrum of sports performance, we think the top is hitting a grand slam to win the game and the bottom is striking out, when in fact the actual bottom is not wanting to be alive."[87]

These same states can occur for anyone who was in the limelight or achieved great success for some time and then stepped back from it all, either of their own volition or not. It isn't just athletes who are willing to go that far to succeed, this mindset applies to all of us to some degree. Our obsession with success in ourselves and others can become so extreme that we forget about our wellbeing and the wellbeing of those we view as most successful, those who "made it" if you will. We need to take a good hard look at what we truly value in life. A good analogy to our response to success is that many of us continue to watch football and support it, even though we know it damages football players' brains over time, causing them possibly severe physical and mental health issues after their career. *I mean what would we do without football?* Some may ask. I'm not interested in what we would do without it, I'm interested in the connection between our obsession with success and performance and our current culture of success in the way we view our own lives in the context of work. *Work hard until you make it* and *Practice hard until you win* really aren't that different. But what does "making it" or winning really mean? What should it mean? If it means a culture where we are too afraid to reach out for help because we think that's a sign of weakness, or if it leads to a culture where we only value the successful at the expense of the perceived unsuccessful, then I want nothing to do with that.

Success culture doesn't just stop there either. We see it in our corporations and government too. We idealize CEOs and politicians under this *hero* guise. It's this culture of heroism, where the really smart and adept CEO will come in and save the company from disaster. This culture leaves many of us perfectly fine with paying them millions or billions in compensation as if the smartest kids at Harvard or somewhere else couldn't do the same job for a tenth of the pay. We look at how our economy has floundered under the current presidential administration and instead of fixing the underlying political and economic systems which lead to these negative outcomes, we tend to champion whichever politician falls on *our* side of the political aisle as if they will fix everything. When in reality it's often just a game of reversal where one administration or member of Congress reverses all of the previous leaders' policies.

Our company's and democracy don't need heroes, they need sound, structural solutions. Our hero culture is a byproduct of our relationship with success, and it is both unhealthy and unsustainable. It's unhealthy and unsustainable for us as individuals and within our work culture. We need a change in culture and a different approach to success. Instead of viewing success as this crazy phenomenon only achievable by a select few talented individuals, we should view it as something that can be achieved by all of us, because we all should have our *own* definition of success- not success based on what *other* people have achieved.

Not to mention that many of us, including famous athletes and celebrities, feel that the success we have achieved is not good enough and that we don't belong. Even when we've "made it"' according to society's expectations and the expectations of those around us, we often feel imposter syndrome. From the American Psychological Association on imposter syndrome:

> *First described by psychologists Suzanne Imes, Ph.D., and Pauline Rose Clance, Ph.D., in the 1970s, impostor phenomenon occurs among high achievers who are unable to internalize and accept their success. They often attribute their accomplishments to luck rather than to ability and fear that others will eventually unmask them as a fraud. Though the impostor phenomenon isn't an official diagnosis listed in the DSM, psychologists and others acknowledge that it is a very real and specific form of intellectual self-doubt. Impostor feelings are generally accompanied by anxiety and, often, depression.*[88]

By definition, most people with imposter feelings suffer in silence and don't talk about it for fear of being "found out." The experience is not uncommon and with effort, you can stop feeling like a fraud and learn to enjoy your accomplishments. A few ways you can do that is to talk to your mentors, recognize your experience, remember what you do well, realize no one is perfect, change your thinking, and talk to someone who can help.[88]

In the end, it is important to choose the right metric(s) of success. If "you are what you measure", and you're measuring your life or your career through money, power, and prestige, then you'll end up stuck on the hedonic treadmill, comparing yourself to others. It's better to measure your success on more healthy, purposeful, and meaningful metrics. This very well may mean moving away from the traditional work structure as well, which places a heavy focus on the American dream and individualism. Or maybe even drop success from your vocabulary altogether. Live a life worth living according to your personal values and purpose, not a life based on success- much of which is subjective and moment to moment anyways.

"Unhappy is he who depends on success to be happy," wrote Alex Dias Ribeiro, a former Formula 1 race-car driver. "For such a person, the end of a successful career is the end of the line. His destiny is to die of bitterness or to search for more success in other careers and to go on living from success to success until he falls dead. In this case, there will not be life after success." Everyone from your average person to your professional athlete experiences the hidden and often accepted costs to living "the American dream", living your life according to an individualistic lifestyle, and having an unhealthy relationship with success.[75]

The True Cost of the American Work Ethic, Individualism, and Success

When you look at how we experience work, we can easily see the costs of this lifestyle. Our system of work has at least in part, led to greater amounts of loneliness, depression, and anxiety. As mentioned earlier, the main sources of stress for Americans were "the future of our nation" (63%), followed by money (62%) and work (61%).[2] But stress isn't the only problem. Loneliness is a problem for many Americans right now, and it has been on the rise over the past few decades. Increased loneliness correlates with early mortality, risk rates similar to those for obesity, and smoking 15 cigarettes a day. Not to mention other adverse health risks and a link to mental health issues such as anxiety and depression. Some of this loneliness has to do with the way we work. We spend most of our hours at work and if we have no meaningful connections at work or the work itself isn't' meaningful, what does that do to us long term?[89]

Cigna conducted a report on loneliness, finding a nearly 13% rise in loneliness between 2018 and 2019. The report surveyed over 10,000 adult workers in July and August 2019, relying on a measure of loneliness called the UCLA Loneliness Scale, used as a standard within psychology research. Rates of loneliness were different between men (63%) and women (58%), social media use played a role with 73% of heavy users considered lonely compared to 52% of light users. And there is also a generational gap, with Gen Z reporting higher levels (50%) and boomers the least (around 43%). "This new research dives deeper into the factors behind these feelings of isolation than the previous report, and it found that conditions in the workplace made a difference in how lonely people felt."[90] According to Cigna, the following workplace scenarios led to less loneliness:

- *Good co-worker relationships*
- *Good work-life balance*
- *Shared goals among colleagues*
- *Being a new employee, not having held your position for long*
- *Having a close friend at work*[90]

Employers have an incentive to address loneliness, as lonely workers are more likely to miss work due to illness or stress, and many of these employees feel like their work isn't up to par.

The survey conducted by Cigna found that "more than three-quarters of survey respondents had close relationships that bring them emotional security and well-being."[90] This made them less lonely compared to those without. You can see why it is important to have close relationships at work, not just outside of work. The source of loneliness doesn't come from just one place, but our work plays a significant role in its occurrence.

Related to loneliness is depression, which is a mental illness associated with higher rates of disability and unemployment. Depression directly interferes with our ability to work and be productive day-to-day. According to the CDC, "depression interferes with a person's ability to complete physical job tasks about 20% of the time and reduces cognitive performance about 35% of the time."[91] Much of this depression goes left unaddressed too. "Only 57% of employees who report moderate depression and 40% of those who report severe depression receive treatment to control depression symptoms."[91] By the end of a three-year assessment of workers by the CDC, employees at high risk of depression have the highest healthcare costs, even after taking into account other health risks such as smoking and obesity.

And the thing is, you don't need to be depressed daily to have similar symptoms and a similar feeling. A mild, chronic cousin of depression is this other long-term feeling called Dysthymia. The symptoms of which are low energy, low mood, loss of interest, and general anhedonia (loss of pleasure). This condition "can last years and often goes undiagnosed because life still goes on, although it feels like the colors are muted."[92]

There are many solutions to addressing loneliness, depression, and anxiety for workers, which can include employers promoting a work culture of health and wellbeing and initiating workplace wellness programs. Not to mention the many solutions available to individuals on a personal level such as seeking out and receiving professional help or doing your best to live a healthy lifestyle. But what we need most is to not simply address the symptoms, instead, we must tackle the issues at their source. Doing so will require changes to our over-all work culture, the way we work, and changes to what and who we prioritize in our society.

What we are seeing now in our culture is the next level after we've accepted the mantra of individual hard work and American success. That next level is acceptance. Acceptance that not all of us can be LeBron James. That not all of us will reach that level of success that society expects from us. That when it comes to your work and your career that there's no point even trying to follow your dreams. That *existing* is the same as *living*. Many of us today are living day to day with this idea that where we're at now, who we are now, and what our career is now will just be what it is and that's *good enough*. Because hard work is good enough. This mindset is pervasive in our communities today, and it's visible through our actions. We have drunk the Kool-Aid and are now passed out on the couch. Our current model of success concerning work is not sustainable and workers have been neglected for too long. We must change our relationship with success, shifting away from an approach to work where we simply *exist* to one where we are *living*. From this change, we can expect to see an increase in the well-being of American workers.

Chapter 8

A Meritnotcracy

Embedded deep into the American culture of hard work and the American dream, is this idea that we have a complete meritocracy in this country. A meritocracy is a system in which the talented are chosen and moved ahead based on their achievement.[93] Having a meritocratic work culture and workplace is important because it allows those who truly *work hard* and are *talented* to succeed and progress in the workplace. We talk a lot about the American dream and achieving success as if merit is the primary and only system that is responsible for our outcomes. The idea of meritocracy is embedded in both our systems of education and work.

The term was first coined by British sociologist, social activist, and politician Michael Young around 60 years ago. The term first appeared in Young's book *The Rise of the Meritocracy*, and the term was meant to employ a democracy that would be ruled by the cleverest, "not an aristocracy of birth, not a plutocracy of wealth, but a true meritocracy of talent."[94] Young, who has been called the greatest practical sociologist of the past century, viewed meritocracy as the type of system that would allow power and privilege to be allocated by individual merit, instead of social origins. He wanted to supplant the old caste-like system of social hierarchy that was very much present in Britain, so he "pioneered the modern scientific exploration of the social lives of the English working class," with the goal of studying class and further ameliorating the damage he believed it could do.[94]

What makes a meritocracy is *merit*, which was originally defined as *I.Q. plus Effort*. But "it has evolved to stand for a somewhat ineffable combination of cognitive abilities, extracurricular talents, and socially valuable personal qualities, like leadership and civic-mindedness."[95] We think that jobs should go to those most qualified individuals, not people with connections and pedigree. We occasionally allow for exceptions, such as positive discrimination, to undo effects from previous discrimination. These exceptions are meant to last until the bigotries of sex, race, class, and caste are gone.[94] Many of us today still think that we have rid ourselves of this class system and its inherited hierarchies. From the Young Foundation:

> He imagined a country in which "the eminent know that success is a just reward for their own capacity, their own efforts," and in which the lower orders know that they have failed every chance they were given. "They are tested again and again.... If they have been labeled 'dunce' repeatedly they cannot any longer pretend; their image of themselves is more nearly a true, unflattering reflection." But one immediate difficulty was that, as Young's narrator concedes, "nearly all parents are going to try to gain unfair advantages for their offspring." And when you have inequalities of income, one thing people can do with extra money is to pursue that goal. If the financial status of your parents helped determine your economic rewards, you would no longer be living by the formula that "I.Q. + effort = merit."[96]

Starting off, we should review meritocracy's role in our school system. That is where American workers find themselves before they start working, and it holds a larger impact on where workers end up than one might think.

K-12 is not personalized and is instead standardized as if we will each be proficient and interested in specific subject areas at specific points in our education. This lack of personalization prevents students from knowing or following their personal skills and interests. And what this ends up doing, is not only killing creativity as mentioned earlier, but it also prevents those students who would truly succeed in a given area from excelling and reaching their full potential. Education in America is not meritocratic when it should be for specific skills and interests. Talented students should be able to move ahead and conduct math or English at higher levels and with greater rigor.

Of course, we should make sure students have a basic understanding of necessary subject materials- but standardizing for that across the board at a certain point becomes unfair to students with their natural abilities, talents, and interests. It's not unfair to let students rise at what they are naturally talented at, skilled in, or interested in. In our schools, we begin educational sorting quite early, placing schoolchildren into "gifted and talented" programs, up into high school where we essentially determine that a student belongs on a vocational track or the standard college track. Sorting is something you do with paperwork, not students, yet we continuously support a system that treats the latter as the former.[95]

We also have expensive preschool programs and private schools in the U.S., which can only be afforded by those well off enough to afford this schooling and are concerned enough about their children's education to send them to the best schools (the roughly 34,000+ private schools in the U.S.).[97] A large problem with private universities is that public schools, and their occupants, actually do worse off as a result of many families pulling their students out of (or deciding against) public schools. When a public school is struggling with its finances, funding, teaching capabilities, education tools, and learning environment, the schools would benefit by having the families who send their kids to private schools *invest* their time and money into the public schools. When some parents have a large impact on whether or not their children and public schools, in general, perform well comparatively, then you have a *voice vs. choice* situation.

Families who are well off in the middle and upper class can afford to use the *choice* option when confronted with a potentially less-adequate public school for their kids, meaning they can usually choose to instead have their children receive a "better" education, one that is essentially "guaranteed." Or they can stay and use their *voice*, where they invest more of their time and money- which they tend to have more of compared to other parents at that public school- into the public schools themselves, building better education outcomes for those students. The point here is that we still have class issues in our school system which from the get-go set up our children for unequal chances in opportunity and success through and post-education. This is not a meritocratic system.

Furthermore, students from wealthier backgrounds are more likely to receive extra tutoring services throughout their K-12 education. As well as enough money to afford the expensive preparation material for the standardized tests (i.e., SAT, ACT) that students would benefit from and can determine their higher education opportunities. Opportunities for greater educational attainment and college opportunities are not only essential to students for their post-education lives, access or lack-there-of to these resources' compounds over time. Receiving extra assistance in your learning, or simply receiving the education all students deserve (the best) isn't included in the merit equation. All students have the potential for developing skills, maximizing their talent, and exerting great effort, yet that is not enough for many students to receive equal access to opportunities for growth, learning, and future career prospects. Still- unmeritocratic.

Without some meritocracy in K-12 education, this sets students up for even less success post-high school. Because if you received little to no skills, are unsure what you are interested in (or not interested in), and don't know which subject or field to apply your effort so by the time you reach college, you are less likely to achieve educational and work success immediately afterward and down the road. We know that K-12 is unmeritocratic and that sets up many students for failure or less opportunity straight out the gate with higher education. But it also holds that higher ed is unmeritocratic too. Of course, this starts with which higher ed institutions students can even get into. When high school students approach junior and senior year, they are again being sorted by the system through standardized tests like the SAT and ACT.

These two standardized tests have been used nationally in college admissions since the fifties, constantly trying to win over greater market share. To take one of the tests as an example, "the SAT was originally designed as an I.Q. test, based on the idea that people are born with a certain quantum of smarts (g, as psychologists used to call it). The purpose of the SAT was not to expand the college population. It was just to make sure that innately bright people got to go. A lot of the debate over the SAT, therefore, has had to do with whether there truly is such a thing as g, whether it can be measured by a multiple-choice test, whether smarts in the brute I.Q. sense is what we mean by "merit," and whether the tests contain cultural biases that cause some groups to underperform."[95]

The real problem with the SAT though is much simpler: SAT scores are not good at predicting college grades, whereas high-school grades (for American applicants) are good at predicting them. So then why are universities focusing largely on these standardized test scores, placing a lot of weight on them? As mentioned earlier, not every student can afford to properly prepare for these highly stressful tests, which over the years has cost many millions of dollars for families. In other words, it costs a lot to administer a standardized test that isn't as predictive of success as high-school grades are- which costs the applicant nothing. Thus, I think it's in our best interest to toss out the SAT and ACT standardized tests altogether. We can certainly have tests for individual skills and subjects to measure education attainment and growth, but the SATs and ACTs create even more inopportunity than they provide.[95]

We must provide equal opportunity to each student in their pursuit of higher ed because we know that receiving a college degree is worth it. Almost every study concludes that a college degree is worth it and leads to greater earnings upon entering the workforce. "What is known as the college wage premium—the difference in lifetime earnings between someone with only a high-school diploma and someone with a college degree—is now, by one calculation, a hundred and sixty-eight percent." Advanced degree holders have a wage premium of two hundred and thirteen percent. The situation is also one in which the more people who get a college degree, the greater the penalty for not having one (roughly a third of the population has a bachelor's degree).[95]

So, the question isn't whether a college degree is worth it, the question should be what role does merit play in our students' success getting into and making it through college? As well as what conditions need to be created to provide equal opportunity for students?

When we look at the lack of merit able to be utilized by students in their pursuit of good higher education, we can immediately see that the unequal opportunities have the potential to compound over time. Thus, education finds itself at the intersection of several problems, including social mobility and income inequality. In the nineteen-fifties and sixties,

Americans didn't have to go to college to enjoy a middle-class standard of living, as the wage premium was small or nonexistent.[94] Also, the income of Americans with degrees was not exorbitantly greater than the income of the average worker. The economy started to change around the 80s though, with a hollowing out of the middle class, and the less-advantaged members taking service jobs that reduced their relative income even more. "The help-wanted ads are full of listings for executives and for dishwashers—but not much in between," Walter Mondale said at the 1984 Democratic National Convention.[95]

The situation has only grown worse since then, with thirty-nine percent of American adults identifying as either lower class or working class. The number of Americans identifying as lower class or working class has gone up over the past few decades, while the number of Americans identifying as middle class has gone down. In the U.S., the top fifth of households enjoyed a $4tn increase in pretax income between 1979 and 2013 – $1tn more than came to all the rest. These numbers hint at both a shrinking middle class and greater amounts of income inequality.[94]

Income inequality could be managed if more Americans had increased social mobility and were supported by an education system that distributed opportunities equally- unlike our current "meritocracy." One example of higher ed increasing social mobility for less-privileged Americans is the role that universities play in selecting students and where those students end up. Elite universities like Stanford and Princeton aren't necessarily looking for future hedge-fund managers when they put together a class. It's the businesses that recruit from those colleges which have obsessed over the Ivy Plus credential. If we truly want different kinds of people to get those jobs, we should ask those firms to take more of their new employees from the bottom quintiles.[95] Doing so would lead to greater equality in career opportunities, and thus greater social mobility for them. Degrees in general should be nice add-ons that help job seekers or those looking to progress in their career, a leg-up. But right now, they act as a leg up- and over- the people without degrees or degrees from non-elite universities. "American meritocracy," the Yale law professor Daniel Markovits argues, has "become precisely what it was invented to combat: a mechanism for the dynastic transmission of wealth and privilege across generations."[94]

Before Young passed away in 2002 at the age of 86, he saw what was happening. "Education has put its seal of approval on a minority," he wrote, "and its seal of disapproval on the many who fail to shine from the time they are relegated to the bottom streams at the age of seven or before."[94] I share Young's concern, but I also want people to know that this issue isn't one where *the elite* are purposefully trying to make life worse for everyone else. I don't think the elite are placing their kids and their families into meritocratic systems which most benefit them for the sole purpose of being exclusionary. It's just that the elite happen to benefit most from the meritocratic inequalities which exist and are simply taking advantage of the system, doing what most humans do on important issues- lookout for their own (and their families) self-interests.

Parents don't choose to send their kids to private schools over public schools or give them the connections they need in higher ed in spite of public schools or non-elite universities. Instead, I think these parents, like most of society, are simply fearful of the unknown. You don't know how your child will fare if they attend a public university with fewer resources, less attention dedicated to them in school, and potentially worse test grades. You don't know how your child will fare by attending a less-known university. When you couple this fear of the unknown with people seeking out their (and their childrens) personal interests (as we like to do), you have a situation where public schools and non-elite universities are bound to be continuously neglected over time by those who have the time, money, and resources to invest in them.

But the problem isn't just class-based issues or education's connection with the economy, it's broader than that. Income inequality would still exist, even with changes to the meritocratic sorting which happens between higher ed and the American workforce. An economy without meritocratic structures would still include sorting and only a fraction of individuals will continue to get those CEO jobs. With greater social mobility you could see a larger share of these positions and opportunities given to people from disadvantaged backgrounds, but even though the faces change, income inequality would still largely persist. "The problem is not that some citizens are lawyers and some work in Amazon fulfillment centers. It's that the economy is structured to allow the former class of worker to soak up most of the national wealth."[95]

It's easy to call out the elite as if they are the ones responsible for these inequalities from a flawed meritocratic system. It's easy to blame large elite universities as corrupt and tainting the very ideal around education for which they stand for. It's easy to call out Jeff Bezos and rich CEOs as perpetuating income inequality or any inequality for that matter which partially derives from what we consider a meritocratic system. But it's the system itself- the way our economy is structured- that holds most of the blame. The problem is not that meritocracy isn't working *properly*, it's just that it wasn't the right approach in the first place.

Others have written about which of these answers is correct, such as Paul Tough who wrote *The Years That Matter Most: How College Makes or Breaks Us* (Houghton Mifflin Harcourt), and thinks that the problem is a broken system. Daniel Markovits, in *The Meritocracy Trap* (Penguin Press), thinks that the whole idea was a terrible mistake. I agree with Markovits that the whole idea is a terrible mistake, but I don't agree with him on everything. If a lack of a real meritocracy leads to vastly different opportunities in our education, careers, and life- and we have a system where the inequalities or gaps between groups are so great, merit-driven systems should only be one part of the whole in which opportunity and success are rewarded. We should evaluate what true equal opportunity looks like and how to best create an environment in which talent, skills, and interests are all afforded their best chance at excelling. The entire idea of meritocracy in its present context places too much emphasis on the individual and plays right into the notion of the American dream and working hard- a culture where we are okay with sacrificing our personal well-being and time, in addition to the well-being of our communities.[95]

Our American ideals around our strong work ethic, individualism, and success are in many ways responsible for meritocracy's shortfalls. We tell students and young professionals entering the workforce that they can succeed, get ahead, and make a good living as long as they demonstrate merit in their endeavors. We believe strongly in an American work ethic where your abilities and effort can propel you forward, but that's not always the reality. I agree that the benefits of an individualistic work culture can be useful, but success at work isn't solely determined by our individual work ethic.

There are other factors at play that prevent a true meritocracy from taking place. Our country, compared to others, is particularly enthusiastic about the idea of meritocracy. We are more likely to believe that people are rewarded for their intelligence and skills, but less likely to believe that family wealth plays a role in getting ahead. Also, despite the previously mentioned growing economic inequality, recessions, and the lack of mobility within the U.S. compared to other industrialized countries, Americans' support for meritocratic principles has remained stable.[98]

The inequalities between classes have deepened not just in the numbers, but also in divisiveness in recent years. Through this divisiveness, many Americans are still holding onto this idea of meritocracy. Many still believe that the US mostly is and certainly should be a society in which opportunities belong to those who have earned them. This idea that opportunities belong to those who have earned them plays right into the previously mentioned idea of American individualism and the American ethic of *hard work* underscores the American dream. A large portion of the U.S. population still has this mindset that opportunities can come to those who manifest them through sheer effort- that America is a *true* meritocracy. As we can see with the large number of inequalities that exist, plus the lack of social mobility, that we do not have a meritocratic system.

It is hard for many Americans to let go of this American work ethic, which consists of a largely meritocratic ideal, because if we don't live in a true meritocracy how can they make progress? How can they find and take advantage of those opportunities which we know are difficult to achieve but worth the effort? If my outlook on work and life is heavily based on a value system of meritocracy and hard work, while I simultaneously am suffering the many inequalities which derive from our current political and economic systems, then I have two options. I can admit that the inequalities are a problem because of our flawed idea of work and opportunity, and then push back against my own values which I was raised. *Or* I can embrace those values and find another cause for those inequalities. More on Young from The Guardian:

> *Young believed, the problem was not just with how the prizes of social life were distributed; it was with the prizes themselves. A system of class filtered by meritocracy would, in his view, still be a system of class: it would*

involve a hierarchy of social respect, granting dignity to those at the top, but denying respect and self-respect to those who did not inherit the talents and the capacity for effort that, combined with proper education, would give them access to the most highly remunerated occupations.[94]

I completely agree with this premise, that the problem isn't that we aren't meritocratic enough, it is that meritocracy and the rewards which it endows are wrong in themselves. Are those who are not smart enough or who do not place enough "effort" (whatever we define that as) in their work, destined for failure? Destined to be left behind? Destined to a sense of indignity and no self-respect? And destined to be void of opportunities in life and work? They shouldn't be. What I am trying to get across in this book is that people are valuable in and of themselves. Our entire idea of an American dream, thinking that we live in a true meritocracy, this idea that hard work and talent will always prevail, fly's right in the face of an equitable and just society. These misplaced and outdated ideals go against what work *should* be: a system where everyone in society is valued because they are human, where we take care of each other as a collective, and where we create an environment in which everyone can follow their purpose in life without being told how "unrealistic" that is, or how "hard work and talent" are the only paths to our flawed ideal of success.

Young shared "this alternative vision, in which each of us takes our allotment of talents and pursues a distinctive set of achievements and the self-respect they bring", and he did so with a profound commitment to social equality.[94] This ideal seems quixotic, yet it demands of us a philosophical picture.

The central task of ethics is to ask what it is for a human life to go well. A plausible answer is that living well means meeting the challenge set by three things: your capacities, the circumstances into which you were born, and the projects that you yourself decide are important. Because each of us comes equipped with different talents and is born into different circumstances, and because people choose their own projects, each of us faces his or her own challenge. There is no comparative measure that would enable an assessment of whether your life or my life is better; Young was right to protest the idea that "people could be put into rank order of worth." What matters in the end is not how we rank against others. We do not need to find something that we do better than anyone else; what matters is simply that we do our best.[94]

A meritocracy confuses two different concerns: a matter of efficiency and the question of human worth.

The capacity for hard work is itself the result of natural endowments and upbringing. So, neither talent nor effort, the two things that would determine rewards in the world of the meritocracy, is itself something earned. People who have, as The Rise of the Meritocracy bluntly put it, been repeatedly "labeled 'dunce'" still have capacities and the challenge of making a meaningful life. The lives of the less successful are not less worthy than those of others, but not because they are as worthy or more worthy. There is simply no sensible way of comparing the worth of human lives.[94]

Meritocracy in the Workplace

In a false meritocracy, workers are often neglected and left out of opportunities for achievement and success. Our "strong commitment to meritocratic ideals can lead to suspicion of

efforts that aim to support particular demographic groups."[98]
There are many initiatives designed to recruit or provide development opportunities to under-represented groups, which
often come under attack as "reverse discrimination." On the
flip side, some companies justify a lack of diversity policies by
highlighting their commitment to meritocracy. "If a company
evaluates people on their skills, abilities, and merit, without
consideration of their gender, race, sexuality, etc., and managers are objective in their assessments then there is no need
for diversity policies, the thinking goes."[98]

The problem is that commitments to meritocracy and ob-
jectivity do not actually lead to more fair workplaces.[99] Emilio
J. Castilla, a professor at MIT's Sloan School of Management,
has explored how meritocratic ideals and HR practices like
pay-for-performance play out in organizations. One study involved examining 9,000 employees who worked for a large service-sector company, a company committed to diversity, and
included merit within their compensation program. High-level
performance would be rewarded, and rewards would be offered
equitably according to their compensation system. Castilla's
analysis revealed non-meritocratic outcomes though. He
found that women, ethnic minorities, and non-U.S.-born employees received smaller increases in compensation compared
with white men, despite having the same: jobs, work units, supervisors, human capital, and performance score. This company stated that "performance is the primary basis for all
salary increases," yet women, minorities, and workers born
outside the U.S. needed "to work harder and obtain higher performance scores in order to receive similar salary increases to
white men."[98]

Organizational culture and practice that promote meritocracy may actually accomplish the opposite of what these organizations set out for, at least that was what Castilla wanted
to find out- if the pursuit of meritocracy could actually trigger

bias. With his colleague, Indiana University sociology professor Stephen Bernard, they designed several lab experiments to find out. Each experiment came to the same conclusion, that "when a company's core values emphasized meritocratic values, those in managerial positions awarded a larger monetary reward to the male employee than to an equally performing female employee."[98] Something Castilla and Bernard termed, "the paradox of meritocracy". More from the Atlantic:

> The paradox of meritocracy builds on other research showing that those who think they are the most objective can actually exhibit the most bias in their evaluations. When people think they are objective and unbiased then they don't monitor and scrutinize their own behavior. They just assume that they are right and that their assessments are accurate. Yet, studies repeatedly show that stereotypes of all kinds (gender, ethnicity, age, disability, etc.) are filters through which we evaluate others, often in ways that advantage dominant groups and disadvantage lower-status groups.
>
> For example, studies repeatedly find that the resumes of whites and men are evaluated more positively than are the identical resumes of minorities and women. This dynamic is precisely why meritocracy can exacerbate inequality—because being committed to meritocratic principles makes people think that they actually are making correct evaluations and behaving fairly. Organizations that emphasize meritocratic ideals serve to reinforce an employee's belief that they are impartial, which creates the exact conditions under which implicit and explicit biases are unleashed.[98]

Castilla's research provides "a cautionary lesson that practices implemented to increase fairness and equity need to be carefully thought through so that potential opportunities for bias are addressed."[98]

Further evidence of gender bias can be seen in a 2012 study by the National Academy of Sciences, where researchers sent identical resumes (laboratory manager job) to over 125 hiring managers at U.S. universities. Half of the resumes had a female name and the other half had a male moniker. Hiring managers, professors of both genders, were asked to rate the candidates and the results were troubling. "Both male and female evaluators ranked resumes with women's names as belonging to people lower in competence, employability, and appeal as potential mentees." Even the salaries offered to the candidates were lower, with women who landed this job offered more than $3,500 less in salary than those offered to males. It appears that unconscious bias is impacting the evaluator's decisions, and of course, this will not happen in every organizations hiring process, but it's troubling enough to warrant a deeper examination of bias on gender bias in the workplace.[99] One study that looked into this suggests mitigating these negative effects by "promoting less managerial discretion, more accountability, and transparency in the workplace."[100]

Our workplaces according to our current meritocratic system, contribute to the accumulation of social inequality. Unfortunately, "initial differences in opportunities and rewards shape performance and/or subsequent opportunities and rewards, such that those who receive more initial opportunities and rewards tend to receive even more over time."[101] Opportunities and rewards, such as what was mentioned earlier in education, compound over time up until students prepare for the workforce and then again as workers. Workplaces can contribute to the accumulation of social inequality. One study used a cumulative social inequality in workplaces (CSI-W) model which indicated that specific "mechanisms interact, such that the social inequality dynamics in workplaces tend to

(a) exacerbate social inequalities over time, (b) legitimate social inequalities over time, and (c) manifest themselves through everyday occurrences and behaviors."[101]

The fact is that even when focusing on merit in the workplace, hidden biases, subtle prejudices, and structural discrimination (e.g., the compounding of unequal opportunities from the beginning of life) all prevent workers from participating in a true meritocracy. One company rebuttal these issues by utilizing a skills-based approach to identify the highest-performing talent through the practice of having hiring managers hold blind auditions for new job applicants. GapJumper, a Silicon Valley startup uses this method and has "about 60 percent of the top talent identified through GapJumpers' blind audition process, [which] come from underrepresented backgrounds... Blind performance auditions are a powerful tool to manage bias and address the pervasive and incorrect assumption that elite pedigree best predicts performance of on-the-job skills."[98]

Meritocratic outcomes can also be achieved through greater transparency and accountability. Following Castilla's study mentioned earlier, that same company asked him to recommend practices that would close the pay gap. Castilla counseled the company on actions they could take, drawing on research that shows transparency and accountability can reduce bias. The company took the advice and made several changes, including the creation of a performance-reward committee to monitor increases in compensation and sharing information with top management about pay. By making these changes to reduce bias in gender, race, and foreign nationality, the company largely reduced its demographic pay gap, according to Castilla's analysis, five years later.[98] The Society for Human Resource Management has some recommendations in addressing these issues around biases and promoting equality in the workplace that follow a similar vein:

- *focus on behavior change, not culture change.*
- *Be transparent about pay. (This is especially important as jurisdictions around the country adopt gender equity laws)*
- *Provide non-threatening training and education to surface and address implicit biases.*
- *Educate stakeholders on how structural bias affects corporate bias.*
- *Enlist allies to support women and minorities at work.[99]*

The U.S. is hardly the only state to abide by meritocratic ideals and claim meritocratic principles, at least in part. Most of the largest economies in the world, such as the United States, China, Japan, Germany, and the United Kingdom, all purport to have a meritocratic education and/or work system. Yet they all relate to the U.S. in having disparities based on socioeconomic status and access to opportunities. "Historical forms of discrimination may differ by country, but the outcomes are the same."[99]

There is no such thing as a true meritocracy, and I am confident that we should not try and create one. I think instead, we should provide the means by which people can apply their interests, talents, knowledge, and skills to whichever type of work they find purposeful and meaningful. There will only ever be a few astronauts, there are only so many slots on an NBA team roster, and there is only one position to be the President of the U.S. It is necessary to shift our focus towards creating the right *conditions* in which we can each maximize our potential for success. And doing so on our own terms, instead of being told as students or workers that we can be whatever we want under the guise of a merit-based system that ignores our realities of poorly distributed opportunity.

Furthermore, we know how to democratize opportunities for advancement in this country, we have done it before for specific issues, primarily during times of crisis. Unfortunately, the current state of politics in the U.S. makes it unlikely that this will be done in the near future, but it's certainly achievable over the next few years. Young envisaged a meritocratic utopia where inheritance holds little sway, but "his deeper point was that we also need to apply ourselves to something we do not yet quite know how to do: 'to eradicate contempt for those who are disfavored by the ethic of effortful competition.'"[96] This is especially difficult in the U.S. as our culture is heavily defined by effortful competition and the *work hard* mantra. This isn't to say that merit should have no place in this utopia.

"It is good sense to appoint individual people to jobs on their merit," Young wrote. "It is the opposite when those who are judged to have merit of a particular kind harden into a new social class without room in it for others."[94] The goal isn't to eradicate hierarchy, as there will always be better writers, faster runners, and so forth. We cannot fully control the distribution of capital in its relation to work and opportunity, but we can see through our individual experience to that of the collective and see the unequal distribution of opportunity based on class. "It remains an urgent collective endeavor to revise the ways we think about human worth in the service of moral equality."[95]

Chapter 9

National Well-being and The Growth Delusion

A problem with work today is based on the idea that capitalism is king, the free market will create the best and most equitable outcomes, and that we have a successful meritocracy. Those who work hard, make it. That's the American dream, right? Well, unfortunately, the American dream is not alive and well, at least not for everyone.

According to a study by Raj Chetty et al, only half of today's 30-year-olds earn more than their parents. "Rates of absolute mobility—that is, the share of children with higher inflation-adjusted incomes than their parents—declined from around 90 percent for children born in 1940 to just 50 percent for those born in 1984...The big drop in absolute mobility for those at the top of distribution occurs between the 1940 and 1950 birth cohorts." This was likely due to large economic growth in the post-war years. "Since then, the middle class has suffered greater losses of absolute mobility than those at the top or bottom."[102] If the American dream was alive and well, then the middle class would stand a much better chance at making more than their parents. Declining rates of absolute mobility are not the only concern.

Inequality plays a role too. Racial inequality is so pervasive that even successful black CEOs are uncommon, and not just by a little. The number of Black CEOs in Fortune 500 companies remains very low, at only 5 as of 2020. This is despite years of diversity programs and pledges by corporate America. That is only 1% of all Fortune 500 companies when African Americans represent 13.4% of the U.S. population.[103] The major theme about work in America has become less about a land of opportunity and more about a land of inequality. Most of the inequality derives from the structures we have set up for ourselves over the years- political, economic, and social. But for a country with such large growth in recent years, wouldn't we expect this dream to be alive and well? Wouldn't we expect our nation to be doing well? The problem is that we are measuring our nation's success based on economic success- and our economic success based on the wrong measure: GDP.

For over a half-century, Growth Domestic Product (GDP) has been a commonly used measure of economic condition by the U.S. and many other countries. A short history of the GDP:

> *GDP is an estimate of market throughput, adding together all final goods and services that are produced and traded for money within a given period of time. It is typically measured by adding together a nation's personal consumption expenditures (payments by households for goods and services), government expenditures (public spending on the provision of goods and services, infrastructure, debt payments, etc.), net exports (the value of a country's exports minus the value of imports), and net capital formation (the increase in value of a nation's total stock of monetized capital goods). Since its creation, economists who are familiar with GDP have emphasized that GDP is a measure of economic activity, not economic or social well-being.*

In the U.S., GDP is "one of the most comprehensive and closely watched economic statistics: It is used by the White House and Congress to prepare the Federal budget, by the Federal Reserve to formulate monetary policy, by Wall Street as an indicator of economic activity, and by the business community to prepare forecasts of economic performance that provide the basis for production, investment, and employment planning." Internationally, the IMF and the World Bank both use the changes in a country's GDP to guide policies and determine how and which projects are funded around the world.

The US Bureau of Economic Analysis' description of GDP states that the purpose of measuring GDP is to answer questions such as "how fast is the economy growing," "what is the pattern of spending on goods and services," "what percent of the increase in production is due to inflation," and "how much of the income produced is being used for consumption as opposed to investment or savings."[104]

Even with these specific uses for GDP clearly spelled out, the measure has been misused and continues to be misused as a scorecard for national well-being.

In 1937, an economist at the National Bureau of Economic Research by the name of Simon Kuznets, presents the original formulation of gross domestic product in his report to the U.S. Congress, *National Income, 1929-35*. His goal with this formulation is to capture all economic production by individuals, companies, and the government in a single measure, which should rise in good times and fall in bad. This measurement? The GDP.[105] It is important to understand that Kuznets, the chief architect of the US national accounting system and the GDP, cautioned in 1934, "against equating GDP growth with economic or social well-being."[104] Kuznets was concerned that the simplicity of GDP made it prone to misuse:

> *The valuable capacity of the human mind to simplify a complex situation in a compact characterization becomes dangerous when not controlled in terms of definitely stated criteria. With quantitative measurements especially, the definiteness of the result suggests, often misleadingly, a precision and simplicity in the outlines of the object measured. Measurements of national income are subject to this type of illusion and resulting abuse, especially since they deal with matters that are the center of conflict of opposing social groups where the effectiveness of an argument is often contingent upon oversimplification.*[104]

It truly started when the measure was used in dialogue and economic reasoning during the great depression and WWII. "President Roosevelt's government used the statistics to justify policies and budgets aimed at bringing the US out of the depression." It was becoming clear that the U.S. was going to get involved in World War II, which may jeopardize US citizens' standard of living, which wasn't ideal considering they were just starting to recover from the Great Depression. "GDP estimates were used to show that the economy could provide sufficient supplies for fighting WWII while maintaining adequate production of consumer goods and services." GDP as a measure of economic progress was further strengthened in 1944, during the Bretton Woods conference.[104]

Much of the lead-up to WWII involved economic instability in a number of countries due to unstable currency exchange rates and unfair trade practices that discouraged international trade. Thus, in order to avoid a recurrence, in 1944 leaders of the 44 allied nations held a meeting in Bretton Woods, New

Hampshire to create a process for international trade cooperation and currency exchange. The intent of the meeting was to "speed economic progress everywhere, aid political stability and foster peace." Increased and sustainable international trade would create many jobs in these countries, jobs which provided income and a greater standard of living among the allied nations. Growing the economy was a firm path towards improving economic well-being and creating lasting world peace.[104]

Two outcomes from the conference were the establishment of the international financial institutions: The International Monetary Fund (IMF) and the International Bank for Reconstruction and Development (IBRD—now part of the World Bank). The former was created to address issues around international monetary exchange, exchange rate stabilization for various currencies. The latter was established as a source of investment funds for reconstructing infrastructure and development for countries negatively impacted by the war or in need of development. Due to the political and economic strength garnered by the U.S. following WWII, the nation dominated the governing structures of these institutions for the first quarter-century, as opposed to the original intent of an equal voice provided to all member counties.[104]

Work done by the US and UK Treasuries with GDP methodologies and economic analysis informed much of the Bretton Woods discussion. As a result of this U.S. dominance in discussion, the US dollar and economic policies became the de facto standards against which other countries were compared. The IMF and World Bank ended up using the GDP as the primary measure of economic progress in the ensuing 60 years until the institutions were restructured in the 1970s. From then on, the US has held a less dominant position within the World Bank and IMF, yet GDP remains the most widely cited measure of economic progress.[104]

In 1962, "Arthur Okun, staff economist for U.S. President John F. Kennedy's Council of Economic Advisers, coined Okun's Law, which holds that for every 3-point rise in GDP, unemployment will fall 1 percentage point." This theory that everything will be just fine as long as we grow the economy informs monetary policy today. In 1978, "writing in Britain's *The Economic Journal*, Irving B. Kravis, Alan W. Heston, and Robert Summers compiled the first estimates of GDP per capita worldwide, with figures for more than 100 countries." Since, GDP per capita is often used to compare the *quality of life* in different countries. In 1999, the U.S. Commerce Department declared GDP "one of the great inventions of the 20th century."[105]

The GDP wasn't without its detractors and concerned individuals. In 1959, economist Moses Abramovitz became one of the first to question whether GDP accurately measures a society's overall well-being. He cautioned that "we must be highly skeptical of the view that long-term changes in the rate of growth of welfare can be gauged even roughly from changes in the rate of growth of output."[105]

Former U.S. Attorney General Robert F. Kennedy on Gross National Product:

> *Our Gross National Product...counts air pollution and cigarette advertising, and ambulances to clear our highways of carnage. It counts special locks for our doors and the jails for the people who break them. It counts the destruction of the redwood and the loss of our natural wonder in chaotic sprawl. It counts napalm and counts nuclear warheads and armored cars for the police to fight the riots in our cities..., and the television programs which glorify violence in order to sell toys to our children. Yet the gross national product does not allow for the health of our children, the quality of their education or the joy of their play.*

It does not include the beauty of our poetry or the strength of our marriages, the intelligence of our public debate or the integrity of our public officials. It measures neither our wit nor our courage, neither our wisdom nor our learning, neither our compassion nor our devotion to our country, it measures everything, in short, except that which makes life worthwhile. And it can tell us everything about America except why we are proud that we are Americans.

- Robert F. Kennedy, speech at the University of Kansas, March 18, 1968 [104]

There were also efforts to steer away from GDP internationally too, with the UN (1990) launching the Human Development Index. The Index measures factors like education, gender equality, and health. In 2006, "China created a new index for "green GDP" — a measure of national economic output that takes environmental factors into consideration."[105] China and other countries started to shift away from a narrow measurement of their economies via the GDP over the past few decades, with some considering similar *green* measures.

There are many examples of the GDP not being an effective tool for measurement of economic well-being and success. Just from thinking about the dismal statistics on economic inequality mentioned in this book, we can see that there are plenty of reasons to steer away from GDP. But to provide more examples, after the temporary tailspin in the U.S. economy from the bursting of the tech bubble and the 9/11 attacks, we had a subsequent recovery where something unexpected happened: Although GDP rose between 2002 and 2006, personal income fell.[105] Furthermore, as RFK mentioned in his speech, most of the indicators of wellbeing within a community, within a country, are not included in GDP. One very large one is ecological impact.

Even though the environment in itself has long-term advantages to being measured as essential to our planet's wellbeing, it's often neglected. GDP measurement even encourages the depletion of the world's natural resources faster than they can renew themselves:

> *In 1997, research by Costanza and colleagues estimated that the world's ecosystem provides benefits valued at an average of US$33 trillion per year. One example is that in GDP terms, clear-cutting a forest for lumber is valued more than the ecosystem services that forest provides if left uncut. These services—including biodiversity habitat, reducing flooding from severe storms, filtration to improve water quality in rivers and lakes, and the sequestration of carbon dioxide and manufacture of oxygen—are not part of the market economy and as a result, are not counted in GDP."There is also the threshold effect: "As GDP increases, overall quality of life increases, but only up to a threshold point.*[104]

Beyond the threshold, an increase in GDP either provides no increase in wellbeing, or it leads to a decline in wellbeing:

> *This is due to the fact that the benefits provided by the increase in expenditures are offset by the costs associated with income inequality, loss of leisure time, and natural capital depletion. In fact, an increasingly large and robust body of research confirms that beyond a certain threshold, further increases in material well-being are poor substitutes for community cohesion, healthy relationships, knowledge, wisdom, a sense of purpose, connection with nature, and other dimensions of human happiness. A strikingly consistent global trend suggests that as material affluence increases, these critical compo-*

nents of psychic income often decline amidst rising rates of alcoholism, suicide, depression, poor health, crime, divorce, and other social pathologies.[104]

Our consumerist culture is great for economic growth, but we live in a finite world and we continue to purchase and collect material that is likely unnecessary and certainly unsustainable. When thinking about all of the previously mentioned inequalities that exist in the U.S., one can see the negative implications of focusing too much on GDP.

When writing this book in the summer of 2020, new GDP numbers for the second quarter of the year came out, which were both dismal and misleading. Numbers came out in July (for the April- June quarter) that GDP was -32.9% which makes one ask the question, so we lost a third of our economy? The answer is no. Instead, the US actually shrunk about 9.5 percent over a few months but the US measures GDP in such a way that it extrapolates the GDP growth out, quarter after quarter, for an entire year. This number can be confusing, which is why I bring this figure up. Unfortunately, it's still a scary number for Americans behind that negative growth.[106]

GDP can be a great indicator of growth, but it mustn't stay the overarching measurement, and nor should it be the only one. A good analogy for using GDP as the only indicator of economic success is that one person who works out at the gym and works on their bench press and is sure to tell everyone how many more pounds, they lift on the bench press. Sure, building muscle by increasing your bench press is a form of growth but is it the ultimate indicator- or only indicator- of success for physical fitness? Hardly so. It's a great short-term indicator and can certainly build someone's strength. But it says very little if anything at all about the longevity of their total physical fitness.

Even though GDP is not a perfect measurement and should not be the only measure of a successful economy, it's still important to know how we ended up with our current model. The term *you get what you measure* certainly had an impact concerning our economic model based on growth. But capitalism as we know it, with not enough of the right government regulations and decision-making by business leaders, has become a model of limitless growth hidden under the guise of consumerism. Our economy also values corporate well-being over the well-being of employees and communities, which is wrong and unsustainable.

This prioritization of the wrong structures within our economy and corporate America has led to greater wealth inequality and concentration of power and influencing ways that can't be sustained. The dynamics involved with these structures are complex but worth running through the history of how they came to be and how they impact us today. Because if we don't understand how our current economic and political structures lead us astray, it will be difficult to address and redesign them for the betterment of this country in the long term.

Chapter 10

American Capitalism

Industrial capitalism created large gains and progress in the U.S. and elsewhere, but not without its caveats. Prominent thinkers and authors throughout history have pointed to the drawbacks and consequences of a capitalist system. Karl Marx, the well-known German philosopher, economist, historian, sociologist, political theorist, journalist, and socialist revolutionary, published his first volume of *Capital* in 1867. In it, he argues against capitalism, that it's inherently flawed, leads to the suffering of the labor classes, and creates a system where *capitalists* profit by paying workers as little as possible to make their products. Products that are sold at a higher price, meaning the worker never receives the real and full value of their work. Marx essentially points out that capitalists make money without doing any actual work.[107]

Soon after in 1905, *The Protestant Ethic and the Spirit of Capitalism* is published by German sociologist, philosopher, jurist, and political economist Max Weber. In his work, he provides some background on the origins of the capitalist system. He argues that capitalism evolved out of Calvinism. "The spirit of modern capitalism is rooted in a Protestant frame of mind that 'strives systematically and rationally in a calling for legitimate profit' in accordance with the virtues of punctuality, industry and frugality and honesty.'"[107]

Then, more recently in 1962, American economist Milton Friedman published *Capitalism and Freedom*. His work argued that economic freedom and political freedom are intrinsically linked. He argues against government regulation of the workplace, government intervention in financial markets, and that the greatest aspects of American society derive from the free operation of the market.[107] Many of us today do generally agree and assume that the free market makes us free. So, we have some thought leaders denouncing capitalism as inherently flawed, others who think an unfettered free market system leads to the best outcomes for everyone, and that capitalism is deeply embedded in our culture, in large part due to religion. To get an understanding of how capitalism impacts America today, let's look at a bit of its history.

First and foremost, American capitalists had an easy time gaining control of what is now the U.S., a land that seems unimaginably rich in natural resources. There are countless examples of economic swindling in this country's history, including the Lincoln Savings & Loan affair and the deregulation which led to the '08 financial crisis and great recession, to name a few. But the largest swindle was that of stealing of Native American land, "which constituted the basis of America's claim to unparalleled economic sufficiency and generosity." Two centuries of colonial history which consisted of massive development would have been impossible without this land grab. Land was the principal means of production in America during the 17th and 18th centuries. "Instead of acquiring wealth by retail means such as piracy on the high seas, European Americans stole other people's wealth wholesale."[108]

This massive production and distribution of land were not distributed equally, and as European colonists moved westward along the great frontier, they repeated a pattern of land grabbing with the choicest parcels of land being distributed to those closest to the seats of political power. A couple of years before the declaration of independence, wealth and income were extremely concentrated.

> To be sure, the European immigrants who were not semi-slaves in the form of indentured servants stood a better chance of becoming landowners than if they had remained in England or Europe. At the same time, distributing other people's land was a perverse form of generosity. Few outside of a tiny circle of insiders received free land. Even during a time of presumed success in spreading ownership, fully half the adult white males owned no land. This, for example, was the case during the decades around the Civil War (1850-1870). The proportion grew in the next generation or two.[108]

In 1776, the Declaration of Independence was issued by the Continental Congress, signifying political and economic independence from Britain. This was the same year that Scottish economist, philosopher, and author Adam Smith (also known as "Father of Economics" or "Father of Capitalism") published his *Inquiry into the Nature and Causes of the Wealth of Nations*. In this work, he suggests labor rather than land as the source of a nation's wealth. He added to the dialogue around government regulation, arguing against government regulation and for free markets.[107] His words marked the beginning of America's transition away from American exceptionalism based on concentrating and controlling land and towards concentrating and controlling labor. This shift underlays the basis for much of our mindset today around the American dream and hard work defining one's individual success. Today we still care about land and property, but labor is where we attach most of our meaning.

In little time after Adam Smith's publication, America's land equals power equation morphed into labor equals power.

By the end of the 19th century, manufacturing, railroads, and new financial industries eventually took the reign of economic production and wealth generation. Thus, the source of wealth was focused on labor instead of land. America had less concentration of wealth and income compared to Europe up until the 20th century primarily due to relatively easier access to land ownership. Before long, the concentration of wealth matched or exceeded that of other industrial capitalist countries. This concentration was so great and the gap between rich and poor so wide that the U.S. became a favorite place for great wealth throughout the world.[108]

Capitalism has never been an equal game and was born out of stolen land and political favors. Sure, there was a great adventure into the west and massive development, but there was plenty of blood spilled on that land in the process. Usually, a just system of government would step in and provide balance to a country that experiences unfettered capitalism- but American culture at the time was one of growth- through the expansion of people across land and the concentration of capital through labor. Our government has had a difficult time working hand in hand with our system of markets and capital, that is at least with hands of transparent and equitable nature.

In a novel concerning Italy during the 1920s and 1930s, Ignazio Silone's Bread and Wine, a character says: "The government has two arms of varying length. The long one is for taking—it reaches everywhere. The short one is for giving—it reaches only to those nearest." This pretty well sums up the role of the capitalist government which has ruled for many years in the United States. It was most generous to those nearest when it came to distributing land and other valuable properties. And it has not hesitated to reach out to collect from the poorest person sufficient funds to extend capitalist rule.[108]

American capitalism has grown over the years to occasionally create conditions where large corporations can gain control of the market and concentrate their power. In 1901, J.P. Morgan and Elbert Gary created U.S. Steel, by merging Federal Steel, The Carnegie Steel Company, and the National Steel Company. It was valued at $1.4 billion ($43 billion today), making it the world's first billion-dollar company. It was at this time that mergers and acquisitions became a popular way of consolidating power. Not all merging is about dominating an entire market though. Around 1965, diversification became a popular form of merger. This meant merging not just with companies within the same industry but with other industries so as to hedge investments and reduce risk.[107]

Mergers, acquisitions, and anticompetitive behavior from corporations can lead to too large of a share of their respective market. At this point, they become a monopoly, which is "the exclusive possession or control of the supply of or trade in a commodity or service."[109] In 1904, Standard Oil controlled 91% of oil production and 85% of final sales in the United States. They had a monopoly over the oil supply, and the federal government was able to step in and break the company up.[107]

A relatively recent example of what used to be a monopoly was AT&T, which was forced to split into six subsidiaries, known as Baby Bells in 1982. Presently in the U.S. we also have duopolies, but we tend to see more oligopolies. The former is essentially where two companies own all, or nearly all, of an entire market for a given product or service, whereas the latter is where "a market is shared by only a small number of firms, resulting in a state of limited competition."[110] Recent examples of duopolies are Amazon and Apple's control of the e-book market and Boeing and Airbus for command over large passenger airplane manufacturing.

Oligopolies are even more prevalent, existing in film and television production, recorded music, wireless carriers, and airlines. "Film and television production in the U.S. are dominated by the film and television production units of five media conglomerates: The Walt Disney Company, Warner Media, NBC Universal, Sony, and Viacom." Disney exceeded $7 billion in box office proceeds in 2018 alone. Of the four major wireless carrier companies here in the U.S.- Sprint-Nextel, Verizon, T-Mobile, and AT&T- their combined market share is over 98%. "In this highly concentrated industry, certain practices that are unfriendly to the consumer have become the norm, including termination fees and sneaky overage charges."[110] One large issue with these different market structures is that they can lead to bad outcomes for consumers, but something that's often not talked about is fewer bargaining rights for workers. If your employer is the only game in town or one of the only companies that would hire someone in your field or positions, then you have less ability to bargain with your employer and demand better working conditions and employee rights.

To prevent companies from getting this big, creating monopolies over an entire market, and practicing anti-competitive behavior which may hurt both consumers and employees, the government has the power to regulate companies with anti-trust laws. They can even break companies up if they get too large and violate these laws. "In the United States, antitrust law is a collection of federal and state government laws that regulates the conduct and organization of business corporations, generally to promote competition for the benefit of consumers."[111] After the Supreme Court ruled Standard Oil was a monopoly in 1911, the company was forced to split into 33 smaller companies. This was the same year that the government tried to break up US steel, but US Steel didn't nearly have as much control of the market as Standard Oil did. So, you can see that it takes a company to have a stranglehold on the market and anticompetitive behavior, for the government to step in. Or at least that was the case in the past. The government is currently unable to address issues of antitrust in the tech and e-commerce industries, which are demonstrating some of the same market-dominating, anticompetitive behaviors.[107]

What allows the government to step in with anti-trust regulation is the passage of ant-trust laws such as the Sherman Anti-Trust Act of 1890. This was passed after a series of large corporate mergers in the 1880s, and it enables "government departments and private individuals to use the court system to break up any organization or contract alleged to be in restraint of trade."[112]

President Theodore Roosevelt was the first President to use the Act in a meaningful way in 1902, by urging his Justice Department to dismantle the Northern Securities Corporation, who was a holding company with too much control over railroading in the northern tier of the U.S. Since this act was initiated, we haven't seen too many more government break-ups of major corporations, but we are in a new age in the 21st century with technology and e-commerce industries potentially requiring some regulation due to anti-competitive behavior. The House of Representatives antitrust committee has recently talked to the CEOs of Amazon, Apple, Facebook, and Google about their role in the market. The underlying issue is that there are concerns that these companies have too much power and may be violating anti-trust laws. Some argue "that Facebook unfairly dominates the advertising market, uses its power to reduce competition, and has harmed consumers by doing so."[113]

They have acquired both Instagram and WhatsApp, which many people say was to reduce competition. There is also concern about Facebook and Google's collective duopoly over digital advertising that may harm consumers by reducing total innovation in the tech industry, not to mention the increase in political concerns by both parties over Facebook's role in political ads and distribution of foreign propaganda. Then you have Amazon, which is an entirely different beast with its sheer dominance of the e-commerce space. There are concerns that the company is participating in predatory lending, which is a long-standing concept in economic thought:

> To get the better of a competitor, a business drops the price of a product to below its cost to produce. The competitor, unable to beat the price, goes out of business. Then the company, now with a monopoly, raises prices, recouping the loss.[114]

This practice may end up becoming an antitrust case if the government can make a case against them under this practice. One example of this happening is when diapers.com (parent company Quidsi), a limited but successful e-commerce company, was given a proposal to be bought by Amazon in the late 2000s. According to "Brad Stone's 2013 book, *The Everything Store*, Bezos tried to buy the company — and when they refused, began rapidly dropping Amazon's diaper prices, including under a newly launched Amazon Mom product."[114] This new venture was a disaster for diapers.com, forcing them to sell their diapers at a loss worth millions of dollars per month. "Quidsi's customer base plummeted and, after a bidding war with Walmart, the company finally sold out to Amazon." Stone suggests that the sale was "made largely out of fear" that the prices would drop even further.[114] Market control and power have become so concentrated that it is increasingly easy for large corporations to invite other companies over for lunch and then have them for dinner.

It can be hard to say whether or not these tech and e-commerce giants are directly responsible for antitrust violations and to what degree, but it is up to the government to step in and figure out if that is truly the case. If so, regulation can prevent consumers and employees from being negatively impacted. Unfortunately, it seems our partisan government is incapable of or doesn't entirely know how to handle much of the antitrust issues. Some of the issues are often technology-centered, which is completely new for the government to intervene in on this scale. We need more experts in the field of technology and antitrust to at least be part of the process of deliberation with these company's or deliberation amongst themselves when making determinations about antitrust.

Right now, capitalism is a system that does not look out for American workers, it simply acts as a means in which for wealth, income, opportunity, and capital to concentrate in adverse directions. The government needs to step in and provide some rules to the game that is capitalism, but right now the government is unable to respond for political reasons. Our two-party system has led to battle lines drawn and daily inaction, all the while the machine of capitalism rolls on, and often right over American workers.

Chapter 11

American Consumerism

The machine of capitalism would not work the way it does or at all if it weren't for the large cog that is our collective consumption. Consumerism is what keeps the wheels turning and is especially prominent here in the United States. Consumerism "is a social and economic order that encourages the acquisition of goods and services in ever-increasing amounts."[115] America's culture of individuality plays right into a social media age where we look at advertisements, celebrities, and our "connections"- giving us this sense that we must have the newest product, whether it's a new outfit or iPhone. Many of us are living a "keeping up with the Joneses" consumer lifestyle as a result.

This lifestyle has become easier to pursue, meaning it has also become easier to partake in conspicuous consumption. That "is the spending of money on and the acquiring of luxury goods and services to publicly display economic power of the income or of the accumulated wealth of the buyer. To the conspicuous consumer, such a public display of discretionary economic power is a means of either attaining or maintaining a given social status."[116] A concern for attaining or displaying a given social status is of course more of a concern when it is easier now to compare ourselves to those around us. The fact is though, this lifestyle and consumption habits are not without their costs to society. To conspicuously consume is to be a passive consumer, as your priority would be status over concern for the many outcomes of your purchasing decisions.

American culture also plays right into a largely consumer-based economy which has especially grown in the past two decades with the rise of e-commerce and this idea that we must have something the moment we buy it. Our expectations of what the marketplace can provide us and when it can provide it have changed drastically, meaning we consume at a much larger amount. Consumer spending in the U.S. generally increases year after year, with 2020 of course having decreased numbers.[117] This shouldn't be a surprise with how accessible and increasingly affordable it is to have goods delivered straight to our doors.

We've made relatively quick progress in the way we consume in a short period of historical time. In 1793, Samuel Slater opened the first factory in America, in Pawtucket, Rhode Island. This factory produced textiles and was a significant moment in American capitalism, as labor started to concentrate in factories and dense locations over a relatively short period. By 1811, construction began on the first federal highway, the Cumberland Road, which connects the Potomac and Ohio rivers. Laying down the pavement for our nation's highway system laid the groundwork for our increasingly robust and interconnected distribution system, which today allows us to almost always have stocked shelves at our grocery stores and receive packages from across the country in a day or two. Becoming a consumer in this country has become increasingly easier due to the aforementioned advancements in industry and distribution, and also in large part because of our nation's culture around private property and individualism.[107]

We shifted from a focus on land as being the central tenet of power in the U.S. to a focus on labor. We have played along with the advancements and changes of industrial society- even through the hardships and poor work conditions because it is easier to sell our skills and save time as opposed to learning how to be skilled in enough skills to the point where we can survive off them alone. In the context of consuming goods and services, we would prefer to have as much of our survival needs and personal desires met as easily as possible with the least amount of time having to be wasted. It would be timelier for us to learn multiple skills that provide the means of which to survive, such as working to make our clothes and produce our food.

If we could instead sell our *individual* skills and labor to the market and industry, then we can use the money earned to buy clothes and food from someone else. We have a culture where being completely self-reliant in providing our own goods and services is seen as a worse deal than working all day towards some other end because we prefer to have domain over our own labor. This has been the American way of life since we increasingly concentrated labor and our respective skills.

The trade-off here is that as we are able to consume more effectively and efficiently- going from buying necessary items downtown to opening an app and clicking a button, we end up becoming more and more separated from the processes- the means of which our goods were provided. We have traded transparency and space (between our purchasing decisions and their impact) for speed and ease of consumption. *Out of sight, out of mind.* It's in this lack of transparency and knowledge of what our purchasing decisions have on the rest of the society, that is troublesome. Sure, our nation's consumption is a marvel to behold due to its speed and ease. But unfortunately, not everyone benefits from this system- many workers are neglected in the process. Countless American workers are affected in profound ways due to 21st-century advances and our nation's consuming habits.

First, the way we consume has shifted in the 21st century. Purchases are increasingly made online, as opposed to just physical retail. Between Amazon and other businesses that can easily send their products to your doorstep, it becomes increasingly less likely that we will buy those same products in-store. A shift in our consumer habits is what's leading to the *retail apocalypse*, or mass closing of retail stores across the country. Some of it is just changes in the way we shop and some of it is because of our shift towards online shopping. Regardless, with more stores closing, that means more people without a job and fewer jobs available altogether. "An estimated 75,000 stores that sell clothing, electronics, and furniture will close by 2026, when online shopping is expected to make up 25 percent of retail sales, according to investment firm UBS." This is in large part due to about 16 percent of overall sales being made online.[118]

America's malls face the same fate, as their business model just doesn't work as well as it used to, especially not during a crisis. This also affects workers and business owners who would otherwise set up shop in these spaces. Brick and mortar retail stores aren't going anywhere in the long term though, it's just that the way we shop is changing. Most of our retail purchases still happen in a physical store, many customers still prefer buying from brick-and-mortar, and some U.S. retailers are opening more stores (location and fit making a huge difference). Thus, we must think about how our consumer habits shifting will impact future businesses and workers. We have a lot of retail space across this country that isn't being used which means it's just a waste in those communities, where instead those spaces could be providing jobs to many of the country's unemployed population. All brick-and-mortar businesses will simply have to think about their location and if they are providing the right type of experience to consumers-including even an online presence on top of a physical one.[119]

There's also the concern of automation at grocery stores and replacing certain positions like cashiers that will increasingly become less necessary. But when there's automation there's also someone working and managing that process as well, so this is just another example where yes- there is a lot of change- but it is change that we can manage if we properly adapt. We can have 21st-century consumption work for us and make sure our workers are trained to take on these new jobs. We need investment in new jobs, investment in the workforce through training, and simply just investing in workers altogether.

Another issue with consumerism today is its impact on environmental degradation and the burdens placed on the workers hidden from our point of view as a consumer. The speed and quantity of which we consume are not suited for a world where pollution is too burdensome on our environment. We often feel powerless in our purchasing decisions because we can't see the tangible impact of decreasing our plastic waste or waste in general. Sure, we can demand more transparency about where our products come from and whether they were sustainably sourced, what alternatives exist, and so forth.

But I think the overarching issue here is that we as consumers are so separated from the process which lets us have an always-stocked grocery store, retail store, or restaurant. Our robust interconnected distribution system is indeed something to marvel at, but there are unfortunately countless workers on the other side of our purchasing decisions who are neglected and treated unfairly. Many of which are completely unknown from the perspective of the consumer.

For all we know, the farmers who collected the coffee beans for our morning cup of coffee are working 12-hour days, are paid very little, and are working in awful conditions. But we wouldn't know this unless we could verify it to be true and we also can't verify whether the ethical standards these companies swear by are truly being adhered to. Not being too involved with the process, being unsure about worker conditions on the other side of our purchases, and having an incomplete picture of what's going on is all by design. It's a feature of our interconnected and globalized system that we don't know where it all comes from, just that we know that it's available. It is a feature for us to be disconnected from what used to be a process that happened before our eyes.

Let's take our food purchases as one example. Right now, much of the food we receive comes from farmers and their crews who are not doing well financially and work in poor work conditions. Most of the meat, dairy, and animal products that you see at the grocery store come from factory farms and large feeding operations. These operations and most of the agriculture industry in the U.S. are controlled by a select few multinational corporations who provide most of the capital that farmers across the U.S. need to start their chicken or pig operations for example. Farmers are often convinced to go into debt to set up their farm operations. But since the corporations who offered this capital also expect a steady supply of animals throughout the year, it only takes a few incidents- natural disaster or sick and dying animals- to put these farmers in a financial hole they can't get out of. Before they know it, they're essentially indentured servants to the animal agriculture industry.

There is also the issue of poor working conditions for workers in the meat industry as a whole. Farmers and their crew who end up treating animals as products instead of sentient beings, also pay a psychological toll. Slaughterhouse workers are often working in poor conditions as well, having to keep up with high speeds of animal slaughter at each stage of the process. This process is of course both psychologically draining and oftentimes unsafe. When we think about our food purchases though, we often don't think about the workers on the other side who make it possible.

Another hidden job from much of our consumer decisions is that of truck drivers, who are part of an industry that is critical infrastructure to our economy. These jobs are not for the faint of heart, as you often have to be away from home for days or weeks at a time. "Trucks move more than 70% of all goods transported around the United States." This industry is the lifeblood of our commerce and our consumption. Most grocery stores would run out of food in just three days if long-haul truckers stopped driving.[120]

They are so fundamental to our nation's infrastructure and consumer lifestyles, yet truck drivers are notoriously underpaid. You would think with how important these positions are, they would be paid a decent salary to go along with the work and strenuous work conditions. "According to the Bureau of Labor Statistics, in 2018, the median income was about $46,800 per year, while median annual wage for truckers was $43,680."[120]

Also, around 30% of truckers are self-employed (aka nonemployer) truckers which means many drivers receive little to no benefits and are forced to maintain their hectic and stressful work schedules to maintain their less than average median income. Truck drivers are less likely to have health insurance compared to other workers too. They are more likely to work longer than forty-hour workweek compared to other professions. We rely on these truckers for most of the goods we consume, yet we don't take care of them and show that we value their crucial work. If we have to pay more for our goods purchased online or physically, for truckers to actually receive solid benefits and an appropriate wage for the sacrifice they make in their work, then I think we should be more than okay with that.[121]

Right now, many "truckers are frustrated with the laws that dictate how they're paid, when they can work, and how their employers can treat them."[122] And many are directing that frustration to the agency that makes those laws — the Federal Motor Carrier Safety Administration (FMCSA). "The Federal Motor Carrier Safety Administration is charged with managing the laws and regulations that control trucking in America... but not one of its four administrators have ever held a commercial driver's license or had any background in the trucking industry."[120] This is unlike other transportation agencies which tend to be led by those who have direct work experience.

> *A 2019 rulemaking from the FMCSA stated that trucking companies in California were exempt from paying their truck driver employees during their mandatory rest breaks. Ray Martinez, the FMSCA administrator, said in December that these rest breaks were "a drag on the economy"; studies from retailers and trucking firms indicated that the breaks reduce productivity.*[122]

Many truck drivers would disagree though, on the grounds that without paid rest breaks, you're putting the safety of truck drivers and other motorists at risk. We should want people on the highway who are not stressed about pay and who are well-rested. Is "productivity'" more important, or is safety for truck drivers and other vehicles on the road? The model of pay for truckers, which is primarily total miles driven, is certainly something worth looking into so that truck drivers don't feel the need to drive an unsafe number of miles. I've seen three or four total incidents where tractor-trailer trucks had gotten into accidents on the highway and none of them looked pretty. I know that's anecdotal, and I don't know what caused those accidents, but regardless it's enough to convince me that safety should be a major priority for truckers across the country. When we think about our purchasing decisions, we often don't think about the distribution workers who make it all possible. As consumers, we have more say in how our goods get to us than we'd like to think. Let's not take for granted key pieces of our economy's infrastructure.

A complete separation from our purchasing decisions and one of the worst outcomes of this modern lifestyle is something we experience all too often, yet it receives almost little press, or once the events are over we tend to forget about it. I'm referring to infectious disease, epidemics, and potentially pandemics like Covid-19. In our current global system of animal agriculture, we treat animals as commodities, as products since the day they are born. They have an expiration date on them essentially from the start. But to provide the amount of meat and animal products we consume daily- more than 200 million land animals are killed daily for food, 72 billion land animals yearly (not including aquatic animals)- we have to have a factory-like system that keeps the animals ("livestock" and "products" as the industry calls them) constantly flowing. The only way to do this is to pack these animals tightly together with sometimes no more room than the plate you eat them on, to produce food at a massive scale.[123]

This environment breeds zoonotic diseases like avian influenza, avian viruses, and swine influenza, plus Coronaviruses such as SARS-CoV, SARS-CoV-2, and MERS-CoV. The associated effects include the recent pandemics Covid mortality rate, which is relatively low compared to N1H5 at 60%.[124] Zoonotic diseases are accused by germs like viruses, bacteria, parasites, and fungi, that spread between animals and people.[125] Now of course the current pandemic is thought to have originated in a Chinese wet market, but many of these other infectious diseases come from what we consider "normal" animal farms. Animal operations here in the U.S., everything from the Concentrated Animal Feeding Operations (CAFOs-

where they feed the animals until slaughter) to their constant transport across states and countries, are breeding grounds for these diseases because you have a bunch of animals close together, who often get sick and are living in conditions that increase the spread of germs.

It's only a matter of time before these conditions, and our purchasing decisions to buy them lead to more contagious and deadly infectious diseases that we'll have to respond to time and time again. We all must understand how our demand for these products leads to the industry's supply. Do what you will with that knowledge, but just know that you have control as a consumer, through your purchases. We pay a price when we receive our goods where we want them and when we want them. Workers suffer and unintended consequences increasingly occur as a result.

Our nation's obsession with consumption (and we're not the only one) is a slow and silent threat that lurks underneath our capitalist system and work culture. 21st-century changes in the way we live are making it easier for us to get what we want, where we want it, and when we want it. But it's also become easier to produce waste, pollute the environment, and hurt both workers and consumers in the long run. I hope we can find ways to bridge the gap of accountability and knowledge that lays between our purchasing decisions and their upstream/downstream effects. It is in our nation's best interest to drop this *passive consumer* mindset and become an *active consumer* instead. A nation of passive consumers has the result of a populace that consumes its own well-being right before its eyes. A path forward around active consumerism is exactly what we need, increasing our collective well-being today and for generations to come.

Chapter 12

Corporate America

Corporations are an interesting development. The concept originated in ancient Rome as *college* or *corpora*, which essentially performed public duties and later became part of municipal administration. "In no meaningful sense could they be regarded as voluntary associations of private businessmen." According to Roman law, a corporation had a distinct personality apart from that of its members or "owners" and existed beyond their lifetime. "Also, the head of a Roman corporation who brought an action in law represented the corporation rather than its individual members."[108] 17th century England saw numerous corporations chartered by the Crown. These monopolies over specific lines of business were reasoned to be carrying out work in the public interest and thus merited government privilege. In the 17th Century, Lord Coke rendered a definition that was for long considered classic:

> *A corporation aggregate of many is invisible, immortal, and rests only in intendment and consideration of the law. They cannot commit treason, nor be outlawed, nor excommunicated, for they have no souls, neither can they appear in person, but by attorney. A corporation aggregate of many can't do fealty for an invisible body can neither be in person nor swear; it is not subject to imbecilities or death or the natural body and divers other cases. Coke's defini-*

tion of a corporation was much like the Roman one. A century later, Adam Smith barely discussed the corporation, pausing several times only to denounce it for conspiring to charge more than the "natural price" for goods.[108]

At the beginning of the 19th century, Americans started to develop the corporate form as we know it, but with little business practice and judicial doctrine to go off of. Before 1789, virtually all firms that came before had failed so there were no best practices. For the first half of the 19th century, other countries looked to America as a storehouse for items like cotton, wool, meat, and grain, and eventually lumber and coal. This required massive transportation efforts, which foreign investors gladly invested in through purchasing shares in American transportation corporations. With this capital to build and manage the transportation enterprise, these corporations and the flow of goods grew extensively, with those involved making a handsome profit. The corporation proved an excellent net too, to catch domestic investment funds.[108]

One issue though was still this question of what a corporation truly was, because the answer has legal implications. Lord Coke asserted that a corporation was a creature of the law, so did it have all the legal rights of natural creatures? "In 1809, the U.S. Supreme Court decided *Bank of the United States v. Devaux*. Georgia had collected a state tax levied upon the Savannah branch of the Bank of the U.S., a federally chartered corporation. The Bank sued in federal court to recover payment. Georgia denied the existence of a federal issue; Section 2, Article III of the Federal Constitution extended the jurisdiction of federal courts to cases "between citizens of different states." Corporations, insisted Georgia, were not citizens and thus could not have access to federal courts. The court agreed.[108]

> *"That invisible, intangible, and artificial being, that mere legal entity, a corporation aggregate," declared Chief Justice John Marshall, "is certainly not a citizen." He held that only real persons could be citizens. The officers of the corporation, being real persons, could sue and be sued. But the corporation itself could not enter into federal legal procedures. The Devaux ruling included a proposition that the firm's owners could sue or be sued provided they lived in a state other than that of the contending side. The corporation's legal rights did not extend to citizenship. The Devaux doctrine was a compromise between traditional law and changing business practice. The law could not conceive yet—although single jurists did—of a totally abstract person possessing full legal rights.*[108]

Over time, the corporate form evolved in response to concrete economic challenges and became crucial to American industrialization and capitalism. Economic pressures combined with American legal thought determined the eventual shape of the modern business corporation. The most recent update in how the U.S. views a corporation came during the 2010 Supreme Court ruling *Citizens United v. Federal Election Commission*. The Supreme Court handed down a controversial 5-4 verdict, which overruled its earlier verdict in *Austin vs. Michigan Chamber of Commerce (1990)* and part of its verdict in *McConnell vs. FEC* regarding the constitutionality of the Bipartisan Campaign Reform Act's (BCRA) Section 203.[126]

Long story short, Justice Anthony M. Kennedy in his majority opinion, "held that the First Amendment protects the right to free speech, even if the speaker is a corporation, and effectively removed limitations on corporate funding of independent political broadcasts." The dissent was strong, with Justice John Paul Stevens arguing in his dissenting opinion "that the framers of the Constitution had sought to guarantee the right of free speech to "individual Americans, not corporations," and expressed the fear that the ruling would "undermine the integrity of elected institutions across the Nation."[126] So, the question of whether a corporation is legally defined as a person seems to be yes-*ish*, or at least enough to be given the right to free speech.

The Stock Market

A large guiding force for our economy today is stocks and the stock exchange. The stock exchange and individual stocks hold a large amount of power and influence over publicly traded companies and investors. Two major stock exchanges in the U.S. today are the New York Stock Exchange (NYSE) and the Nasdaq, the former of which is arguably the most powerful stock exchange in the world.

The path to stocks and the stock exchange was initiated in the 1300s when Venetian moneylenders began to sell debt issues to other lenders and individual investors. These "Venetian lenders would carry slates with information on the various issues for sale and meet with clients, much like a broker does today."[127] "A broker is an individual or firm that acts as an intermediary between an investor and a securities exchange."[128] Then, in the 1500s, you had Belgium's exchange which dealt exclusively in promissory notes and bonds, because there were no real stocks at the time. The Antwerp-based exchange was a place where "brokers and moneylenders would meet to deal with business, government, and even individual debt issues."[127]

Soon after "in the 1600s the emergence of various East India companies that issued stock led to a financial boom, which was followed by a bust when it was revealed some companies conducted very little actual business."[127] Shares for various East India companies were issued on paper and investors could sell these papers to other investors. Since there were no stock exchanges at the time, investors would have to track down a broker to carry out a trade. Interestingly enough, in England, coffee shops were the primary place of business between brokers and investors. "Debt issues and shares for sale were written up and posted on the shops' doors or mailed as a newsletter."[127] We have come a long way from relying on coffee shops to do investments, now we can open up our investment apps anywhere we want- coffee shop, or not.

Finally, we end up in relatively modern stock exchange history. The first stock exchange in London was forced in 1773, 19 years before the NYSE. The latter came about when 24 stockbrokers signed an agreement under a buttonwood tree on Wall Street. The agreement stated that they would only deal with each other, charging a commission of 0.25%. They rented a room at 40 Wall Street. The London Stock Exchange (LSE) was handcuffed by the law restricting shares, whereas the NYSE had dealt in trading stocks since its inception. It's important to point out that the first U.S. stock exchange was actually the Philadelphia Stock Exchange, but the NYSE quickly became the most powerful primarily due to its location:

> *It was in the heart of all the business and trade coming to and going from the United States, as well as the domestic base for most banks and large corporations. By setting listing requirements and demanding fees, the New York Stock Exchange became a very wealthy institution.*[127]

Over the next two centuries, the NYSE faced little serious domestic competition. It became the most important stock exchange in the world, having its international prestige rising in tandem with the burgeoning American economy. Of course, the exchange experienced ups and downs such as the Great Depression and the Wall Street bombing of 1920, the latter of which left 38 dead and scarred many of the buildings.[127]

It wasn't until 1971 when an upstart emerged in competition with the NYSE- Nasdaq. Nasdaq was created by the National Association of Securities Dealers (NASD), which is now called the Financial Industry Regulatory Authority (FINRA). Since its inception its been a different type of stock exchange, where it doesn't inhabit a physical space, such as Wall Street. Instead, the exchange operates using computers that execute trades electronically- a process introduced to make the trading process more efficient. "The competition from Nasdaq has forced the NYSE to evolve, both by listing itself and by merging with Euronext to form the first trans-Atlantic exchange, which it maintained until 2014 when Euronext was spun off to become an independent entity."Today, the Nasdaq has larger quantity of companies listed, but the NYSE holds the upper hand with market capitalization- larger than Tokyo, London, and the Nasdaq exchanges combined. Other stock exchanges will have a hard time and will likely never unseat the NYSE with its massive role in the global economy.[127]

The stock market today is very powerful and holds a lot of sway in our economy. So just as it has a lot of potential to do good for economic growth, businesses, and investors, it also has the potential to do bad. Right now, only 55% of Americans own a reasonable amount of stock. That means about half of the country isn't participating in the stock market with all of its financial benefits like investing and saving for retirement. Matter of fact, "the top ten percent of households had 84% to 94% of stocks, bonds, trust funds, and business equity."[129] And in general, "the top 20 percent of households actually own a whopping 90 percent of the wealth (homes, land, financial assets) in America."[130] I don't think most of the onus for this inequality lies on the stock market itself, I think it's primarily a result of the other inequities we have in our political and economic structures. We have a large challenge in front of us in addressing this inequality, and I will break down some ideas to do just that later in the book.

Quarterly earnings and targets

Something that impacts how much investors invest in a company's stock is how well they are performing. Right now, a large determinant of a company's performance is its quarterly earnings report. This quarterly filing made by public companies includes items such as net income, earnings per share, earnings from continuing operations, and net sales. "By analyzing quarterly earnings reports, investors can begin to gauge the financial health of the company and determine whether it deserves their investment."[131] Every quarter, analysts and investors wait for the earnings announcement.

These reports generally provide a quarterly update of all three financial statements, including the income statement, the balance sheet, and the cash flow statement. Investors must be provided in this report, an overview of sales, expenses, and net income for the most recent quarter. Sometimes, this includes a yearly or quarterly comparison with past performance. Also included in some reports are "a brief summary and analysis from the CEO or company spokesman, plus summary of previous quarterly earnings results."[131]

There are limitations to the quarterly earnings report though, especially since a lot of emphases is placed on it, quarter to quarter, without as much concern for long-term company goals and objectives. For one, the entire market can move when a company's earnings are reported, especially for well followed large-capitalization stocks. Stock prices can fluctuate wildly on days when these reports are released, leading to some instability. Instability is actually quite common. If a specific company's stock doesn't beat earnings *estimates* projected by analysts or the firm itself, it's very likely to experience selloffs. So instead of having a system that emphasizes a company's ability to grow earnings over the prior year, instead the system emphasizes earnings that beat projects quarter to quarter. "In many ways, analysts' earnings are just as important as the earnings report itself."[131] This is very problematic in that it doesn't encourage companies to focus on long-term growth and earnings, which are likely to be more sustainable and equitable for all stakeholders involved.

Investors deserve a system where they can feel confident in investing in a company whose values, mission, and long-term goals they share and appreciate. And everyone in a firm, from the low-level employees to the company's leadership, deserves to be able to focus on long-term growth and wellbeing of their company and employees, instead of short-term quarterly earnings- which are likely to lead to a lack of sustainable and equitable prioritization. Unfortunately, the attitude in many businesses is fatalistic about changing this short-term culture, whether they would benefit or not. Short-term gains, massive investment growth due to high interest and demand, and the resulting increase in stock prices are very enticing for companies as well. So, it shouldn't be too much of a surprise that the status quo hasn't changed much from this short-term model of quarterly earnings and growth.

Another large reason this short-term model stays in place is that it has been common practice over the past few decades to focus on providing shareholder value. "A shareholder, also referred to as a stockholder, is a person, company, or institution that owns at least one share of a company's stock, which is known as equity." Shareholders, who are essentially owners in a company, benefit from a company's success. They reap rewards in the form of increased stock valuations or from dividends, which are financial profits distributed to shareholders. Conversely, the share price invariably drops when a company loses money, likely causing shareholders to lose money, or at least suffer declines in their portfolios' values.[132]

Shareholder value then, "is the value delivered to the equity owners of a corporation due to management's ability to increase sales, earnings, and free cash flow, which leads to an increase in dividends and capital gains for the shareholders."[133] Corporations are not required by law to maximize shareholder value, it still is common practice in the marketplace. Providing shareholder value is quite often a concern of a firm's management and directors, with many CEOs having stock-based compensation tied to their leadership positions. When your compensation is tied to how much shareholder value you provide, as opposed to how much value you provide to your employees, your customers, or the communities in which you deal, then you are likely to see these other stakeholders neglected over time. And that is exactly what we've seen.

Shareholder Value and Corporate Mindset

But where did this focus on shareholder value come from? Well, over time we have had a pushback against the broader interests of society. The Business Roundtable (BRT) is a non-profit association based in Washington, D.C. whose members are chief executive officers of major U.S. companies. Unlike the U.S. Chamber of Commerce, whose members are entire businesses, BRT members are exclusively CEOs. The BRT is one such organization that has pushed against our broader interests, such as in 1975 when it helped defeat anti-trust legislation. Then in 1977, BRT played a role in defeating a plan for a Consumer Protection Agency, successfully blocking labor form. It successfully lobbied for reducing corporate taxes in 1985, and in 1997, it issued a policy of "maximizing value for shareholders as the sole purpose of a corporation." Now, this policy is already accepted throughout business culture, but it did cement in place this shortsighted policy.[134]

This shareholder model was widely accepted in large part due to Nobel Prize-winning economist Milton Friedman's article in 1970, published in the New York Times: *A Friedman Doctrine-- The Social Responsibility Of Business Is to increase its profits.* This article was much of an echo of Friedman's book *Capitalism and Freedom*, published eight years earlier. In this ferocious article, it is argued that any business executives who pursued a goal other than making money were "unwitting puppets of the intellectual forces that have been undermining the basis of a free society these past decades."[135] They were guilty of "analytical looseness and lack of rigor," turning themselves into "unelected government officials" who were illegally taxing employers and customers. The article assumes its conclusion before it begins: "In a free-enterprise, private-property system, a corporate executive is an employee of the owners of the business," namely the shareholders. We all know the executive is truly an employee of the corporation, but this didn't stop Friedman's message or the business world from nodding along.[136]

"A corporate executive who devotes any money for any general social interest would", the article argues, "be spending someone else's money... Insofar as his actions in accord with his 'social responsibility' reduce returns to stockholders, he is spending their money." According to Friedman, the corporation's money = the shareholder's money. But then he states "Insofar as his actions raise the price to customers, he is spending the customers' money."So now the corporation's money = the customer's money. Which one is it then? "Insofar as [the executives] actions lower the wages of some employees; he is spending their money" Now suddenly, the organization's money has become the employees' money. It can be very difficult to ascertain this article's premise because there really is none.[136]

The success of the article was not because the arguments were sound or powerful, but rather because people desperately wanted to believe. At the time, private sector firms were starting to feel the first pressures of global competition, and executives were looking around for ways to increase their returns. The idea of focusing totally on making money, and forgetting about any concerns for employees, customers, or society seemed like a promising avenue worth exploring, regardless of the argumentation. In fact, the argument was so attractive that, six years later, it was dressed up in fancy mathematics to become one of the most famous and widely cited academic business articles of all time. In 1976, finance professor Michael Jensen and Dean William Meckling of the Simon School of Business at the University of Rochester published their paper in the Journal of Financial Economics entitled 'Theory of the Firm: Managerial Behavior, Agency Costs and Ownership Structure.[136]

This paper argues the same false assumption as Professor Friedman. "Namely, that an organization is a legal fiction which doesn't exist, and that the organization's money is owned by the stockholders."[136]

Unfortunately, this idea of shareholder value caught on and became conventional wisdom. Executives weren't going to turn down generous stock compensation being offered. Add political support to this corporate 'wisdom', and you have a recipe for skyrocketing executive compensation and shareholder value. Ronald Reagan was elected in 1980 partly due to his message that government is "the problem." Across the way in 1979, Margaret Thatcher became UK's Prime Minister, who also had no problem urging *economic freedom*, with making money as a solution. Corporate greed became all too common thanks to the combination of this political rhetoric, increased focus on shareholder value, and the executives who exemplified this movement. General Electric CEO Jack Welch- rightly or wrongly- came to be seen as a large implementer of this shareholder theory during his 1981-2001 tenure. He excelled at increasing shareholder value, hitting numbers with precision.[136]

Yet, in a short matter of time, this theory proved to be built on unstable ground, as underlying reality became apparent. The Shift Index, a study of 20,000 US firms, shows that the asset rate of return and invested capital of US firms had declined by three quarters between 1965 and 2009. The theory failed, with the period of shareholder capitalism since 1976 seeing executive compensation explode next to a decline in corporate performance. The logic continued through books like *Hardball* (2004), where "winning" in the marketplace was described as the optimal goal for firms. The idea was that firms should be "mean" to their rivals, an approach that has clearly led to poor outcomes for nearly all other stakeholders not valued in the shareholder equation. Scandals and shady business practices have been all too common in corporate America. Everything from accounting scandals like Enron ad WorldCom to the 2005-2006 options backdating scandals, and of course the 2007-2008 subprime meltdown. When focusing squarely on profits, you end up having corporations conduct shady but not strictly illegal activity, where it's only a matter of time before they move into criminal activity.[136]

Even Jack Welch came to criticize shareholder value as a business theory. On March 12, 2009, he gave an interview with Francesco Guerrera of the Financial Times:

> *On the face of it, shareholder value is the dumbest idea in the world. Shareholder value is a result, not a strategy... your main constituencies are your employees, your customers, and your products. Managers and investors should not set share price increases as their overarching goal...*

Short-term profits should be allied with an increase in the long-term value of a company.[136]

Maximizing shareholder value has led to a variety of corporate, economic, and social issues. An increasingly wide gap between executive pay and their employees, growing inequality, stagnant median income, the occasional massive financial crash, slowing productivity, and an increasingly large distrust in business. When you see the younger generations call out capitalism or even want to dismantle the entire enterprise, that's a symptom of something much larger. Most people don't take on that view unless they're deeply concerned about the way business has carried itself, its environmental impact, and so forth. Quaker Oats president Kenneth Mason (1979) said it best when he declared Friedman's profits-are-everything philosophy "a dreary and demeaning view of the role of business and business leaders in our society... Making a profit is no more the purpose of a corporation than getting enough to eat is the purpose of life. Getting enough to eat is a requirement of life; life's purpose, one would hope, is somewhat broader and more challenging. Likewise, with business and profit."[137]

Maximizing shareholder value is still a problem with corporate America today, but for many, there has been this shift away from shareholder value to customer value. In Peter Drucker's classic book *Management* (1974), he argued against shareholder value, saying that "There is only one valid definition of business purpose: to create a customer. . . . It is the customer who determines what a business is. It is the customer alone whose willingness to pay for a good or for a service converts economic resources into wealth, things into goods. . . . The customer is the foundation of a business and keeps it in existence." Peter Drucker's argument about customer primacy took greater effect with 21st-century globalization and the internet changing everything.

Marketplace power shifted from the seller to the buyer with customers now able to insist on "better, cheaper, smaller, quicker" in their consumption, along with a more convenient, reliable, and personalized purchasing environment.[136] The change in consumerism at the turn of the 21st century is made easier by what many are calling the *Fourth Industrial Revolution*, which is essentially our current technological revolution that fundamentally alters the way we work, live, and relate to one another.[138] And as I mentioned earlier, this transformation really set off a demand-driven movement which many companies have been successful in fulfilling. Company's like Apple and Amazon figured out how to shift from shareholder value to both shareholder value *and* customer value model that takes advantage of 21st-century advances and consumer preferences.

The large problem with this transition is that *employee value* has been entirely left out of the value equation throughout the business environment and business theory over the past few decades. Ignoring the needs of employees and American workers has been a topic of discussion throughout this book, and it's something that needs to be addressed. As the lifeblood of our organizations, it seems to me it only makes sense to prioritize employee value just as much if not more than customer and shareholder value. Employees are the ones who work directly with the customers.

Of course, not all employees have been neglected throughout corporate America, it's just that those who benefit and see the most value are upper-level management- through salary, bonuses, and stock compensation. All the while, low-level and many wage-based employees (especially those making at or near minimum wage) have been left out of the value equation. Employees are often neglected concerning their work rights, their benefits, their labor representation, and the lack of a living wage. We see this throughout our business environment, meaning workers all over the U.S. are suffering as a result. Our culture continues to pay executives millions and billions worth of stock compensation while simultaneously paying many workers less than a living wage. That is unfortunately the status quo.

Customers aren't just essential; they are literally the lifeblood of a company; thus, it makes no sense to value them over the organization as a whole. Stakeholders are also important to the enterprise, but considering Americans use the stock market as an investment tool to save up for retirement, why do we continue to buy into this system of corporations and shares that is primarily staked in short-term success? Investing for retirement is *long-term*, the life of a corporation (or any organization) depends on the *long-term*, employees like to work for companies that value them and their *long-term* success, everything is *long-term*. Yet most of corporate America hasn't quite figured that out.

The BRT has in recent years stated that this focus on shareholder value, which they supported for years, is no longer defensible and has brought to the table a new corporate purpose. This purpose is to deliver value to customers, invest in employees, deal fairly and honestly with suppliers, support communities, and protect the environment, all of which are equal in generating long-term value for shareholders. Their statement moves away from maximizing one value at the expense of others, instead promising greater balance and compromise. Yet, the BRT statement is just as easily seen as a defensive reaction to complaints around big business, much of which comes from the younger generations. Not much will likely change from the BRT's statement, with most well-known and public businesses already picking up on these concerns and tailoring their strategies accordingly.

We have already seen and will continue to see companies emphasize all the good things they claim to be doing while hiding many of the outlined issues under the rug. It's hard to see corporate purpose statements around equal focus on all stakeholders as serious, actionable content when our current system still emphasizes short-term goals over long-term ones. It's great that a prominent business donated a few million dollars to a cause or planted a million trees, but if they're still paying their executives millions in stock compensation and their employees less than a living wage, it's hard to take them seriously.

We have seen the priorities of corporate America play out during the Covid pandemic and it's become harder for them to hide their underlying approach to employee and community well-being. It's safe to say that many small businesses had little options in their decision to lay off workers when it came crunch time because many small businesses already exist on the margins and it's hard for them to afford to pay employees without recurring revenue. Large corporations though have less of an excuse, especially those who operate with much higher profit margins and who've had time to prepare for an economic downturn, regardless of whether it came from a pandemic or not. But many of these large organizations and industry giants consider themselves "too big to fail", understanding that if their financial situation plummets, the government can bail them out. We have seen this play out during the government's response in bailing out a few different industries via Covid response and stimulus packages.

These taxpayer-funded bailouts and our usual government subsidies are nothing but corporate America *privatizing the profits and socializing the losses*. This refers "to the practice of treating company earnings as the rightful property of shareholders, while losses are treated as a responsibility that society must shoulder... In other words, the profitability of corporations is strictly for the benefit of their shareholders. But when the companies fail, the fallout—the losses and recovery—are the responsibility of the general public."[139] As long as the government can print money and continue to bail them out, there are fewer short-term incentives for industries to change their ways. Overall, this isn't a sustainable form of capitalism. Instead, it's more of an ersatz economy that pretends to be the best possible outcome for every American taxpayer. The idea of privatizing profits and socializing losses isn't new either, it *supposedly* dates back to Andrew Jackson's closing of the Second Bank of the United States in 1834:

> *I have had men watching you for a long time and I am convinced that you have used the funds of the bank to speculate in the breadstuffs of the country. When you won, you divided the profits amongst you, and when you lost, you charged it to the Bank. ... You are a den of vipers and thieves.*

Market economies are essential to our lives and the economy but without the right rules and referees, the game doesn't work.

Corporate America will be less likely to change in totality until the underlying model of business changes towards a focus on the long term. You might have a lot of great managers out there who want to prove they are not maximizing one stakeholder's value to the exclusion of all others, but without clear direction around long-term goals, it will be difficult for them to pursue that end. Management theorists have come to call corporations frequently operating based on inconsistent and ill-defined preferences, goals, and identities as *garbage can organizations*.[134]

These organizations were commonplace between the 1930 and 1970s, due to a large corporate focus on trying to balance the needs of all stakeholders. This balancing was the approach to managerial capitalism at the time, and this approach is in part what led to Friedman's shareholder value theory, claiming that shareholder value gives management something to work towards. The problem is that Friedman chose the wrong variable. It's not just shareholders, customers, or employees whose value should be maximized, the priority should be on long-term goals and objectives tied to a timeline and past yearly performance. You can have a system where long-term goals and objectives can be broken down into short-term goals, objectives, and a managerial approach that encourages competing against yourself (individually or as an organization) over time. This approach doesn't focus on one stakeholder, at the expense of others. Instead, the result will mean fewer stakeholders being shortchanged in the process of conducting business.[134]

Chapter 13

A Concentration of Power and Wealth

When capitalism, consumerism, and corporate America work against the wider interests of Americans, the conditions for equal opportunity narrow, and the spoils become unevenly distributed. The result is a system of wealth and power that accumulates over time until it is concentrated by fewer and fewer people. The very same system will also create conditions that allow the minority of Americans with wealth and power to maintain their positions and status, for as long as these structures stay in place.

American institutional economist John Commons wrote, "Economic power is simply power to withhold from others what they need."[108] Capitalism relies on economic power, thus before Europeans arrived in America there was no economic power. Before, there was equality of condition, but that soon changed. You have economic power when you can choose not to share, a condition which became well embedded within capitalism as America transformed into a place of wealth and power thanks to industry.

Since the beginning of American economic power, you've had a minority of the population concentrating most of the wealth and power, thus since the beginning, we have had mechanisms in place for those individuals to maintain their advantages. This required that power and political rule join forces. Lawrence Friedman writes: "A plan of government is a plan for distribution of the power and wealth of a society," but we must not fool ourselves into thinking the powerful will make a habit of relinquishing this power. That was especially the case during constitution-making, where it made sense to consolidate power and set up power structures to the advantage of the wealthy and powerful.[108]

"By 1850, America was a commercialized society, [where] it had become normal for men to conceive of themselves as producers and sellers for impersonal ends." In a short matter of time, the corporation as mentioned earlier became the primary institution responsible for much of this nation's growth and international prowess. The combination of corporate America with its concentration of labor and our country's culture of self-worth *tied* to our labor, over time created a nationwide acceptance of economic power as we know it today and its underlying power dynamics. As the economic labor machine grew, the more that average workers came to accept the difference between themselves and the economically powerful. Understanding this difference has created an atmosphere over time where those who are not economically powerful have accepted their circumstances as mere circumstance. We see this today with our American culture of hard work, placing the onus of individual economic success on the individual; so much so that we forget about the power dynamics at play which makes it more or less likely that we experience economic opportunities.[108]

Economic, and even political power in the U.S., has dominated to the point where those with less power in society, have become dependent on the possessors of power and the very structure itself. As seen through much of this book, political and economic power go hand in hand. Ideally, they would balance each other out, providing an overarching system of checks and balances of our nation's power dynamics. Unfortunately, that vision has yet to fruition.

These power dynamics have led to a separation of class and that separation or gap between the haves and the have-nots have increased drastically over the past few decades. As mentioned earlier, the middle class has hollowed out to a large degree and you can see much of the distaste for one class from another playing out in real-time. Talk about "the elite" happens in multiple instances, referring to multiple groups of individuals, not all wealthy, but generally, much of this rhetoric is based on class. Late American economist and sociologist Thorstein Veblen writing in 1919, observed:

> *The population ... now falls into two main classes: those who own wealth invested in large holdings and who thereby control the conditions of life for the rest; and those who do not own wealth in sufficiently large holdings, and whose conditions of life are therefore controlled by these others.*[108]

Research into the history of class and wealth in the U.S. has become a major field of investigation recently, and its subject is hard to avoid when looking at the inequities now present.

> *During more than 150 years before the American Revolution, an economic and political elite held sway in just about all the colonies. Bureaucratic capital accumulated as offices in government became a main avenue for acquisition of land. Prodigious land grants were assigned by top officeholders to themselves or handed over to family, friends, and business associates. The elites treasured such golden connections and closely superintended access to official positions in county- and province-wide government. Almost invariably, large-scale merchants, landown-*

ers and slaveholders, and occasionally professionals occupied the top rungs of colonial society. Even where politics was more democratic, as in colonial Boston, concentration of economic power did not fade away.[108]

Wealth and power were consolidated even during the Revolution and when drafting the Constitution. It's hard to comprehend capitalism in its entirety, never mind how it grew in the U.S. as a dominant system. Adam Smith once explained that "a system is an imaginary machine invented to connect together in the fancy those different movements and effects which are already in reality performed."[140] The reason we can't just *change* the system is that it's made of multiple moving structures that are best addressed individually.

Today, power and wealth are concentrated at the top of our polity and economy through the previously mentioned systems- including our misaligned capitalist system, ever-increasing, and damaging consumerism, and corporate America which benefits the most at the intersection of these structures. Great power and wealth are being concentrated thanks to our corporate design. It is the intersection between corporate America with capitalism and corporate America with government where we find most of the gains occurring- at the detriment to those without much power.

One example of power and influence being concentrated has to do with lobbying. Lobbying is "any attempt by individuals or private interest groups to influence the decisions of government; in its original meaning, it referred to efforts to influence the votes of legislators, generally in the lobby outside the legislative chamber. Lobbying in some form is inevitable in any political system."[141] Lobbying takes many forms. From Brittanica on lobbying:

Group representatives may appear before legislative committees. Public officials may be "buttonholed" in legislative offices, hotels, or private homes. Letters may be written, or telephone calls made to public officials, and campaigns may be organized for that purpose. Organizations may provide favored candidates with money and services. Massive public-relations campaigns employing all the techniques of modern communication may be launched to influence public opinion.

Extensive research into complex legislative proposals may be supplied to legislative committees by advocates of various and often conflicting interests. Substantial election campaign contributions or other assistance may be supplied to favored legislators or executives. The persons who lobby in those ways may be full-time officials of a powerful trade or agricultural association or labor union, individual professional lobbyists with many clients who pay for their services, or ordinary citizens who take the time to state their hopes or grievances. Cities and states, consumer and environmental protection and other "public interest" groups, and various branches of the federal government also maintain staff lobbyists in the United States.[141]

Most legal scholars and judges consider lobbying to be protected by the First Amendment, which guarantees the right "to petition the government for a redress of grievances."[141] Nonetheless, the federal government and the majority of states regulate lobbying, including the Federal Regulation of Lobbying Act (1946). This law requires lobbyists to register and report contributions and expenditures and the groups whom they represent make similar reports. The efficacy of these laws is doubtful as there are still forms of indirect lobbying.[141]

"In 2019 alone, lobbyists spent \$3.47 billion on influencing political policy, representing the highest sum spend on lobbying since lobbying spend peaked in 2010."[142] This is more than it costs to fund both the house and senate.[143] The largest companies today have more than 100 lobbyists representing them, allowing them to be essentially everywhere they need to be. "For every dollar spent on lobbying by labor unions and public-interest groups together, large corporations and their associations now spend \$34." The organizations which spend the most on lobbying consistently represent business.[144]

In the 1950s and 1960s, political representation did tilt towards the well-off, yet lobbying was still more well-balanced by today's standards. Labor unions and public-interest groups around this time were more important, and very few companies had their own Washington lobbyists before the 1970s. Before this, businesses that did lobby were for the most part quite ineffective at it. Business lobbying built itself over time though, and business' interaction with the government changed along with it. "Rather than trying to keep government out of its business (as they did for a long time), companies are now increasingly bringing government in as a partner, looking to see what the country can do for them."[144]

In 1972, the BRT was formed against the backdrop of a poor business environment. This organization, as mentioned earlier, devoted itself to explicitly cultivating political influence. This group of CEOs and their messaging around the business climate motivated many leading corporations to engage in serious political activity. This meant hiring their first lobbyists, and before long "they killed a major labor law reform, rolled back regulation, lowered their taxes, and helped to move public opinion in favor of less government intervention in the economy."[144] The work didn't stop there though, businesses kept getting involved with politics, some even deepening their commitments. So, lobbying became a tool of both keeping the government away (e.g., lobbying to avoid regulation) and keeping them close (e.g., making them partners).

One example of working closer to the government is when the pharmaceutical companies moved from opposing the government adding prescription drug benefits to proposing and supporting (around 2010) Medicare Part D- a prescription drug benefit that benefitted companies to around $205 billion over ten years. The companies were concerned that a government-added prescription drug benefit to Medicare would give the government bargaining power through bulk purchasing, reducing industry profits, but industry lobbyists were able to step in and dreamed up the Medicare Part D plan, which explicitly forbade bulk purchasing.[144]

Money in politics doesn't stop at lobbying though. You also have Political Action Committees (PACs) or super PACs. The former raises money privately to influence elections or legislation, especially at the federal level, and the latter can raise funds from individuals, corporations, unions, and other groups without any legal limit on donation size. The super PAC's appearance is a result of the Citizens United and SpeechNow.org decisions. Super PACs have become a great way in the past ten years for influence in politics to increase substantially.

It's a win-win for companies to invest in specific candidates for office who have their bests interest in mind, and for those candidates to receive campaign money in return for not acting or acting on specific issues. The loser in this equation is often smaller interest groups who can't afford large amounts of lobbying or campaign contributions, and Americans in general who would benefit from electing specific candidates with government policy that matters to them. This policy often never sees the light of day due to your average American's inability to spend as much as these other groups.

Greater transparency is needed so American voters can see potential policy options on or off the table due to lobbying and influencing efforts. There's also the problem of Congress not having enough staff to conduct their policymaking, meaning they often have to rely on lobbyists for that role. Investing more in government "would give leading policymakers resources to hire and retain the most experienced and expert staff and reduce their reliance on lobbyists."[144] Another problem is that many of the problems this nation faces and would best be solved right now, often don't have any representation in Washington or through these large interest groups. These less well-resourced positions could certainly use more support.

My concern about lobbying isn't so much that it allows Americans and groups of Americans to practice participative democracy, but that some wealthy individuals, groups, and corporations have too much influence over the election process, and incentives to pass specific legislation start to fade for many politicians over time. The fact is that the more control lobbying has over government policy, the more we should think about how that impacts the vote of individual Americans who may not have their interests considered. That includes American workers whose representation has gone down over the years. With less labor union participation and less representation in Congress through politicians or legislation, American workers will continue to see their interests ignored.

Now that we've seen one example of how power and influence are developed and concentrated in the U.S., we should illustrate how wealth concentration comes into the picture. Stock price appreciation and dividends are the most common ways to share the wealth with a company's shareholders, but stock buybacks (or share repurchase) have also become common.

A stock buyback, also known as a share, repurchase, occurs when a company buys back its shares from the marketplace with its accumulated cash. A stock buyback is a way for a company to re-invest in itself. The repur-chased shares are absorbed by the company, and the num-ber of outstanding shares on the market is reduced. Because there are fewer shares on the market, the relative ownership stake of each investor increases. [145]

In other words, greater shareholder value is being provided. A firm's management will likely say a buyback is the best use of capital at that time and it's an efficient way to return money to shareholders, with a typical line being 'we don't see any bet-ter investment than in ourselves.' This certainly may be the case, but often isn't true. It was uncommon before the 1980s for corporations to repurchase shares of their stock. When they started to, it was typically a defense mechanism against raiders, who were drawn to cash piles on a company's balance sheet. "By contrast, according to Federal Reserve data com-piled by Goldman Sachs, over the past nine years, corporations have put more money into their own stocks—an astonishing $3.8 trillion—than every other type of investor (individuals, mutual funds, pension funds, foreign investors) combined."[146]

By reducing the number of shares outstanding in the market, a buyback lifts the price of each remaining share. But that spike is often short-lived: A study by the research firm Fortuna Advisors found that, five years out, the stocks of companies that engaged in heavy buybacks per-formed worse for shareholders than the stocks of compa-nies that didn't. [146]

Managers who initiate buybacks and are privy to their exact scope and timing benefit greatly from temporary price jumps that come with it. An analysis by the SEC "revealed that in the eight days following a buyback announcement, executives on average sold five times as much stock as they had on an ordinary day." Thus, executives capture most of the benefit from short-term stock-price pops created by these announcements. A large tenet of shareholder value is that a manager's interests should be aligned with shareholders' interests. To achieve this goal, boards started to grant CEOs large chunks of company stock and stock options. This compensation shift was originally intended to encourage CEOs to maximize shareholder returns.[146]

In practice though, this rise of incentives coincided with a loosening of SEC rules that governed stock buybacks. The SEC considered such a rule change in 1967, '70, and '73 and when they finally loosened the rules, it became even more tempting for CEOs to conduct market manipulation.[146] The abuse of stock buybacks today is so widespread it's not useful for us to single out any one CEO, but it is important to illustrate just how wrong this practice is.

Take the CEO of Home Depot Craig Menear as one example. In February 2018, he announced with his team on a conference call, their "plan to repurchase approximately $4 billion of outstanding shares during the year." He sold 113,687 shares the next day, netting $18 million. One day later he was granted 38,689 new shares which he wasted no time in selling over 24,000 of them for a $4.5 million profit. According to SEC filings, Menear's compensation was stated to be $11.4 million for 2018, but stock sales provided him an additional $30 million that year. Compare this to the median worker pay for Home Depot at $23,000 a year and you can see the problem with that. According to the Roosevelt Institute and the National Employment Law Project, each worker could have made an additional $18,000 a year had the buyback money been used to boost salaries.[146]

Buybacks are often short-sighted and unfair, and it's the long-term wellbeing of the company (including its workers) that is often sacrificed. Many companies who are flush with cash will repurchase stocks, but many of these same companies aren't taking care of their employees. Over time, practices like these end up concentrating wealth for those in positions of power. To stop the increasing gap in income and wealth inequality (which plays right into other inequalities) we need to think about how we structure our political and economic systems. Creating structures that provide incentives for those in power to focus on long-term outcomes as opposed to the status quo will certainly go a long way in preventing the unequal distribution of wealth. These structures need an across-the-board redesign, which is what the rest of the book gets into.

III

Redefined and Redesigned

I went to the woods because I wished to live deliberately, to front only the essential facts of life, and see if I could not learn what it had to teach, and not, when I came to die, discover that I had not lived. I did not wish to live what was not life, living is so dear; nor did I wish to practice resignation, unless it was quite necessary. I wanted to live deep and suck out all the marrow of life, to live so sturdily and Spartan-like as to put to rout all that was not life, to cut a broad swath and shave close, to drive life into a corner, and reduce it to its lowest terms, and, if it proved to be mean, why then to get the whole and genuine meanness of it, and publish its meanness to the world; or if it were sublime, to know it by experience, and be able to give a true account of it in my next excursion.

-Henry David Thoreau

Chapter 14

A New Corporate Model

For the past four decades, the power of workers has declined. This is the power of workers to negotiate with their employers for better pay, better benefits, and better working conditions. What we see is that workers have been receiving a smaller and smaller share of the money their company makes, due to this power imbalance. This is essentially a redistribution of income and power from workers to shareholders. A Brookings study by Anna Stansbury and Lawrence H. Summers explaining this decline came out during the pandemic. Within their study, they estimated that "the decline in worker power is big enough to explain the entire decline in the labor share of income in the United States over the past four decades." They illustrate how the largest declines in worker power by industry match the largest declines in the share of income going to workers. This happened alongside the largest increases in corporate profitability, signifying that shareholders' gains came at the expense of workers' loss.[147]

There are many causes for this decline in worker power. "Declining unionization, increasingly demanding and empowered shareholders, decreasing real minimum wages, reduced worker protections, and the increases in outsourcing domestically and abroad have disempowered workers with profound consequences for the labor market and the broader economy." When looking at the decline of unions, we see that a third of private-sector workers belonged to a union in the 1950s (the peak) compared with 6% today. And the wage premium for workers who do belong to unions has fallen. The study finds that the changes in the U.S. economy can be explained better by a decline in worker power, as opposed to increased monopoly or monopsony power. Thus, policy solutions should focus on worker power instead.[147]

How to address this issue of worker power in the American workplace involves many moving parts but it is important to start at the basic level of employee-employer relationships. That is first, we must fix employment contracts. This is the contract that many employees sign when starting a job at a new company, and it includes provisions relating to compensation, benefits, scope of employment, and grounds for termination and length of contract. These physical contracts are often laden with social pressure mechanisms that give workers fewer rights and force them to work longer or harder than they should. Understanding the contract is not always easy and requires a lot of work on the employees' part. And negotiating parts of the contract is certainly possible, but more so if you have more power in the negotiating process due to your talents, skillset, and the type of position involved. Someone working a job that can be filled by almost anyone at any time has very little negotiating power when it comes to their employment contract.

Once compensation and benefits have been worked out between both parties, the scope of employment is often overlooked. This part of the contract is more than the job title and responsibilities. The employer can designate "the place of employment and whether the employee can be relocated; If the employee can be demoted or have their responsibilities reduced or modified; and If the employee will have influence over other facets of the company's operations." Many of us go into a role not understanding the scope of our employment, which dictates several crucial facets of the job. A large problem with employment contracts is that employees don't know what the grounds for termination are. Depending on which state you live in, you may fall under "at will" employment which means the employer can fire you at will without any real reason at all, or if they can only terminate you "with cause" for actions such as "breach of contract, criminal charges, or refusal to perform reasonable duties."[148]

The distinction here is very important because being at will means you may be out of a job and unable to pay your bills in a very short period for essentially no reason at all. In this type of work environment, workers aren't being valued as they should. I understand that some workers are bound to be more efficient or effective than others but being able to terminate someone who relies on your paychecks and likely healthcare to survive, all in the blink of an eye is destructive to the employee-employer trust relationship. Employers have way too much power here- if someone isn't doing their job and this lack of work is being documented, that is understandable, but it's not right when workers are just tossed out with no explanation. At least not under our current environment where workers' human needs are neglected through a lack of government-provided healthcare (which means if you have no job you likely have no health insurance) and other laws that might protect unemployed workers.

Next, within the scope of employment section, you also may have arbitration and dispute resolution clauses for employment grievances. Many of these arbitration agreements are mandatory and standard practice in American workplaces. Unfortunately, these agreements take away workers' right to take their employer to court, even in important cases. Workers aren't able to sue their employers for racial discrimination, sexual harassment, or even stealing their wages.

Given a more legalese name such as "Alternative Dispute Resolution Agreement," an agreement buried deep in your employment contract, workers are signing to essentially agree to take any claims they have to private arbitration. This private arbitration is a quasi-legal forum with no judge, no jury, and next to no government oversight. This system sets workers up to be less likely to win their cases or earn less money if they do win than they would in court. "About half of non-unionized workers at US companies are subject to these agreements — more than double the share in the early 2000s." Rising mandatory arbitration has led to workers finding it impossible "to seek legal justice for wage theft, overtime violations, and job discrimination."[149] The judicial system has become privatized and mostly favors the employer. Multiple Supreme Court rulings have allowed businesses to expand the use of arbitration, and there are a lot of changes that need to be made with arbitration and dispute resolution so that workers can start to get their rights back.

The #MeToo movement and minority workers have been particularly impacted by mandatory arbitration, with these workers finding it difficult to receive legal justice through the courts. To fix employment contracts, Congress will have to step in and make laws here, and some bills have been introduced. In October 2018, Rep. Beto O'Rourke (D-TX) introduced the Mandatory Arbitration Transparency Act, which prohibits businesses from including a confidentiality clause in their arbitration agreements related to discrimination claims. You also had a bipartisan group of senators and representatives in December 2018 who introduced the Ending Forced Arbitration of Sexual Harassment Act, which would exempt sexual harassment cases from required arbitration. Several months later, all 56 state attorneys general (including those in five US territories) urged congressional leaders to vote on the bills. They submitted a letter, stating that forcing sexual harassment cases to go to arbitration perpetuates the "culture of silence that protects perpetrators at the cost of their victims." They also questioned the process itself:

> *While there may be benefits to arbitration provisions in other contexts, they do not extend to sexual harassment claims. Victims of such serious misconduct should not be constrained to pursue relief from decision-makers who are not trained as judges, are not qualified to act as courts of law, and are not positioned to ensure that such victims are accorded both procedural and substantive due process.*[149]

Come March 2018, Sen. Richard Blumenthal (D-CT) and a group of Senate Democrats proposed an even better idea through their bill, the Arbitration Fairness Act. Instead of letting businesses force employees and consumers to take their claims to arbitration, their bill would let workers and consumers decide where to pursue their legal claims. "Mandatory arbitration undermines the development of public law because there is inadequate transparency and inadequate judicial review of arbitrators' decisions," they wrote. Unfortunately, thus far, these proposals have been ignored by Republican leaders in Congress.[149]

Other issues that arise through employment contracts involve the number of subcontracting that is done by employers. Instead of hiring employees who are entitled to benefits and certain legal rights in the workplace, employers will often contract out certain work or tasks so that they can save money, avoid paying benefits, and avoid risks. We have seen this very practice happen on a large scale through gig work and the gig economy. Gig workers, such as those working for ride-sharing companies, are often considered contractors which means they receive little to no benefits, at least not the ones afforded to normal employees. By hiring gig workers as contractors, employers are often exempt from paying them minimum wage and overtime too. Fixing this problem may mean classifying gig workers as employees, instead of contractors. But there are other concerns related to this decision from a legal standpoint. Thus, I'm sympathetic to both sides of the contractor vs. employee argument.

Overall, it would be most useful to classify this new, different, and increasingly common type of work under some new way of classifying employees altogether. Having a new classification that allows these workers to still receive needed benefits and living wages is crucial, but the details can certainly be worked out. Maybe referring to these workers as floating workers, who receive real benefits throughout their career, regardless of which gig work is being done. There is a problem when as a country we tie so many of our essential benefits to employees doing specific work. Tying benefits to employment provides less of an ability for workers to switch jobs and work according to their individual schedule, purpose, and needs in life. No one should have to stay at a job only because without it they wouldn't have healthcare. Especially considering the large health crisis this country faces.

Furthermore, addressing employment contracts to provide more rights to workers and getting rid of (or altering) at-will employment are steps that should be taken to make work equitable and fair for workers. We need to demand rights in the workplace, because work is our livelihood, and we rely on it functioning properly for us to survive and thrive.

What this talk about workers' rights boils down to is the process of creating a more equal system and power-dynamic between employees and their employers. Fixing that power dynamic is the point of organized labor, something that has been declining over the years in the U.S. Organized labor, labor unions, and so forth are often frowned upon or seen as unnecessary by certain industries, and a chunk of the general public. But it is important to remember that workers' rights have always had to be fought for overtime. Working conditions used to be truly awful or forced upon people over time, but during the late nineteenth century and much of the twentieth century, organized labor took off and much of the system we have now is a result of that progress.

The U.S. labor movement grew from a need to protect workers' common interests. We had the beginning of sustained trade union organization among American workers in 1794 Philadelphia with the formation of the Federal Society of Journeymen Cordwainers (shoemakers). Strikes also occurred more frequently around this period, with the earliest recorded strike in 1768, when journeymen tailors protested a wage reduction. The Great Depression finally created the conditions for which the labor movement would then grow. Industrial worker discontent combined with New Deal collective bargaining legislation brought the large mass-production industries within reach of real labor reform. "By the end of World War II, more than 12 million workers belonged to unions and collective bargaining had taken hold throughout the industrial economy." Workers in the industrial sector organized into labor unions which fought for better wages, reasonable hours, and safer work conditions. Also included were efforts to stop child labor, provide health benefits and aid to injured or retired workers. In recent years though, labor unions have declined drastically.[150]

Several forces swept through unionized industries from the 1970s onward. A large number of foreign goods, industrial restructuring, and deregulation in transportation and communications set the tone. "As oligopolistic and regulated market structures broke down, nonunion competition spurted, concession bargaining became widespread and plant closings decimated union memberships." The prized National Labor Relations Act increasingly thwarted the labor movement, with a major reform campaign to amend the law failing in 1978. Ronald Reagan was then elected in 1980, bringing with it a very anti-union administration.[150]

What are labor unions like today? According to the Bureau of Labor Statistics:

> *In 2019, the percent of wage and salary workers who were members of unions—the union membership rate—was 10.3 percent, down by 0.2 percentage point from 2018, according to the U.S. Bureau of Labor Statistics. The number of wage and salary workers belonging to unions, at 14.6 million in 2019, was little changed from 2018. In 1983, the first year for which comparable union data are available, the union membership rate was 20.1 percent and there were 17.7 million union workers.*[151]

So, you can see that union membership has been on the decline over the past few decades and only covers a small percentage of American workers. Who are these unions made of? 7.1 million public sector employees belonged to a union in 2019, compared with 7.5 million private-sector workers. The highest unionization rates as of 2019 belong to *Protective Service occupations* (33.8%), and *Education, Training, and Library occupations* (33.1%). The lowest rates occur in *Farming, Fishing, and Forestry occupations* (2.1%), *Sales and Related occupations* (2.8%), and *Food Preparation and Service-Related occupations* (3.5%). Geographically, "over half of the 14.6 million union members in the U.S. lived in just seven states (California, 2.5 million; New York, 1.7 million; Illinois, 0.8 million; Pennsylvania, 0.7 million; and New Jersey, Ohio, and Washington, 0.6 million each), though these states accounted for only about one-third of wage and salary employment nationally."[151]

The decline of American workers in labor unions is not for lack of worker preference. For the most part, Americans broadly support workers' right to unionize. According to a 2018 Pew survey, a majority (55%) hold a favorable view of unions and a third of Americans hold an unfavorable view. Most of us believe important professions that are crucial to our communities and economy, deserve union representation yet many of them don't have it. Large majorities in a 2015 survey said that workers in *Manufacturing and Factory* (82%), *Public Transportation* (74%), *Police and Firefighters* (72%), and *Public School Teachers* (71%) should have the right to unionize. As mentioned earlier, union members have the potential to be paid more if they belong to a union, many of which may not be making a living wage if it weren't for this representation. Union members generally earn more than non-union members, where in 2018 they respectively made a median of $1,051 compared to $860, among full-time workers. "The gap in earnings reflects many factors, including differences in industry and occupation, firm size and region."[23]

Unfortunately, employers are still too powerful when it comes to major issues of workers' rights such as conditions of employment, wages, workplace conditions, and so forth. You could see this power imbalance and the issues at stake during the Covid response when workers were protesting work conditions, matters of pay, problems around PPE, and so forth. For example, Amazon workers at one point were calling out sick in protest of the company's treatment of workers during the pandemic. There was also the case of slaughterhouse workers being forced to work in poor conditions, in a close environment, and at a fast pace for Smithfield Foods and other similar operations. These poor work conditions were already happening before the pandemic, it is just that these conditions and worker exploitation were brought into the light for us to see when COVID-19 cases spilled over. When a crisis hits, we see an increased amount of the conditions that were already in place. This means if work conditions were not ideal beforehand, it should not be surprising that conditions will get worse, forcing employees into a tough situation. It is important that businesses take risks seriously and not leave employees on the hook during difficult times.

A lack of American labor rights can be directly tied to much of the inequality we are seeing. America has some of the worst labor rights in the developed world, which is certainly harmful to the economy and well-being of workers. As labor has been suppressed, inequality has soared. Looking at the chart below (top 1% income share line drops in the middle), you can see as union density increased, the top 1% income share declined, and as union density decreased (much so after Reagan controls NLRB), the top 1% income share increased. The resulting income inequality, as we know, intersects with and increases the likeliness for other forms of inequality as well. To combat this, we should bring back labor unions and expand labor union access across more industries and through government legislation.[152]

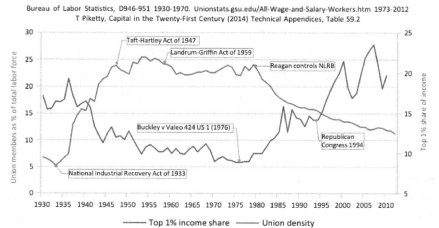

US union density and income inequality, 1930-2012

Bureau of Labor Statistics, D946-951 1930-1970. Unionstats.gsu.edu/All-Wage-and-Salary-Workers.htm 1973-2012
T Piketty, Capital in the Twenty-First Century (2014) Technical Appendices, Table S9.2

But labor law reform will be difficult to achieve without corporate governance reforms. Workers can be given representation by having one or more of a company's board be an employee of the company or a position that represents the employees. This person (or multiple people) would represent the best interests of the employees and could essentially communicate/coordinate with other board members, communicating needs and changes to work conditions for employees. That way if a decision is being made or proposed by the board, employees will have more of a say in what happens. The idea of worker representation on corporate boards is not new and has already been implemented in specific industries and several countries.

According to Ewan McGaughey, corporate law is past overdue in putting workers on boards, stating that: "(1) the evidence shows worker voice is embedded in American tradition and would expand economic prosperity, (2) worker voice now represents best corporate governance practice in the majority of OECD countries, and (3) there is no credible defense for 'shareholder primacy' because asset managers are voting on 'other people's money': those people are usually employees saving for retirement." Workers presently have no part in decision making regarding the very corporations they work for, decisions that will determine that corporations future. That includes issues such as "who to hire and how to compensate a CEO, whether to merge or acquire another firm, what kind of shareholder payments to authorize, and a wide variety of other key decisions."[152]

A Harvard paper from Lenore Palladino titled *Worker Representation on U.S. Corporate Boards*, "argues that workers should have representation on corporate boards of directors, and explores the policy choices in the U.S. economy of the 21st century to achieve" this goal. Effectively implementing this reform will require consideration of several key issues:

"how many corporate directors should represent employees; how they should be chosen and who counts as a worker when the choice is made; how they should meaningfully represent workers, and what information the board owes the workforce; how these choices are different in a unionized or non-union context; and the relationship between a worker's role as director and employee, in terms of pay, time, and protection from repercussions at work."[153] Corporations could voluntarily include workers on their board of directors, but as that is unlikely, the assumption is that this practice should be federally legislated, mandating this practice within all large corporations. States could take the lead on this issue, but that would inevitably lead to state legislation becoming entangled with federal labor law. That is why federal legislation mandating worker representation on corporate boards is essential.[153]

Various stakeholders, including workers, contribute to the success of a corporation, so it is only right that these stakeholders share representation on the board and are provided decision-making capabilities. This practice would lead to business decision making which increases worker visibility and considers the effects of decisions on workers. "Freeman & Lazear (1995) find that increased worker voice can allow more effective information transfer from board to worker, which reduces monitoring costs, creates motivation for workers, and promotes convergence of interest between shareholders and employees." Real participation in this process may encourage employees to increase company-specific investment, taking a longer view of the companies time horizon. "The challenges of actually implementing such a policy should not stand in the way of such a common-sense and fundamental reform that is necessary—though insufficient on its own—to rebalancing power within the corporation and ensuring long-term economic and social prosperity."[153] Many companies and specific industries have already had success in placing workers on boards, oftentimes state by state. These few and small wins were just about always met with pushback from the state or federal government.

The next step after worker representation in the boardroom is to make the entire board room employees. What I mean, is that another great idea for a business to consider is moving to- or starting- a worker cooperative. Workers having greater representation on the board of a company allows for more decision-making on the part of workers, but with only a few decision-makers representing the workers, workers still only have *some* input. A worker cooperative shifts from *some* employee input to *all* employee input. Alana Semuels from The Atlantic describes it as follows:

> *Worker cooperatives are equally owned and governed by employees, who also earn money from the profits of their labor. There are no CEOs here making multi-million-dollar salaries while workers receive minimum wage. Nor are there CEOs with decades of experience and education to successfully guide the company through the up and downs of the dog-eat-dog business world. In worker cooperatives, decision-making is democratic, so each worker has one vote, and policies can't be determined by an investor whose only priority is profit. (Most profit-minded investors probably wouldn't touch a worker cooperative with a ten-foot pole anyway).*[154]

Instead of a traditional top-down hierarchy, a worker cooperative is one where ownership takes the form of a democratically governed organization that is equally owned by consumers, producers, workers, or any combination of the three (multi-stakeholder).

According to the U.S. Federation of Worker Cooperatives, there are over 400 democratic workplaces or worker coops in the U.S.[155] Worker coops are fairly new in the U.S., but they are more established in other countries such as Spain. In Spain, the coops have proven to lead to larger growth than non-cooperatives due to employees having more financial stake in the company. At the same time, progress at these organizations can be slow since you need most if not all stakeholders to be on the same page for decision-making. Even though progress can be slow at these organizations, a great perk is that you have more people to listen to which means creative and unique solutions are easier to come by.

There is less likely to be a situation where some small board is unable to determine a good solution to a problem because it's the same old wheels turning, not to mention that many CEOs or leaders of an organization are making decisions away from the front lines. Furthermore, workers in a coop feel empowered to bring up and work on new ideas to improve the success of the organization because they have an actual stake in the outcome as opposed to traditional businesses where workers get paid regardless of how performance is.[154]

According to the Atlantic article, it may be the case that not everyone is meant to work in a cooperative. "Worker co-ops need people who are willing to compromise, give others the benefit of the doubt, and, most of all, who are invested in participating in a worker co-op." The former and Oregon-based worker-coop Burley is a bicycle trailer business that was pressured by global competition and had to sell the business to a single investor. How this business came to fail as a coop was due to not hiring the right people for a democratic system like they were successfully running for a few decades. At first, it seemed that worker coops may not be able to compete in the private market, but it turned out that over time Burley started hiring worker-owners who were not a good fit for that system, which caused the system to break down.

One lesson here is that even though it may take extra time and effort to make sure a new worker-owner is a good fit for the organization, it is worth the time because the system only works when everyone involved has buy-in for the democratic process. Another problem with coops is securing financing because it is a nontraditional company that investors and banks don't see as normal businesses. Not every worker-owner will have good credit and investors tend to be wary of nontraditional organizations. So, financing these types of businesses may require extra work but for those who truly want the democratic process, it can be worth it.[154]

If you think about it, it is weird that our democracy only applies to government, but we don't think to have any form of democracy in our workplace. Why is that? Why shouldn't we have at least some democratic measures in our work? We spend much more time at work, most of our waking hours are spent there, as opposed to only a few elections a year where we voice our democratic opinion in politics. I would argue that one large solution to our current punch-in, punch-out system of work is to make work more democratic, allowing for workers to be financially and mentally invested in the outcome of their work and the work of everyone else in the organization. Instead of paying millions of dollars in salary to one or a few people on the top to make decisions that often negatively impact workers down the totem pole, let's spread that wealth around and focus on making the organization a place *everyone* is proud to work at. More democracy can lead to more buy-in for a business that stakeholders are proud to work for and makes it much easier to achieve a work-life balance as a worker. As Semuels says,

Life at work is, after all, tiring and uninspiring for most employees. Life at a cooperative has the potential to be something different.[154]

Worker coops are certainly great options for many small to medium-sized businesses, but it's not for every business. Most large corporations wouldn't be able to implement this set-up just due to the sheer size of their organization, but even a large corporation can democratize some of the decision-making.

Along with changes in workers' power, there must be changes in the way businesses are run from the top down. As mentioned earlier, we have a large culture around idealizing hero's in business, especially with CEOs. We have this idea that a CEO can come in and fix everything or that all of the problems of a business fall solely on the CEO's shoulders. Sure, you have the 'Steve Jobs' out there who can make or break a company if they are or are not working as the CEO. But for the most part, most businesses should be looking for a solid leader, who can look after the long-term goals of the organiza- tion- not be the sole linchpin to its success or existence.

A hero mentality can be both ineffective in the short term and even dangerous to an organization that relies solely on one individual for decision-making. This hero culture is also what propagates our current culture around who controls and runs a corporation. The employees are the ones who make it all work, they are the lifeblood. Workers are not afforded much if any control over the operations of a business in large part *because* of this hero mentality. We are left to think that problems will and have been solved by CEOs and management teams and that we as workers or even consumers have no control over the decisions that are being made. We should be asking ourselves how much of the decisions and what type of decisions within an organization should be democratized. There are of course benefits to your average corporate or business hierarchy, as

214 ~ CHRIS RUDKOWSKI

greater interdependence can lead to more inefficiencies. Having said that, a hierarchy of positions doesn't necessitate a hierarchy of decisions.

Lorna Davis, who ran big companies like Danone, had a Ted Talk in which she brought up many of these points.

> *In a world as complex and interconnected as the one we live in, the idea that one person has the answer is ludicrous. It's not only ineffective, but also dangerous because it leads us to believe that it's been solved by that hero, and we have no role. We don't need heroes. We need radical interdependence, which is just another way of saying we need each other. Interdependence is a lot harder than being a hero. It requires us to be open and transparent and vulnerable, and that's not what traditional leaders have been trained to do. I thought being a hero would keep me safe. This is an illusion. The joy and success that comes from interdependence and vulnerability are worth the effort and the risk. And if we're going to solve the challenges that the world is facing today, we have no alternative, so we had better start getting good at it.* [156]

Davis argues that we should include those around us, including workers, possibly even competitors, in our day-to-day approach to leadership and running a company. When CEOs set goals for their corporation, many of those goals most likely can't be solved by them alone. But when you set that goal, you should announce to everybody that you don't have all the answers and seek input from others inside and outside the organization. It's not weak to do that, it's being honest, realistic, not to mention smart considering you'll likely receive critical feedback you otherwise would have missed. Bringing everyone into the process is true leadership. It's often in these open en-vironments where more ideas and creative thinking flows.

Part of moving to this new approach to leading a company involves placing employees and customers first. Many CEOs make decisions that impact the lives of workers across the world, while only viewing those workers as numbers on a spreadsheet. There are alternatives to this approach, which one CEO calls the *anti-CEO playbook*. Chobani CEO Hamdi Ulukaya took over a yogurt factory in upstate New York against traditional knowledge of the situation and others' advice telling him to do otherwise. That's because a very large food company had previously owned the factory and wasn't able to make their yogurt business work. But Ulukaya saw something in the workers who had been laid off and the surrounding com-munity, that made him take the leap- he took out a loan and made it into one of the most successful food brands in the country.[157]

He acknowledges in a TED talk about his story about what is wrong with traditional CEO leadership and that CEOs have their workers suffer for them, while they make more and more money. His anti-CEO playbook involves dropping the notion around shareholder primacy, calling it the dumbest idea he's ever heard in his life. He goes on to say a business should take care of its employees first. In 2016, Chobani announced it would give shares to all 2,000 of its employees. Some people viewed it as a PR stunt, others a gift. But he was sure to point out that the shares were earned by the employees through their hard work. The playbook also emphasizes the importance of community and giving back to the community, instead of the status quo around business which is to ask communities "what kind of tax breaks and incentives can you give me?" He says that businesses should be going to their communities, many of which are struggling, and ask "how can I help you?"[157]

Ulukaya took the same approach with the companies second yogurt factory. He built a plant in rural Idaho, where there weren't many trained employees who could work that job and the location didn't have many incentives, but that didn't stop him. He went from breaking bread with local Idaho farmers to building the plant to partnering with the local community college is training people in advanced manufacturing, to having one of the largest yogurt factories in the world. He goes on to explain that businesses traditionally stay out of politics, but should really take a side, and that side should be about responsibility and accountability. Responsible to the communities your business relies upon and accountable to consumers.[157]

Being accountable and listening to consumers should make up a large part of how corporate America runs its businesses and makes decisions. Ulukaya again:

> Today's playbook says the CEO reports to the corporate boards. In my opinion, CEO reports to consumer. In the first few years of Chobani, the 1-800 number on the cup was my personal number. When somebody called and wrote, I responded personally. Sometimes I made changes based on what I heard, because [the] consumer is in power.[157]

His greater point here is that businesses should report to the consumer, not to the corporate boards.

> You see, if you are right with your people, if you are right with your community, if you are right with your product, you will be more profitable, you will be more innovative, you will have more passionate people working for you and a community that supports you. And that's what the anti-CEO playbook is all about.[157]

I absolutely agree with his anti-CEO playbook, I think it is inspirational and I hope businesses across the world follow suit. When it comes to the power relationship between consumers and business, I will say it's worth bringing up. We as consumers and citizens have a vote when choosing to purchase or not purchase specific products and brands. We should not only vote with our purchases but also demand more transparency for the products and services we receive.

Of course, we don't have all the power in our relationship with the business world. If you look at the tech sector and what is happening with our data- being sold so we can be advertised to- there does appear to be a monopolistic market going on. Yogurt and other food products are of course different, but only to a degree because even food products aren't always transparent about how the food is made, what the ingredients are, what those ingredients do to our bodies long term, and whether animals are truly treated ethically by various companies. The key here is that we *should* use our purchasing decisions as votes, and we should take more control in these relationships if we can afford to. We should also demand greater transparency so that corporate America is forced to make the necessary changes to their businesses. Considering the ethics, environmental impact, and business effects of our purchasing decisions will lead to more workers being valued, thriving communities, and a more sustainable planet.

Part of consumers taking control is this understanding that we are all in this together, that your decisions as a CEO, as a company directly impact our shared environment as employees and as consumers. That is why corporate America needs to approach business in a full-circle, community, and environmentally conscious way. Lorna Davis explains this point from her perspective:

*I want to give you an example from the clothing in-
dustry, which produces 92 million tons of waste a year.
Patagonia and Eileen Fisher are clothing manufacturers
– both of them B Corps, both of them deeply committed
to reducing waste. They don't see that their responsibility
ends when a customer buys their clothes. Patagonia encourages you not to buy new clothes from them and will
repair your old clothes for free. Eileen Fisher will pay you
when you bring back your clothes and either sell them
on or turn them into other clothes. While these two companies are competitive in some ways, they work together
and with others in the industry to solve shared problems.*[156]

To clarify, a certified B-Corporation can be defined as follows,
according to bcorporation.net:

*Certified B Corporations are businesses that meet the
highest standards of verified social and environmental
performance, public transparency, and legal accountability to balance profit and purpose. The B Corp community
works toward reduced inequality, lower levels of poverty,
a healthier environment, stronger communities, and the
creation of more high-quality jobs with dignity and purpose. By harnessing the power of business, B Corps use
profits and growth as a means to a greater end: positive
impact for their employees, communities, and the environment.*[158]

To receive the certification, a company is required to have
*verified performance, legal accountability, and public trans-
parency.* The non-profit B Lab administers the certification,
and part of the process involves assessing the overall positive
impact of a company. Certified B corporations receiving a min-

imum verified score on the B Impact Assessment- "a rigorous assessment of a company's impact on its workers, customers, community, and environment—and make their B Impact Report transparent on bcorporation.net. Certified B Corporations also amend their legal governing documents to require their board of directors to balance profit and purpose."[158]

If more businesses work to receive this B-corps certification, we can truly start to see what a full-circle approach looks like on a much larger scale. Right now, there are over 2,500 certified b-corps globally, and that number could increase drastically if corporate America decided to take a stance on what matters most to our country. Shifting away from shareholder value and towards the greater end that is a positive impact on employees, communities, and the environment is exactly what we need right now. Part of our relationship with corporations as consumers is to look for these certifications in our purchasing decisions. That is what it means to be an active consumer, making the conscious choice to shop at one place over another for ethical and just reasons. It takes practice and a little extra work to align ourselves with the right businesses that stand for the same principles that you stand for, but it's worth the effort.[158]

As we move away from shareholder value towards a more long-term approach to corporate leadership with greater emphasis on all stakeholders instead of just one, we need to also think about incentives. Because it's fine and dandy to talk about redesigning our businesses for the better, but there has to still be the financial incentive to keep going and make long-term progress a reality. We can't completely get rid of shareholder value as it's an essential part of our corporate structure, but we can create a stock exchange that allows for greater unison between investors' goals (usually retirement) and a company's goals (to progress and increase its value over time).

There has been this idea floating around recently, referred to as the Long-Term Stock Exchange (LTSE). It would be the same regulatory category as NYSE or Nasdaq. But to be listed on this market (as a public company), companies would have to meet specific, long-term transparency requirements and listing standards that are focused on the long-term well-being of a company. This idea of an LTSE comes from NYT Bestselling author and entrepreneur Eric Ries, who is the founder and CEO of ltse.com. Eric is well-versed in business and providing value to others in this environment, and he is also the author of *The Lean Startup*, *The Startup Way*, and *The Leaders Guide*.[159]

If you go to ltse.com, you can learn all about the LTSE, but their vision is "a public market that supports investment, experimentation and scaling that companies can use to find continuous success; one that can open the way for innovation and value creation far into the future."[158] More on what an LTSE would provide:

> *We believe an ecosystem reflecting this relationship is critical for the continued growth of American companies. Today's companies deserve a public market where they are rewarded for making smart choices that embrace their futures – choices to innovate, to invest in their employees, to seed future growth. A market that reduces short-term pressures and encourages a steady cycle of innovation and investment in long-term value creation would benefit companies and their investors alike. Our vision is a market designed to support the methods of experimentation and scaling that modern companies use to find continuous success; one that can open the way for innovation and value creation for all companies, far into the future.*[158]

So, in essence, we're talking about longer time-horizons which is exactly what corporate America needs to focus on. A long-time horizon means having long-term shareholders, which inherently makes sense considering most Americans who invest in stocks and companies, are doing so they can re- tire- a long-term goal in itself. This exchange leads to a greater alignment between business goals and personal investment goals.

But how do you create a long-term stock exchange or any new stock exchange? Believe it or not, there's actually a form for that- SEC form 1. It's the U.S. Securities and Exchange Commission's (SEC) very first form, created as a result of Sec- tion 5 of the Securities Exchange Act of 1934 ("Exchange Act").[160] And what about accountability for companies who wish to be a part of the LTSE? Well, "companies that list their shares for sale on the Long-Term Stock Exchange will be re- quired to publish a series of policies that focus on long-term value creation and are designed to provide shareholders and other stakeholders with insight into the way that companies operate and build their businesses for the long term."[159]

A great benefit of using something like a long-term stock exchange is that you could require these businesses to treat their employees, their customers, and their communities like the shareholders that they are. Only allowing businesses who demonstrate their duty to all of their stakeholders, to be listed in this stock exchange, would be a great way of expanding the idea of a shareholder. Shareholders really should be stakehold- ers, because if you have a stake in the outcome of a business then you should at least be a part of the discussion or bene- fit from the decisions that this business makes. Ries says that the LTSE "will serve as inspiration to a new generation of civic entrepreneurs who will say: We don't have to take the insti- tutions of our society as a given. We could try to build new and better ones."[161] When you think about alternatives to running a business in America today, everything from a b-corps to an LTSE, we can start to build a picture of a more equitable and opportunistic design of American business and American work.

So far, we have talked about work in the context of corporations, CEOs, employees, and redesigning work up and down traditional hierarchies. Yet, there is also the hierarchy of human value and what we traditionally view as *real* work or work worth valuing in our society. Many workers in our culture of work are neglected, essentially invisible. I'm referring primarily to domestic workers, home care professionals, home cleaners, nannies, babysitters, elder care workers, and so forth. Activist and Director of the National Domestic Workers Alliance, Ai-jen Poo, gave a TED talk on this topic which strives to make the listener rethink our perspective of domestic work and the value we place on it.

> *You see, the cultural devaluing of domestic work is a reflection of a hierarchy of human value that defines everything in our world – a hierarchy that values the lives and contributions of some groups of people over others. Domestic workers live in poor neighborhoods and then they go to work in very wealthy ones. They cross cultures and generations and borders and boundaries, and their job no matter what is to show up and care, to nurture, to feed, to clothe, to bathe, to listen, to encourage, to care no matter what. It's the work that makes all other work possible, and it's mostly done by women – more than 90% women, disproportionately women of color. And the work itself is associated with work that women have historically done, work that's been made incredibly invisible and taken for granted in our culture. But it's so fundamental to everything else in our world. It makes it possible for all of us to go out and do what we do in the world*

every single day knowing that the most precious aspects of our lives are in good hands.[162]

It's not as if this lack of appreciation and devaluation of domestic workers is new either.

> *In the 1930s, when Congress was discussing the labor laws that would be a part of the New Deal, that would protect all workers, Southern members of Congress refused to support those labor laws if they included protections for domestic workers and farmworkers. That history of racial exclusion and our cultural devaluing of work that's associated with women now means that millions of women go to work every single day, work incredibly hard, and still can't make ends meet. They earn poverty wages without a safety net so that the women that we're counting on to take care of us and our families can't take care of their own, doing this work.*[162]

There has been some progress in this area recently, during the Obama administration. Over two million home care workers were brought under minimum wage and overtime protections for the first time since 1937. But the work is far from done.[162]

Ai-jen has been fighting for the rights of domestic workers for years, fighting for them to have the kinds of rights that more traditionally employed people have like health care, time off, and safety nets. She argues that the way we treat this group of people is really our moral compass, and I absolutely agree. We don't even talk about domestic workers as doing actual work, we often refer to them and their work as *help*. But this work is fundamental to our communities, and as such should be compensated and valued.

That is why it would be in *everyone's* best interest to provide these workers with affordable and quality healthcare, among other benefits- all of which would go a long way in showing that we value them and their work. I've argued about more time off and an overall appreciation for time throughout this book, and the same applies here. These workers should be given the time off they deserve, while also being paid enough so they can truly afford time off. The key here is that everyone, regardless of the work, deserves to have their time and work valued and respected. There are no jobs that someone should feel shame about.

There is a lot of work where workers feel a lack of dignity in what they do, and we simultaneously take them for granted, ignore them, or "look down at" their positions in our work culture. This is the wrong approach to work in general because we all rely on one another's work for us to do ours- and for us to just live our lives. If work is to be done, then let's not make it even harder for those who have to do it.[162]

Some business and government leaders say that these changes to work and our work system need to be systemic and happen all at once if they are to ever happen. Any organization who on one hand claims to care about its workers, but on the other abdicates its responsibility to take care of those workers because *other* organizations are not, should rethink its value statement. Why not be one of the few who step up to do the right thing and treat your employees as if they are individuals spending most of their working hours putting in work for your business, cause, etc.? I would argue that any organization that did this, would actually gain more long-term support and respect from the general public, including both current and potential employees. Redesigning American businesses around the needs of 21st-century work and the type of world we'd like to see, would lead to significant inroads against many of the inequalities and injustices surrounding our work culture today.

Chapter 15

A New Governance Model

Corporate America has a lot of work to do and plenty of opportunities to redesign our work here in the U.S. But changing business won't be enough for American workers, we need new approaches to American governance. Our nation's politics is very divisive right now and there has been little meaningful legislation around most issues, never mind legislation that could benefit American workers and our culture of work writ large. To make legislation we certainly need changes to our political structure and more of an active democracy, but even still the way we have governed and regulated around work has been minute- often specific policies that are conditional-based and are done without viewing work from the broad lens it deserves. I think these issues start with our approach to the economy and workers' place in it. As mentioned earlier in the GDP section and elsewhere, our economy is one based on growth and an infinite-resource view of the world. *What's good for the economy is growth, and thus what's good for workers is to be a part of that growth*, as it goes... but that approach to the economy and its resulting negligence towards communities and workers' well-being is unsustainable.

Instead, we should be spending less time on trying to create growth and more on operating within our planet's limits with a long-term approach to our communities and workers' well-being. English economist Kate Raworth, who works at the University of Oxford and the University of Cambridge, in her Ted Talk *A healthy economy should be designed to thrive, not grow* brings this valuable point about growth into light. Kate, along with some other economists, recommends a more sustainable view of our planet and the economy. "We have economies that need to grow whether or not they make us thrive," says Raworth. "And what we need, especially in the richest countries, are economies that make us thrive, whether or not they grow."[163]

She goes on to talk about the history of Gross Domestic Product (GDP) and our obsession with it. Not only are we economically addicted to growth, we are socially addicted to growth, possible through years of consumer propaganda. Her solution involves a Doughnut of Social and Planetary Boundaries, as seen in the image below. This doughnut economy, an economy un-reliant on growth, is one that lives between the social foundation and ecological ceiling as illustrated below.

The Doughnut of Social and Planetary Boundaries (2017)

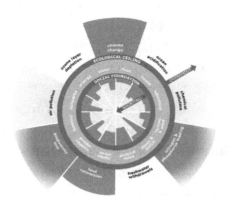

Source: *The Lancet Planetary Health* 2017 1e48-e49 DOI: (10.1016/S2542-5196(17)30028-1)

Dark green circles show the social foundation and eco-logical ceiling, encompassing a safe and just space for humanity. Red wedges show shortfalls in the social foun-dation or overshoot of the ecological ceiling. The extent of pressure on planetary boundaries that are not cur-rently being overshot is not shown here.[164]

The number of resources is finite on the planet. Thus, a model of growth and endless consumption will not work. Many paradigms of inequality exist and are perpetuated when our resources become used up. Once something is rare, it costs more. And thus, excludes others from accessing said item. In other words, our current model does not work. There is no room for exponential growth in a finite system.

Humanity's 21st-century challenge is to meet the needs of all within the means of the planet. In other words, to ensure that no one falls short on life's essentials (from food and housing to healthcare and political voice) while ensuring that collectively we do not overshoot our pressure on Earth's life-supporting systems, on which we fundamentally depend – such as a stable climate, fertile soils, and a protective ozone layer. The Doughnut of so-cial and planetary boundaries is a playfully serious ap-proach to framing that challenge, and it acts as a compass for human progress this century.[164]

A shift to a new model, one based on regenerative and dis-tributive design, is exactly the kind of model that works best for organizations, communities, and individuals in the short *and* long term. This shift has the potential to create a more sustainable work system for everyone. If American employ-ers and organizations focused and invested less on limitless growth, then they would be freed up to invest their profits in the employee's wellbeing. Organizations who are concerned less with their bottom line and more with *sustaining* their current operations should gladly invest in their employees and the communities in which they exist.

Shifting to a new model means shifting what we measure. As I said earlier, *you get what you measure*, so it's time we move away from GDP and towards alternative measurements of economic and national success. The following alternatives to GDP are meant to get us thinking about what sort of measurements should be included in future decisions around the economy and our workforce. Not to mention acting as a benchmark against ourselves year after year. Which alternative provides the greatest benefit will be a subjective matter, as we all have different priorities.

The one thing that GDP has, that these alternatives lack, is consensus. This is certainly a barrier in replacing or measuring alongside GDP, but the U.S. doesn't have to choose just one, it could create a dashboard of indicators. This could be done at each level of government too. I would argue that a federally led approach would be most useful as it would set the tone about which type of indicators matter- even allowing states and local governments to benchmark off the nation as a whole. An international consensus would certainly prove useful too, but that would likely require another meeting similar to the Bretton Woods Conference or other recent gatherings between nations related to these concerns.

One alternative to GDP is Gross National Happiness (GNH). In 1972, King Jigme Singye Wangchuck of the Buddhist kingdom of Bhutan, guided by Buddhism and mindfulness principles, decided that a more spiritual and holistic approach reflected his country's needs. Instead of only looking at the money put towards products and services, GNH takes 9 variables into account: living standards, health, good governance, ecological diversity, resilience, time use, psychological well-being, cultural diversity and resilience, and community vitality. "To measure these factors, government officials interview a random selection of 8,000 households, who are *compensated a day's wage* for answering an in-depth questionnaire." This measurement is great because it is very in-depth with 148 questions (including many sub-questions). With respect to cons, "answering these questions takes about three hours, and Bhutan has to pay both the workers interviewing residents and the residents themselves for their time."[165]

Not to mention that Bhutan's GNH is heavily focused on spirituality with questions about meditation and praying included. It has yet to be implemented in most other countries. I think the time it takes to pay for a random sample of citizens to take a three-hour survey is most worth it because we gain so much from being able to collect and measure this data. Tracking the progress of measures we truly care about over time allows decision-makers in government and business to act on them accordingly. Other countries such as the US could certainly adjust questions to be less spiritual and more tailored to agreed-upon indicators if desired. If you remember the happiness curve from the beginning of the book, it is safe to say we have much progress to gain in measuring national or global happiness. We can only go up from here, right?[165]

Another alternative is the Thriving Places Index (TPI), created by the UK charity *Happy City* to provide politicians and local organizers a better view of the welfare of their people. "Since its first run in 2016 assessing 9 cities, it's grown significantly – as of 2019, TPI generated scores for 351 English and 22 Welsh councils." Focusing primarily on sustainability, equality, and local conditions, the categories are then broken down into 60 indicators. TPI does not do country-wide rankings, instead asking three questions about a specific area: Is it a fair and equal place to live? Is it sustainable enough so that future generations can flourish? Are the conditions present for everyone to do well? What's neat about Happy City is that they also created a Happiness Pulse, "which is a micro index for communities, teams, and organizations – kind of like TPI for your workplace." Imagine if we measured workplace happiness, sustainability, and equality here in the US regularly? Talk about some solid feedback. The benefit of a TPI is that you can see how local communities are impacted by changing economies, which means it is much easier for local leaders to provide more locally informed decisions.[165]

Next is the Happy Planet Index (HPI), founded by the New Economics Foundation. This index seeks to measure wellbeing in a new way. "By factoring in the ecological footprint, inequality, wellbeing, and life expectancy of a country, the HPI provides a simple but rounded glance at the wealth of a country." The foundation compiles their data from a Gallup World Poll, the U.N.'s data on life expectancy, and the Global Footprint Network. "Unlike GDP, this index measures equality by investigating how evenly distributed life expectancy and wellbeing are across a country." Each country's score is determined via the following equation: (life expectancy * experienced wellbeing) * inequality of outcomes / ecological footprint.[165]

This is great because the HPI is easily measurable, flexible, and applicable to many countries. As I mentioned earlier, having an index that has consensus is a large problem when deciding upon international measurements, something that HPI works around. The index also divides people's health and happiness by the size of their country's carbon footprint, putting the country's environmental impact into perspective and dramatically shifting the ranking results. Unfortunately, there is little nuance due to assessing only 4 factors. The U.S. is 108th right now, to give you an idea of how much work we have in front of us.[165]

Another alternative is the Human Development Index (HDI). This is a United Nations Development Program, which was made with a focus on opportunity and capability, rather than just economic growth or environmental sustainability. Interestingly, the U.N. encourages nations to use it alongside their gross national income data. They say that it can help governments assess national policy by "asking how two countries with the same level of GNI per capita can end up with different human development outcomes." The benefit of this index is that it looks at both education and income per capita together, which allows a country to see if money and opportunities are being funneled to the people. On the flip side, this indicator misses a few key factors of human wellbeing.[165]

The Chinese government developed the Green Gross Domestic Product (GGDP), which is essentially the normal GDP but "adjusts the measurements by monetizing environmental damage factors to help countries better understand exactly where they stand environmentally." This measurement was created "in an attempt to understand the consequences of their carbon emissions and account for the losses they experience from climate change." This measurement is great in that it puts a number on environmental negligence. One large barrier here is that it can be very difficult to place a price on factors like the loss of biodiversity, with the price's accuracy being debatable. It is easier to assign a price on CO2 emissions because they are much easier to measure in our atmosphere.[165]

Next is the Genuine Progress Indicator (GPI), which was created in the US as a possible replacement for GDP. It "takes into consideration all the same factors as the GDP, while also accounting for things like the cost of crime, ozone depletion, and lost leisure time, to paint a more rounded picture of the success of a country." Whereas GDP is boosted by issues such as environmental destruction and natural disasters and perpetual systems like mass incarceration, the GNP provides a more well-rounded assessment of welfare in that it factors in environmental, social, and economic indicators together. We'll have to wait to see how this measurement pans out because only a few U.S. states have implemented it.[165]

Moving into an index that focuses primarily on human lives instead of the economy is exactly what the Better Life Index (BLI) seeks to do. This index "was developed by the Organization for Economic Cooperation and Development (OECD), a group founded in 1961 with one goal: to help governments design better policies to improve lives." They identified 11 facets that are essential to well-being: housing, income, jobs, community, education, environment, civic engagement, health, life, satisfaction, safety, and work-life balance.[165]

If you haven't noticed, we have talked about many of these facets in this book already, these issues are very intertwined. Data on BLI has already been collected since 2014, "plans to compare current conditions to conditions over time" with enough data available. The interesting part of this measurement, and which separates it from the others, is that it doesn't come with a pre-imposed value system. Instead, the index lacks a cut-and-dry assessment or ranking, with a site that lets users navigate a country's BLI depending on the factors they value most. But its greatest strength here is also its greatest weakness. "When a measurement can't be broken down into easily digestible raw data, it often fails to gain traction."[165]

The Gross National Happiness and the Better Life Index seem to be the most useful due to their all-encompassing and detail-oriented approaches. A well-rounded approach in measuring the economy as well as both human and planetary health provides a lot of information from which to work. Not to mention that this measure covers most of the major issues discussed earlier, including work-specific indicators like *number of jobs*, *work-life balance*, and most importantly (in my opinion) *time use*. These measures fit within a more equitable, just, and sustainable framework, unlike GDP and its limitless growth/consumption-focused framework. Concerning the

U.S., I think which alternative or indicators you focus on depends on which level of government.

It makes much more sense for a Mayor or CEO who resides in a specific city, to focus on TPI due to its localized approach. Whereas it would be advantageous for a state to collect and compare the TPI of cities within the state as well as look at other major indicators. The federal government should most certainly be concerned with big picture measurements, allowing policy decisions to be made which benefit American citizens and workers. Compiling and analyzing this data wouldn't be difficult either. There are multiple approaches one can take but offering to pay a random sample of citizens to take a detailed survey seems like the best approach to me. The government could easily stand up a commission that looks at these or any new indexes worth measuring. The data which comes from this commission could then be used by other government agencies and entities in making decisions.[165]

When it comes to using new indexes though, it helps to know if any of them proved useful to countries that have already decided to replace or supplement GDP. Luckily, a group of countries formed together to create The Well-Being Economy Governments Partnership (WEGo). WEGo is a "collaboration of national and regional governments promoting sharing of expertise and transferrable policy practices... [that aims] to deepen their understanding and advance their shared ambition of building wellbeing economies."[166] WEGo is currently composed of Scotland, New Zealand, Iceland, and Wales, with an understanding that development in the 21st century involves delivering human and ecological well-being, which is exactly the thesis of the doughnut economy mentioned earlier.

Scotland's First Minister, Nicola Sturgeon, who gave a TED talk *Why Governments Should Prioritize Well-being*, talks about the shift away from GDP and towards a well-being economy. According to Nicola, placing a larger emphasis on factors like equal pay, childcare, mental health access, and green space, would lead to a greater resolve in tackling global challenges. Nicola starts her talk by mentioning how close the physical location of her talk was to the home of world-renowned Scottish economist Adam Smith.

> *In The Wealth of Nations, Adam Smith argued, amongst many other things, that the measurement of a country's wealth was not just its gold and silver reserves. It was the totality of the country's production and commerce.*[167]

To a degree, this described what eventually became the GDP. But Nicola goes on to say that Adam Smith likely would not have wanted GDP to become the most important measurement of a country's overall success. What we choose to measure matters because it drives political focus and public activity. *You get what you measure.* GDP places value on illegal drug consumption, but not on unpaid care. "It values activity in the short term that boosts the economy, even if that activity is hugely damaging to the sustainability of our planet in the longer term." That has been the predominant mindset for countries in modern human history and Nicola's point here is that it is unsustainable and on a deep level, missing the mark on what makes a country- which is just a group of people- successful. Nicola's argument is what WEGo represents, showing a sense of unity between countries that are deciding to focus on the right measures. She is asking others, including other countries, to rethink *success* on a fundamental level. One of the themes of this book is that our time isn't valued in our current system of work, and how could it be if we're not measuring the right factors or even asking the right questions? [167]

> *When we focus on well-being, we start a conversation that provokes profound and fundamental questions. What really matters to us in our lives? What do we value in the communities we live in? What kind of country, what kind of society, do we really want to be? And when we engage people in those questions, in finding the answers to those questions, then I believe that we have a much better chance of addressing the alienation and disaffection from politics that is so prevalent in so many countries across the developed world today.*[167]

I couldn't agree more with Nicola here. Answering all of those questions will also tell us how we should shape our culture and system of work. Once we understand what matters to us in our lives, what we value in our communities, and what kind of country or society we wish to be, we can create a system that values both workers and the value they bring to society every single day. Right now, the network of countries which created WEGo also has women in positions of leadership. Something tells me that it's not a coincidence that fighting for more equitable measures of a country's success has been initiated in large part by women leaders. And we have already seen with the response to Covid the benefit of having women in positions of power.

Partway through the pandemic response, data showed that countries led by women suffered six times fewer confirmed deaths from Covid-19 than countries with governments led by men. "Moreover, female-led governments were more effective and rapid at flattening the epidemic's curve, with peaks in daily deaths roughly six times lower than in countries ruled by men."[168] The point here isn't to say gender equality inherently leads to more equitable outcomes for a nation's success or health, but to say that more gender equality on the world stage is long overdue and can lead to a shift in priorities from defining a country's success via growth to general wellbeing. It is important now more than ever to shift our focus away from short-term measures of limitless growth, production, and consumption towards short *and* long-term measures of *total* wellbeing.

It would behoove the U.S. to join this network of global leaders focused on an economy of wellbeing. Without properly measuring the most important facets of American living and wellbeing, we will continue to make decisions based on limited data and a limited understanding of the real American experience for our citizens. It is in the best interest of the US to replace GDP with more equitable, just, and sustainable measurements which we as a country value in ourselves and our communities. Doing so will allow those in charge- such as politicians and CEOs- to chart a path forward that seeks to improve *specific* measures, not just growth.

Shifting into actual government policies that create an environment where American workers can thrive, there are plenty of policy ideas available. But given the scope of the issue, we're dealing with- many Americans working purposeless jobs and wasting much of their time at work- I would argue we need large, innovative policies. One such policy involves creating more opportunity and work-life balance for many Americans, by providing a sum of money at the beginning of a young adult's career or professional journey. We often assume that balance is something that everyone has an equal chance of pursuing, but reality doesn't back that up.

That is why Professor of economics and urban policy at The New School, Darrick Hamilton, is pushing for the U.S. to tackle wealth and equality by starting a new type of federal cash-flow pipeline. An "ambitious trust-fund scheme that would endow each American baby with a nest egg of cash, retrievable when they reach adulthood." This fund would essentially work like social security in reverse, and Darrick describes it as "an economic birthright to capital for everyone." This is an idea that may seem very progressive or even extreme, but I would like to mention that what opportunities we receive in life are not distributed equally and that everyone deserves to have an equal chance in deciding how their future will unfold- including their career.[169]

Hamilton points out the usually ignored narrative of success in the country, where the wealth gap in the U.S. is so large and disproportionately affects people of color. This inequality trickles down generations and makes the process of building wealth and creating opportunities for work-life balance more difficult to come by. And as mentioned earlier, American workers' wages have stagnated, leaving many struggling to stay afloat. When you're only focusing on making enough money to pay the bills by the time you enter the workforce, it can become very difficult to get out of that cycle. Hamilton believes that adding cash to the equation for every American will make the American dream more attainable. This cash could be used to pay for better (or more) education, healthcare costs, and other large but often necessary purchases such as a car or home.

Under Hamilton's plan:

> The average endowment would be about $25,000 per kid, rising to $60,000 for the poorest children in America. Those born into the wealthiest tax brackets would not be excluded from the trust-fund scheme, and every child in the US would get at least $500. The money would be set aside in federally managed coffers, growing at about 2% a year (to adjust for inflation) until a kid reaches adulthood. At that point, they'd decide what kinds of "asset-enhancing activity" they want to invest in for themselves, whether it's higher education, a new home, or their own business.[169]

Hamilton admits there are plenty of details to be worked out but this is the type of solution that makes work more manageable at the beginning of an adult's career, creating a situation that allows for more time, money, and opportunity. All of which are important for a work-life balance. If a young adult receives some initial money and has access to greater opportunity, they will not only find themselves in a better position to work, they will also have increased opportunities at a young age- which compounds over time. It's also possible that many youths may start planning for and thinking about their actions before adulthood if they know money is on the table when they become an adult.[169]

Another policy proposal that has been floated is similar in design but different in impact. A smaller investment could be made by the federal government at birth for every American, but instead of being taken out at adulthood, it doesn't get taken out until retirement. It involves less capital up-front from the government and works to solve the retirement issue, as many Americans are forced to continue working into retirement without a choice because they have no retirement funds. In other words, it tries to solve the opportunity issue on the opposite side of the equation. Pershing Square Capital Management Chairman Bill Ackmen has proposed this idea in an attempt to solve the increasing inequality gap. His plan would have each child born in the US receive $6,750 in a government-funded basket of index funds, which could only be tapped at retirement. "Assuming 8% returns over 65 years from birth to retirement, that total would ultimately exceed $1 million, and it would cost the government about $26 billion a year if the birthrate holds."[170]

Now of course other ideas would also combat inequality such as stopping rising CEO salaries, taxing top earners at a higher tax rate, closing tax loopholes for the wealthy, and others, but none of these mainstream solutions tackle our outdated system of work where a lack of opportunity happens essentially from birth. Hamilton's proposal would cost about $100 Billion a year and has the potential to act as a social safety net that allows for greater financial flexibility for many Americans. This safety net creates an environment where our new definition of work can thrive, and where a greater work-life balance can be achieved. Hamilton and Ackmen's solutions are the innovative types of solutions we should look at when trying to achieve a balance so that we are no longer working to make a "living", but simply living in and of itself.[169]

A Guaranteed Income

This issue of providing capital to people before they enter the workforce and increasing opportunities across the board, begs the question of the government's role in our lives. The point of taxation is to distribute services to every American that creates the conditions for us to live our lives. Not to mention provide for the public good, which is something out of the purview of businesses and requires us to ask what services truly fall under the public good category. When I think about the government's role in our lives, I look at the large amounts of inequality that exist in the U.S., and I ask myself what the government can do to create the conditions for us to not just live but thrive. Right now, the conditions in America are not looking good. The top-down approach from our government on economic, political, and social issues has not been enough to give Americans the *means* of which to build opportunity and success into their lives. So, I think it's about time we look into bottom-up solutions. The baby-bond idea just mentioned is one example of this, but I think we can do one better that addresses even more of the problems that we're faced with today.

A crisis like Covid demonstrates the need for continuous long-term assistance to Americans. A little money would go a long way. In recent months more Americans were evicted from their homes and small businesses were forced to shut down, lay off their employees, and many even went completely out of business. Considering that many Americans and storeowners are living on the margins with respect to their wages and profits, this shouldn't be a surprise. When it comes to large companies that can weather a storm like an economic downturn, many of them still laid-off employees and told them good luck, without any assistance. Some industries were bailed out by the government as well, deemed "too big to fail" yet again. If these corporations and industries started to put money aside in an emergency fund for instances like this (since we always know an economic downturn is around the corner), then many American workers could have had paychecks (or most of it at least) still coming in, keeping these workers afloat.

That's what it means to take care of your employees and do the right thing. Our economy is just too fragile to maintain the status quo of short-term priorities over the well-being of our own workers. Ideally, Americans shouldn't have to feel forced to work through a pandemic because that's the only way they can pay their bills (since their employers won't pay them a living wage), and work shouldn't be the only thing keeping Americans from falling into poverty or homelessness. We saw how well unemployment benefits and a $1200 stimulus check helped Americans over a few months, allowing them to pay bills and other necessities. If these benefits proved so useful and it was able to be done on a massive scale, then that only confirms our need for this type of assistance long-term. If corporate America won't or is unable to help Americans weather a crisis, then the government could address these problems, along with the way we work (and view work) as a whole, by providing a guaranteed income.

The idea of guaranteed income for every American is known as Universal Basic Income (UBI) or annual income, or Freedom Dividend. For the sake of clarity, I will refer to this idea as UBI in this chapter. The basic idea behind UBI is that every citizen would receive money from the government every year, one payment a month, which would essentially move power within the economy to the citizens (trickle-up) as opposed to top-down measures such as tax breaks for companies and the wealthy. Not only was a trickle-up economy discussed in great detail and advocated for in the past, but this idea has been floating around for some time. Trickle-up and demand-side economics were brought into mainstream economics when UK economist John Maynard Keynes discussed it in detail through his work during The Great Depression. The idea here is that aggregate demand created by households, businesses, and the government is the most important driving force in an economy, as opposed to the dynamics of a free market.

Without going too far into macroeconomics, it is clear to see that UBI would place more money in the hands of the lower and middle class, creating opportunities for these individuals to become debt-free, pay their bills and provide for basic necessities, start or continue to develop savings, and spend more money in the economy. These outcomes, at the least, are possible for many if not lower- and middle-class families. Even from an economic standpoint, where providing people enough money to survive isn't the first priority, we can still see the benefit of someone in the U.S. not being kicked out of their apartment during a crisis (such as a pandemic).

If someone can afford to pay rent, then the landlord continues to be paid without having to waste time or money bringing in a new tenant. Now both the tenant and the landlord can continue to provide demand for other items and businesses that would otherwise be difficult had the tenant nowhere to go and the landlord less money. Everyone including policy ex-

242 — CHRIS RUDKOWSKI

perts will point out how bad the homelessness crisis is, but when it comes to preventing it from taking place to begin with, there's less concern or talk about the issue.[171]

I am not the only one who thinks a guaranteed income is a good idea, but also an imperative solution to the way we view equality of capital and people in our society. MLK said during a speech at Stanford (1967) "now one of the answers, it seems to me, is a guaranteed annual income, a guaranteed minimum income, for all people and for all families of our country."[172] MLK could see the value of providing a *financial floor* if you would, so that no one who is struggling to get by is forced into an even worse situation. Senator Elizabeth Warren echoed these words concerning the Covid crisis, stating "Americans needed an income floor before the crisis, they clearly need one during the crisis, and they need one after the crisis."[173]

UBI would not only provide this floor but over time it would allow American workers to work part-time or full-time at any point in their lives, so they are not struggling to get into the right type of employment, staying employed, and retiring from employment at the right age. It furthermore provides a cushion for workers, and it buys them more time in their career and life decisions. Unlike changes to which Americans and businesses pay taxes that seem to occur with every presidential administration, UBI has the potential to not favor any one person over another.

Guaranteed income would provide for and demonstrate that we value every member of society, regardless of race, gender, age, and so forth. As mentioned earlier, numerous jobs are forgotten about or looked down upon by others- including domestic workers, stay-at-home parents, and many service jobs. A guaranteed income would provide for these members of our society who we know provide valuable, necessary work within our communities. Everyone contributes to creating wealth, regardless of whether they work a traditional job or not, and everyone deserves a share in that wealth.

The most important question of this policy is how much would it cost? "According to Hilary Hoynes, an economist at the University of California, Berkeley, the annual cost of a truly universal federal-basic-income program in the U.S. would be around three trillion dollars, which is approximately three-fifths of current total federal expenditures."[174] You could have a more financially viable model structured like the relief acts passed by Congress during the pandemic, where the income cutoff is set higher than most current welfare programs. This model wouldn't be universal of course but it would certainly address economic inequality to a large degree. I think universal income is more efficient for the government to manage and it also demonstrates to every American that we value all of them. UBI would also prove helpful during a crisis where more Americans are jobless since many assistance programs in America are conditional on employment. Crisis or not, there is always a large group of Americans dealing with economic concerns and unpredictable financial situations (like sudden, major health bills), so providing unconditional assistance across the board would be essential.

Some might think accountability is important for getting Americans to work, but as previously illustrated with the cost of living, Americans already need to work. Thus, it is unfair and overly cumbersome to add conditional requirements to social welfare and public assistance programs such as work requirements and tedious documentation for health insurance, food stamps, and a program like UBI. Unfortunately, the Trump administration, Congress, and specific federal agencies had already proposed and passed more of these conditional requirements during his years as President, based on unsubstantiated claims that doing so would "ensure that [requirements] are consistent with principles that are central to the American spirit — work, free enterprise, and safeguarding human and economic resources, [while also] reserving public assistance programs for those who are truly in need."[175]

Now of course to pay for such a program the U.S. would have to make changes to the way our government taxes. It is in our best interest to ensure everyone pays their taxes and make it difficult for corporations or wealthy individuals to utilize tax evasion regarding American dollars. This means passing legislation making it illegal or at least regulating these practices to some degree. Money that was made off of the backs of American workers should be taxed and go right back to workers and the country writ large. For workers to be paid less than a living wage and then have much of that company's or CEOs profits find its way overseas is not right or sustainable. For the richest Americans, those who are in the top 1% of earners, many have openly said they don't mind paying taxes if taxes are efficient, and the government spends tax revenues on proper government services. It is certainly feasible and in our best interest for the federal government to fix its tax system and capacity to budget without taking on more national debt in the long term.

One problem with making sure everyone pays their taxes is that the IRS must be able to handle auditing on a large enough scale. At the moment, the IRS does not have enough personnel to handle that many audits. This brings me to the next change, which is to beef up the IRS. Every administration has just about dismantled the IRS' capabilities and capacity to do its job, which is the last thing you want when an entire country relies on them to do their job during a crisis (i.e., doling out stimulus checks). Also, it would be useful if the IRS operated more efficiently like other developed countries. Many other developed countries track their citizens' pay stubs and then do the math for them come tax season. So instead of our inefficient system where the IRS says you must figure out how much money you owe or should receive (and if you get it wrong you'll pay a penalty), the IRS would say *this is how much money you made, this is how much money you will pay (or get paid), and if it's not correct, please submit the appropriate documentation.*

The system is much simpler in other countries and we would be doing ourselves a favor by following suit. Not to mention this could all be done online, where most of us do our taxes anyway. There is likely a correlation between the number of groans made during tax season and the number of "taxation is theft" bumper stickers driving around- people hate the IRS and they certainly don't enjoy the day or week-long process of filing. If we made it more customer-focused, the IRS might just win some brownie points, making its budget less likely to be slashed if people respect it more.

Furthermore, having enough funding means having enough workers in place to handle any large, federal, policy solution that would require quick and easy dispersal of funds- such as UBI or stimulus checks during a crisis. Having a large enough IRS means they can handle more of the load, allowing them to handle the dispersal of funds more effectively. We saw how difficult it was trying to rely on mailing out stimulus checks to millions of Americans across the country when and where they needed it. People move all over the place or become evicted- as we saw during Covid- so having enough employees to handle that more effectively and move more fund distribution online, would go a long way.

Another benefit of beefing up the IRS is you would have enough auditors to make sure those who owe money are paying the right amount and not getting away with tax avoidance. The IRS hasn't been effective at preventing or finding tax avoidance for quite some time, so they need assistance there. Preventing tax avoidance- especially among top earners- has the benefit of increasing tax revenues as well, which is money that belongs to Americans. Another important change to our tax structure is that of simplifying the current tax code. Right now, there are so many exemptions and stipulations attached to the tax code that it is not only inefficient, it also prevents what could be a simple method of levying taxes.

When we simplify the tax code, we need to address the tax structure and tax rates. That means keeping a simple progressive income tax rate on personal income. What the exact rates are can be debated but it should be progressive enough so that the more you make the more you pay, especially for anyone close to the top 1% due to the very large increase in earnings between the top 90th percentile and top 1% of earners.[176] A wealth tax is also an option, but it has failed in much of Europe. Out of twelve countries that had one in 1990, only three have them now. This is in large part for the following reasons: "it was expensive to administer, it was hard on people with lots of assets but little cash, it distorted saving and investment decisions, it pushed the rich and their money out of the taxing countries—and, perhaps worst of all, it didn't raise much revenue." U.S. Senator Elizabeth Warren proposed a wealth tax and much of the policy was designed with the European failures in mind. That includes not being able to escape national taxes, limiting the tax to only the "super-rich", and a "significant increase in the IRS enforcement budget."[177] Another barrier is that a wealth tax may be unconstitutional, so there may need to be a constitutional amendment to let it stick.

We also need to reform corporate income tax. This tax provides the third-largest source of federal revenue, although substantially smaller than the individual income tax and payroll taxes. "It raised $230.2 billion in fiscal year 2019, 6.6 percent of all federal revenue and 1.1 percent of gross domestic product (GDP)." Right now, the U.S. taxes the profits of U.S.-resident C-corporations at 21%, reduced from 35% due to the 2017 Tax Cuts and Jobs Act. As you can imagine, the $230.2 billion corporate income tax raised was less than years prior, down 9% since 2017. Having a stable corporate income tax rate so corporations are paying their fair share of money, is necessary for strong and stable tax revenue. Companies that do business in the U.S. sometimes skip out on paying taxes because they find loopholes and are good at tax avoidance. We need to remove all of these loopholes and make sure American-made dollars are taxed and go back to providing services to citizens and funding for communities.[178]

Another type of tax is a speculation tax, which has been proposed by U.S. Senator Bernie Sanders. This is "a small levy on every stock, bond or derivative sold in the United States." It is essentially a tax on Wall Street, where we see a lot of money exchanging hands and most Americans not benefitting from the exchange or resulting impacts on American companies and investors. As mentioned earlier, only around half of Americans have a reasonable amount of money in the stock market, in terms of investment, yet the stock market has so much sway in the form of power and the worth of businesses across the country. "Under the Sanders proposal, trades would be taxed at a rate of 0.5 percent for stocks and 0.1 percent for bonds. A stock trade of $1,000 would thus incur a cost of $5."[179] There would likely be mixed effects from this tax such as raising the cost of investment (which is a cost to the economy) and discouraging unproductive trading (which is good for the economy).[179]

Finally, another method of paying for large government policies is tossing out the inefficient sales tax and replacing it with a Value-Added Tax (VAT). A VAT is "a consumption tax placed on a product whenever value is added at each stage of the supply chain, from production to the point of sale. The amount of VAT that the user pays is on the cost of the product, less any of the costs of materials used in the product that has already been taxed." Value-added taxation is used by more than 160 countries around the world and is most common in the European Union. So, we know it's certainly possible to implement here in the U.S. Of course, there are advocates and critics of this tax too. "Advocates say it raises government revenues without punishing success or wealth, as income taxes do, and it is simpler and more standardized than a traditional sales tax, with fewer compliance issues." Critics charge that a VAT is a regressive tax, which adds bureaucratic burdens for businesses and places an increased economic strain on lower-income taxpayers.[180]

It's important to point out though, that you can tailor the VAT to exempt common household goods like diapers for example and increase the percentage taxed on luxury items (usually purchased by high earners). Thus, it can be tailored to be progressive, not regressive. A VAT is based on taxpayers' consumption, not their income. It's estimated that a "VAT might raise between $250 billion and $500 billion [annually] in revenue for the government" depending on how you run the numbers and whose estimate you use.[180] The fact is that there are certainly some pros and cons to this policy, but it can be tailored to have the right effect.

In the end, regardless of which changes we make to how we tax, there do need to be *some* changes, not the status quo of a back and forth game on tax rates for individuals and corporations. Fixing U.S. taxation has the potential to increase revenue both short and long term, allowing us to afford large policy initiatives such as UBI.

There are other contentions about a guaranteed income, unrelated to the government's ability to pay for it. One is that by itself, it won't directly solve inequality and provide the largely missing opportunity this country needs. I would like to state that I completely agree that it won't solve inequality overnight. But UBI would decrease financial inequalities through direct cash payments, and many of the other inequalities such as race, gender, age, etc. are directly tied to whether or not Americans have money. UBI also provides the conditions in our environment which lead to increased opportunities for Americans, especially low and middle-income. At the same time, increased opportunities and greater equality still don't address the concern of workers taking pride in their work or finding purposeful, meaningful jobs. The work that workers do daily must be work that these individuals and their communities find value in. When a worker is forced to work in these conditions or is simply working to make money and not working for a *purpose*, money can only go so far. What is required are more purposeful jobs and meaningful work provided across the entire country, accessible to everyone.

Workers want to feel like they are providing value to their families, their communities, and the country. According to clinical psychologist and Professor of Psychology, Jordan Peterson, what people want most is to be "provided a place where they can accept social and individual responsibility in an honorable manner."[181] This statement was in the context of discussing UBI, and his overall point was that UBI is certainly an option, but the primary concern should be providing work in which people can accept that responsibility and feel pride in what they do. "Most men would feel insulted if it were proposed to employ them in throwing stones over a wall, and then in throwing them back, merely that they might earn their wages," Henry David Thoreau once wrote about work in the nineteenth century. "But many are no more worthily employed now."[182]

This is still true in America. I completely agree with both Peterson and Thoreau's premise and I think a form of guaranteed income can certainly be a part of the solution, as it would empower citizens in their pursuit of greater personal and career goals. Unfortunately, we have stripped much of the dignity, pride, purposeful, and honorable work away from many workers, and some have never had this type of work in the U.S.

Shifting to a 21st-century economy, a more international and interconnected economy, and an economy that prioritizes profits over American workers has led to this stripping away of American jobs along with the purpose and identity they provide our workers. We have seen more factories shutting down or becoming automated- which requires different skills for many workers. We see farmers struggling to make ends meet, relying on government subsidies to get by. Much of which is due to multinational agricultural corporations having a monopoly over their businesses and the work and lives of farmers. We have and are transferring away from traditional 20th-century work towards an information economy that doesn't benefit every profession or geographic location equally. The list goes on, but the fact is that entire communities have lost their sense of identity, entire groups of individuals- whether it's by race, income, geographic location, and so on- have lost (or never had) that sense of purposeful work.

Real people are suffering, and we have no problem blaming it all on capitalism or saying capitalism is the solution, but what we need now are real policy solutions. As we experience massive change to the way we live our lives and the way we work, it is only natural that our systems change with it- political, economic, and social. We shouldn't view the flaws in these systems as a reason for throwing them out, without first shifting our priorities (i.e. emphasis on workers) and devising necessary solutions, some of which are new and considered "bold". I think a policy solution like UBI provides what this moment in American history needs. It prioritizes Americans as a whole and creates the conditions to live out our new vision of American work life.

Another contention with any form of guaranteed income is that it would incentivize people to stop working. They would become lazy and unproductive to society if we guaranteed them an income. Two things on that. First, can someone really survive off of $1000 a month (to pick a number) in and of itself? That's only $12,000 annually, barely enough for a decently used car. When you consider the costs for rent and other major purchases such as food and transportation, it becomes quite clear that this money would provide enough for only *some or most* major expenses, but not all of them. Thus, people would still have to work in some capacity. Furthermore, the economic and psychological factors behind the idea that welfare makes people lazy are plain wrong.

Economists have known for a while now that well-planned anti-poverty programs, like the Earned Income Tax Credit, increase labor participation. "A 2015 meta-study of cash programs in poor countries found "no systematic evidence that cash transfer programs discourage work" in seven different countries: Mexico, Nicaragua, Honduras, the Philippines, Indonesia, or Morocco. Other studies of cash-grant experiments in Uganda and Nigeria have found that such programs can increase working hours and earnings, particularly when the beneficiaries are required to attend classes that teach specific trades or general business skills."[183] There's also the striking finding from a new paper from researchers at Georgetown University and the University of Chicago that welfare programs led to greater employment and health prospects for low-income children. "They analyzed a Mexican program called Prospera, the world's first conditional cash-transfer system, which provides money to poor families on the *condition* that they send their children to school and stay up to date on vaccinations and doctors' visits. In 2016, Prospera offered cash assistance to nearly 7 million Mexican households."[182]

"The researchers found that the typical young person exposed to the program for seven years ultimately completed three more years of education and was 37 percent more likely to be employed. That's not all: Young Prospera beneficiaries grew up to become adults who worked, on average, nine more hours each week than similarly poor children who weren't enrolled in the program. They also earned higher hourly wages."[182] And for basic-income programs, if opportunity isn't directly reflected in employment, it proves useful in other areas of our lives that are essential to living and future career prospects. "In research based in Canada and the U.S., the economist Ioana Marinescu at the University of Pennsylvania has found that even when basic-income programs do reduce working hours, adults don't typically stay home to, say, play video games; instead, they often use the extra cash to go back to school or hold out for a more desirable job."[182] From a psychological perspective, most people do not enjoy feeling shame or a lack of dignity by barely making it by, and most of us certainly have an innate desire to improve our conditions in life.

According to PEW, eight-in-ten adults consider themselves hard workers, and even though some people are likely to overestimate their amount of hard work, that depends on how you measure work.[184] Like I've said before, work is more than just your traditional nine-to-five job- there are other untraditional types of work that someone can be hardworking at. Would anyone dare say a stay-at-home parent isn't hardworking? Or a family caretaker who isn't paid but takes care of disabled family, children, or the elderly? The point is that most Americans tend to work hard, and desire that sense of individual and social responsibility. If guaranteed income were to be provided to Americans with no strings attached, I wouldn't even consider it welfare, it would be an investment in American workers from the time they're an adult to the point where they retire, and even afterward.

Another point worth mentioning is that if we talk about guaranteed income in the context of capitalism and free-market economics, the goal of a capitalist society is to have people spend money. So what if someone uses their extra $1000 a month to buy a Lamborghini (as if that would happen)?

That money ends up in the pockets of some business and a wealthy individual (or multiple)- both of which would be taxed anyways. And when they're taxed properly, that money would make its way back into the hands of- or invested into- Americans through UBI, government healthcare, or some other policy. That constant flow of money at the bottom of the marketplace and investment in Americans would just become a cycle that repeats itself. That's not capitalism, it's sustainable capitalism. Also, any money spent by a consumer goes *somewhere*, it doesn't simply vanish into a void because it wasn't spent on something we personally deem as more important or valuable to *us*.

When reviewing if UBI or something similar works in the U.S., it helps to see if it's already been done to some degree, and what the outcomes were. Fortunately, several local leaders have taken the initiative here in the U.S. to pilot such programs. In a first-of-its-kind pilot last year, Stockton, California Mayor Michael Tubbs launched the *Stockton Economic Empowerment Demonstration* (SEED), which provided over 100 low-income Stockton residents with $500 per month over 18 months. Due to Coronavirus, Tubbs extended SEED through January 2021.[173]

According to the program's research plan, providing basic income could "lead to reductions in monthly income volatility and provide greater income sufficiency, which will, in turn, lead to reduced psychological stress and improved physical functioning." Stockton was an ideal location for a pilot of this kind due to it being the most diverse city in the country (as of 2018) and is historically the foreclosure capital of the U.S. This program has been studied, with residents who received payments compared to a control group who did not receive payments. Throughout the study and during the pandemic, you can see types of- and changes in- purchasing behavior. During the pandemic, for example, participants cut back on non-essential purchases and spent more on essentials like food.[173]

"Participants have also put the money toward rent, car payments, and paying off debt, as well as one-off expenses for themselves or their children: dental surgery, a prom dress, football camp, and shoes. They've also been able to cut back on working second and third jobs; one participant, a forty-eight-year-old mother of two who works full time at Tesla, was able to stop working as a delivery driver for DoorDash. Alcohol and tobacco have accounted for less than one percent of spending per month."[173] Results for a year-long study on this UBI program were published in March 2021, with great results for proponents of the policy. Results supported the positive results previously mentioned and "recipients of the monthly payments were twice as likely to gain full-time employment than others, according to data analysis by a pair of independent researchers, Stacia West of the University of Tennessee at Knoxville and Amy Castro Baker of the University of Pennsylvania."[185]

If this type of set-up for a guaranteed income was implemented at the federal level, the federal government could set up a commission and (anonymously) track spending habits, similar to what we already do in our economic analysis. Doing so would illustrate that Americans on average do not spend their money on unnecessary purchases; instead focusing on personal well-being and meaningful goals (e.g. food, bills, medical, debt, education, important one-off purchases).

Other cities have explored the idea of guaranteed income as well, especially for in-need residents. "The Angeleno Campaign in Los Angeles raised over $10 million from private donations to be distributed to residents via prepaid debit cards, and the City of Compton, CA partnered with the nonprofit Give Directly to distribute $1 million at random to families impacted by COVID-19."[186]

Not only has Mayor Tubbs pushed for UBI piloting in his city, but he and ten other mayors also formed a coalition recently dubbed the *Mayors for a Guaranteed Income* (MGI). This coalition was formed in an effort to boost economic security nationwide, which is especially helpful during a pandemic. "Michael Tubbs worked with the nonprofit *Economic Security Project* to develop this network that will advocate for a monthly guaranteed income — also known as a universal basic income (UBI) — at all levels of government. The coalition will also invest in "narrative change efforts" to highlight the issue of economic insecurity and will invite other cities to join MGI and support new pilots."[184]

As we can see, non-profits are getting involved, but so are private individuals. Jack Dorsey recently invested three million dollars in MGI so that cities such as Pittsburgh, Atlanta, Seattle, Los Angeles, Compton, Stockton, and more can test the feasibility of a guaranteed income across the nation. There is something really neat about local governments taking it upon themselves to act as testbeds for new and innovative policy solutions that could later be implemented at the state or federal level.[187]

Not only have local government leaders been interested in UBI, the National League of Cities (NLC) and the U.S. Conference of Mayors (USCM) are also looking into it. The idea of UBI is no longer a fringe one, with guidelines about piloting UBI in cities across the country created by NLC. Recommendations from the report include:

- *Identifying goals of a UBI pilot;*
- *Choosing stakeholders and partners, and deciding when they should get involved;*
- *Deciding who should qualify for the pilot;*
- *Implementing a successful program; and*
- *Creating a communications team and strategy.*[188]

It may seem like wishful thinking on behalf of local government leaders, but it is steps like these which provide data and information on improving and eventually initiating state or countrywide UBI. Further providing the efficacy of UBI is what's happening on the international stage. In 2017, Finland tested a pilot of UBI, with the researchers who conducted the study stating that it led to people out of work feeling happier, but it did not lead to increased employment. Right in the middle of year one of Covid, in August of 2020, Germany announced that it would start a UBI pilot. The pilot started in August and will last for three years. During this period, 120 Germans will receive €1,200, or about $1,430 in monthly payments, which is right above Germany's poverty line. Researchers will compare this group's experiences with a control group of 1,380 Germans who will not receive payments.

A staggering 140,000 private donations are being provided to the German Institute for Economic Research to conduct the study. Throughout this period, "all participants will be asked to complete questionnaires about their lives, work, and emotional state to see whether a basic income has had a significant impact."[189] Hopefully, the data that comes out of Germany will shed some empirical light on more outcomes of a UBI policy.[172]

Another benefit of UBI to workers is that many workers are in a transition period between positions, careers, locations, and stages of life. Having a steady flow of basic income can assist workers in this transition stage, acting as a buffer between these events that we all naturally experience. This is especially true for workers living in poverty or with low income, in trying to advance their professional aspirations. As mentioned a few chapters ago, the amount of sick leave for most workers is extremely low, making it difficult to provide care to loved ones or take necessary time off to heal during a medical crisis such as a pandemic. If the government provided a steady flow of guaranteed income to Americans, then we could simply use that system as a means to help keep afloat these individuals who need sick leave.

More employees would be able to afford to quit their job or take a furlough if they had this steady stream of basic income. Unfortunately, household expenses for most Americans in the lower and middle class are so high that a mere $1000 a month may not provide enough for workers who have lost their job, have emergency medical expenses, and find themselves in a dire situation. With a system like UBI already in place, the government would only have to increase the amount of money paid to its recipients during a crisis such as an economic downturn, natural disaster, or global pandemic. The possibility of providing funds to Americans more effectively and efficiently in a very short period is not only necessary during these situations, but also a better use of the government's responsibility.

Another serious life event that would become easier with guaranteed income is that of childbirth. Having a child should not be such a burden for workers that they feel inclined not to have the child to begin with, give the child up for adoption, or quit their job entirely. Many workers living in poverty are faced with these decisions constantly because many part-time and low-paying jobs are not required to provide FMLA coverage. Coverage includes providing certain employees with up to 12 weeks of unpaid, job-protected leave per year. FMLA applies to all public agencies, all public and private elementary and secondary schools, and companies with 50 or more employees. But employees are only eligible for leave if they have worked for their employer at least 12 months, at least 1,250 hours over the past 12 months, and work at a location where the company employs 50 or more employees within 75 miles.

Unfortunately, many workers do not meet these stipulations for FMLA coverage, meaning childbirth and the care for children at a very crucial point in their (and the child's) lives becomes a burden and hardship as opposed to the amazing gift that we all recognize childbirth to be. Having a form of guaranteed income during this crucial moment would help many of these workers afford time away from work, not to mention the expensive medical and childcare costs. Do we not value newborn children and their parents enough to care for them in our society?

The homelessness crisis is also one that is difficult to solve. "In January 2018, 552,830 people were counted as homeless in the United States. Of those, 194,467 (35 percent) were unsheltered, and 358,363 (65 percent) were sheltered. The overall homeless population on a single night represents 0.2 percent of the U.S. population or 17 people per 10,000 in the population."[190] Rates of homelessness are highly uneven across states, with the four states of New York, Hawaii, Oregon, California, along with the District of Columbia containing 45% of the homelessness population- yet only 20% of the overall population. This crisis has both a marketing problem and a capital problem. The marketing problem is that we refer to it as a homeless crisis, where in reality it's a lack-of-money crisis. Providing shelter to the homeless, and even providing social or mental health services is a great first step and that's exactly what many local governments have been doing. Yet shelter does not provide the homeless the means to get them back on their feet or reintroduce them into society and the economy. That is where the capital problem comes in.[188]

Without providing actual cold hard cash to the homeless- a financial floor- they will always find it difficult to get a job and land back on their feet. Local governments, unfortunately, are unable to tackle these issues by themselves because not only is homelessness a byproduct of multiple issues, including poverty, these cities and towns can't afford to invest the necessary amount of resources or funds to the cause that is required to address the problem. That is why the federal government needs to step in, they can provide a guaranteed income and financial floor to the homeless. They can even stand up a commission to tackle the issue nationwide. UBI would provide this much-needed financial floor.

It's great that the homeless are often provided a temporary place to stay, but they need the means of which to put food in their stomach, clothes on their back, and the ability to slap a piece of paper on a potential employer's desk- asking them for a job. Without this actual monetary investment, our approach to tackling homelessness will *always* fall short. Full stop. Homeless people in our country should not be neglected, nor should anyone, and providing them a financial floor will allow them to develop their means for making a living through a support structure and work.

Another group that would benefit greatly from a financial floor are those working 21st-century jobs of distributed work, jobs in low-wage industries (which have increased in recent years), and even gig work. When more and more workers are becoming self-employed or contracted through gig jobs, these workers are likely to have slim to no benefits such as healthcare, 401K matches, pensions, etc. It is important that we provide a financial floor such as UBI because it will allow these workers to invest in their personal health and financial well-being, in addition to more time- a buffer- when switching between gig work and trying to create opportunities for themselves in the modern economy. That same opportunity and investment would also prove useful to those working in low-wage industries such as the service industry, who are not only paid less than a living wage but are the most likely to become homeless or fall back on debt if an emergency arises.

As you can see, our country would certainly benefit from having a dialogue around an idea like guaranteed income. Luckily, some well-known individuals on the political stage have discussed and called for UBI. Actually, it's really just been one individual who initiated the dialogue on UBI in recent years. Former U.S. Presidential candidate and entrepreneur Andrew Yang entered the political scene when running for the 2020 presidential election. He calls his plan for UBI a Freedom Dividend. His entire campaign was built on this promise and he continues to this day advocating for a dividend for all Americans. Yang's Freedom Dividend includes $1,000 a month- $12,000 a year- to every American adult, regardless of income. "Our economy functions much better when we have money to spend, where we can participate in the market, where businesses are responsive to us," he said. "We'll start more businesses. We'll be able to change jobs more easily. So, the money doesn't disappear in our hands. It creates a trickle-up economy from our people, our families, and our communities up."[191]

One large and important reason that has driven Yang to advocate the Freedom Dividend is the increasing amount of automation and corresponding job loss happening in our economy- not to mention the many changes and disruptions we are seeing as a result of the 4th Industrial Revolution. We can add these concerns to the reasons for implementing a guaranteed income here in the U.S. Yang also mentions that many people in our country are not measured in today's economy. Examples include stay-at-home parents and caretakers who, as I mentioned earlier, provide essential work to our communities and our economies- without them our economy struggles to function.

He is also adamant about the GDP problem mentioned earlier, that we focus too much on GDP as a measurement of economic and national success. GDP does not value every part of the economy that we understand as providing value. So naturally, we end up excluding a lot of essential work, whereas measures and costs related to negative outcomes like war are included. You can see the disconnect here, which is why I agree with Yang that we should create a new measure for our economy. One that measures and includes every person and part of our economy that we as a people value.

At the end of the day, there are many ways to conduct guaranteed income or a Freedom Dividend, whether it's universal or for every American up to a specific income threshold, and whether it starts at $500 or $1000 a month for every recipient. Regardless, the point is to provide a base level of freedom for Americans to pursue a life worth living, not a life where they are stuck in a cycle of poverty or a life that's less of a life and more of an existence. Freedom is an American value through and through. But how we've viewed that freedom in the context of work and living no longer meets the needs of America today or the demands of 21st-century living. We can have freedom, but it's the freedom to choose. The freedom to choose our own vocations that will inevitably provide value to not only ourselves but those around us. The freedom to choose how we spend our money and what we spend that money on because let's face it- only you know what your needs and career goals are over time, and only I know mine. Having the personal freedom to choose how we spend our money allows us to work our way through these needs and goals, on our own timeline.

We've all had those days where we feel like our work or contribution to society is not valued or appreciated. We have all had those days where our energy levels are so low because we feel little to no purpose or fulfillment in our work. Having the freedom to find our purpose, develop a work-life balance, and live a life worth living is not something only a few should be able to afford, it should be the basis of our day-to-day existence. Yes, there will be jobs that many of us work as stepping-stones on our path to more purposeful and meaningful work, but it should be our long-term goal to automate as many of these jobs as possible, while simultaneously lessening our dependence on these jobs to make ends meet.

Chapter 16

The Intersection of
Time and Work

Time. This is a structure that arguably plays the largest role in how we go about work, yet it's often never addressed. Our perception of time and the best way to spend it is deeply rooted in the status quo of traditional work. I touched on time earlier when I brought up flexible and reduced work schedules, as well as productivity, but there is a lot more to time besides moving away from a forty-hour workweek. The way most of us spend our time working day-to-day and over our entire life is not the best way to spend our time. Much of it is wasted and it's in large part due to our culture around work ethic. This culture leads to an unequal distribution of time throughout our population. Thus, I find it fascinating that we seldom talk about *time* as a form of equality... why not? Is it not the most important type of equality?

When we think about time's relationship with work, we first need to make sure we understand what *work* is. We know that there is a lot of work that is being done in our communities that we value yet is not measured or compensated within our economy. Our definition of work can be expanded to include this type of work and any type of work that our traditional system doesn't acknowledge. If we want our culture of work to be just, equitable, and sustainable, I think we owe it to ourselves to examine our thoughts on work, compensation, and work's relationship with time.

Work in its entirety really is about how we spend our time and what we see as the most valuable or worthwhile use of it. Yet we have a culture of work that is okay with many of us just going through the motions of work to get by, without considering that our energy and effort isn't all that's being used up- so is our time. Our common path of working towards retirement so we can then enjoy the remainder of our life is our common approach to work. This approach emphasizing sacrifice today for the benefit of a non-guaranteed outcome later in life is entirely backward. The outcome, the success we are obsessed with, matters only in part.

What matters is that you feel a sense of purpose and meaning behind your work. That you find meaning *in* your work, in the *process*. The *process* is where most of your life happens. That is where most of your time is spent every day. So why are we placing such a large emphasis on the *outcome* and the temporary feeling of accomplishment it provides? Sure, we need goals and goals are important but neglecting the actual process, the actual day-to-day work itself, only creates a situation in which we don't value and appreciate the time we are given each and every day. In other words, we tend to and even encourage disrespecting our *time*.

As mentioned earlier, in ancient Greece work was considered both virtuous and necessary, idleness was condemned, and the craftsmen were held in high esteem.[21] That says a lot about how time was prioritized in the past with respect to work. How much has work changed since then? In America today, do we view work in a different light? Something to ponder for sure. I really don't think much has changed since then. We certainly have no problem spending some portion of our life doing work that isn't purposeful because we view it as necessary. Craftsmen in ancient Greece often included *demiourgoi*, or men who worked for the people. This included professions such as doctors and singers. These professions were viewed as honorable then, and I would argue are still viewed that way today. We certainly appreciate doctors and singers in this country, and we glorify their work and success.[21]

If you look at Aristotle's views about work and leisure and you read some of his material, you will see a general belief that it's not right for people to work their lives away conducting manual work; that leisure is the type of work that should be maximized and prioritized. Leisure is "the use of free time for enjoyment."[108] Aristotle believed that work was not an end in itself. "The end which man aims at is happiness: "Happiness seems to depend on leisure; we work in order to enjoy leisure, just as we make war in order to enjoy peace."[21] There is an interesting phenomenon one can see about the way work was viewed in ancient Greece between classes. Why did Aristotle view leisure as essential and view work in a different light than other Greek members of society? He was born into great wealth and had plenty of it, so is it surprising that he viewed leisure with utmost importance? It can be assumed that he spent much of his time in leisure, whereas the working class during his time would likely have spent most days working hard, having less time for leisure.

One could argue that if you belonged to a higher class in ancient Greece or most periods and places throughout history, you were likely spending more time in leisure, which would have skewed your perception of work and time altogether. The adverse is likely true, with most working-class people viewing work as virtuous and necessary when in reality more leisure would likely have been of great benefit to these members of society (better health, work-life balance, etc.). Spreading out both work and leisure equally throughout a population would likely lead to a more balanced view of work today in America and across the world- and in some places it has.

But instead, work-life balance is often a privilege for those who can actually afford to spend more time in leisure as opposed to working class' often strenuous, non-purposeful work. Likely, this viewpoint of work and the surrounding culture around work in America today is in large part due to this class-separation of labor and leisure. How time is spent over generations is likely to compound over time and form our individual perceptions of it personally and culturally. I would argue that our relationship with work and time today- one that is okay with sacrificing working class Americans' times and lives, but not that of wealthier American's (the leisurely class)- is in large part a cultural impression of the aforementioned compounding of class's relationship with work overtime.

To further drive this point, if you pay attention to our remarks about work, leisure, and balance today, you are likely to spot the difference in class when you view who's making the remarks.

Working-class Americans are likely to justify their personal sacrifice of effort and time in pursuit of *the American dream*, an idea which itself emphasizes the importance of hard work, which is both virtuous and necessary. To make the sacrifice of one's time acceptable in this situation, it makes sense to claim that work is virtuous and necessary. Yet the working class is not as vocal about this lifestyle or its justification. Wealthier Americans are likelier to espouse the same American dream, yet simultaneously partake in more leisurely activities. This class is *more* vocal about the benefits of the hard-working American who can achieve anything as long as they're willing to *grind* and *do whatever it takes*.

So we have a situation in which those who reap the benefits of a proper balance between work and leisure (work-life balance if you would) are more vocal about our traditional culture around working in America, which ends up playing into and encouraging working-class Americans (and the rest) to continue to work at the expense of their own time, their own lives, and as we've seen throughout the book their own health. It's easy for the wealthy and well-off to tell everyone else to work hard as if the onus of every worker's situation falls only on them and not the environment or culture around work. Even though upper-class Americans may benefit from playing into this very American ideal around work, I don't think they are necessarily doing it on purpose as it's grained into our culture.

Another class-related aspect on this topic- one that we consciously partake in- involves the idea of conspicuous leisure. Coined by American economist and sociologist Thorstein Veblen in *The Theory of the Leisure Class: An Economic Study of Institutions* (1899), conspicuous leisure "is the application of extended time to the pursuit of pleasure (physical and intellectual), such as sport and the fine arts. Such physical and intellectual pursuits display the freedom of the rich man and woman from having to work in an economically productive occupation."[192]

This ability to work less and spend more time in leisure still occurs today, with most working-class Americans unable to receive that balance between work and leisure. Again, this phenomenon is not classist as much as it is based on American culture. We have bought into this idea that the wealthier you are, the more you deserve to conduct leisure. I think this is in large part the reason many of us feel the need to display our leisurely activities to the world, such as what we do online with social media (i.e. our continuous habit of posting travel pictures and the underlying message from many online influencers). We value leisure to such a large degree but instead of fighting for more time to partake in it, we are satisfied with posting pictures of the few times we can do it.

My thoughts are that manual work and leisure should all be balanced in a way that is aligned and at peace with one's purpose in life. Neither of them is worthy of too much of our energy because neither is an end within themselves. Purposeful work, meaningful work, is work where you are immersed in action and a state of contemplation. Between people, the line between manual work and leisure may be thin. You may despise painting, you may find no meaning behind it, thus painting is a form of manual work to you. But for me, maybe I enjoy painting. Maybe it provides me with a feeling of immersion, enjoyment, or contemplation. In this case, I may not see the enterprise as one of manual work but instead as leisure.

If you and I can both conduct the same activity, yet for one of us it is a form of manual work and for the other it is leisure, this has broad implications for us as a society in how we spend our individual time, and furthermore in how we structure our system of work. Not to mention, activities that can be either manual work or leisure- such as painting- can also provide value to the rest of society. Value that can be monetized. I am of the mind that this either-or type of work should be experienced by and provided by those who enjoy it and who can reap both the enjoyment and the associated monetary value. This to me, would be considered work. Your "work" should be an activity you find purposeful and provides you compensation because your actions provide value to others. Those who do not enjoy it, who see it as manual work, should be free to partake in other forms of manual work that we value as a society; work which may or may not be monetized, and that provide purpose and meaning to them.

American work ethic today is unfortunately too focused on manual work as providing value, as if it's an end in itself, whereas leisure is also a type of work, done in contemplation which provides value for us as individuals but also as collective people. We have shunned leisure at the expense of manual work, even manual work that provides no meaning to us.

If you think about some of the greatest work you've done, there is likely a specific state of mind that you commonly found yourself in, in those moments. It is a state of total immersion. Being immersed in the task at hand that you almost feel lost in it. This is the state that you may find yourself in when conducting deep work. Remember that deep work is work where you are *in the midst* of it all. You are immersed in the work at hand. This state of mind of being immersed in your work or favorite activity is often referred to as being in *flow*. The psychological term, "flow", is the term coined by Mihaly Csikszentmihalyi to describe the state of optimal experience gained from complete immersion in one's activity. Csikszentmihalyi conducted a study amongst professionals in which their flow experiences were compared in two major settings: work and leisure time.

> Csikszentmihalyi and his team gathered over a hundred working professionals during a weeklong period, equipping each of them with a pager that 'beeped' at eight random points throughout the day and evening. At each randomly scheduled 'beep,' the participant would write down what they were doing and how they felt at that very moment. The findings of the experiment can be best summed up by the following quote from Csikszentmihalyi. 'What was unexpected [from this experiment] is how frequently people reported flow situations at work, and how rarely in leisure.[193]

"The necessary factors that must be present to achieve a flow state include the presence of some sort of challenge for which your skills are adequate, clear goals, and feedback."[191] What's interesting is that there are leisurely activities that match these factors, so what does that say about our perception of leisure?

People found optimal experience at work, more so than leisure. This makes sense when you consider how fleeting leisurely activities are or that in the U.S., we don't perceive leisure as this type of experience. Leisurely activities are enjoyable, but they tend to lack a sense of individual or social responsibility that you would find in your work. It makes sense intuitively that if we didn't have to work and we could leisure all day, that we would do just that. But that's usually not the case, even for those who are able to. There is something about being actively engaged with work and feeling flow that is satisfying and rewarding in the moment, often leaving us with a sense of pride in the productive work we did that day.

Some might imagine that if work wasn't necessary that we would all just be sitting around in leisure all day when in reality we'd likely be conducting some form of work, something that puts us in that state of flow. Whether that activity is considered traditional work or leisure, is beside the point. On a fundamentally human level, we embrace the responsibility that comes with work. Not only do we want work that provides value to ourselves, but we also want work where we can provide value to others. The issue is that our definition of work is too narrow. Work should be something that is natural, and where we have intention in what we pursue.

Leisure right now, is something most of us do when we're not working, but what if we incorporated leisure with work itself? British Writer Tom Hodgkinson talks about the idea of *idling*. This concept seeks to combine play and work.

> *A characteristic of the idler's work is that it looks suspiciously like play. This, again, makes the non-idler feel uncomfortable. Victims of the Protestant work ethic would like all work to be unpleasant. They feel that work is a curse, that we must suffer on this earth to earn our place in the next. The idler, on the other hand, sees no reason not to use his brain to organize a life for himself*

where his play is his work, and so attempt to create his own little paradise in the here and now.[194]

This idea of not just being a worker but being an idler would require a large shift in the way we view work. Why shouldn't we organize a life where our play is our work? A large obstacle to this approach to work in the U.S. is our culturally derived sense of shame around being idle. If you're incorporating play into your work, it's often stigmatized as purposeless, unserious, or a lack of hard work. This disdain for mixing play into work or idling isn't a new phenomenon. In ancient Greek literature, work is seen by the general populace as "ordained by the gods and approved by men, [where] idleness is condemned by both alike."[21] There was no shame in work but there was in idleness.

Work already takes up most of our waking hours, so as I see it, we have three options here. We can either incorporate more of this idle time or idler lifestyle into our work, we can be given more time off of work so that we can idle, or we can do both. You and I might have completely different ideas of incorporating our sense of play into work and finding the right balance between work and leisure, and that is perfectly okay. The reason for that is because what I might see as boring manual labor you might find fulfilling and a form of leisure. We all know how to dawn the hat of the idler, but we don't all idle the same.

Now some might find it problematic if everyone is afforded the opportunity to be more idle because there are plenty of jobs that no one would want to do, given they had a choice. And most of these jobs are necessary to our communities (e.g. cashiers, agricultural fieldwork). If people become idlers, then no one will be willing to work these jobs. But that is precisely the point of this change. Since the foreseeable future is filled with jobs that simply aren't playful (until we can automate them) then that leaves us with option two which is giving workers enough time off to be idle until they can afford to be a full-time idler. But the only way these workers can make this transition into a greater work-life balance is if they make enough money.

Right now, these essential positions we understand as necessary, yet most people wouldn't do if they didn't have to, need to be respected. And we respect these positions and their workers by paying them a living wage. Not only will a living wage allow these workers to pursue more meaningful work-work of the idler- increased pay will give them more bargaining power so that they can demand a work environment more cohesive to the idler mindset. *Everyone* deserves to have their work and their time respected, and the opportunity to pursue a better, leisurely, idle lifestyle.

When we try and live up to society's expectations around work, we end up not respecting our time or the time of others. It's to the point where we feel unproductive and negatively about ourselves if we don't provide the type and amount of work relished by American work culture. Even though we're not suited to continuously work nonstop eight hours a day and then repeat that most of our life, many of us do it anyway. The result is that we find ourselves so strapped for time that we are increasingly willing to "buy" some of it back. This can take the form of purchasing fast food instead of cooking because it's quicker or paying for a moving company to handle all of our moving instead of doing it ourselves. We tell ourselves 'It's just easier' to do these things, but a prominent reason behind buying our time back is that it's a response to something called *time famine*.

This term arose from the scientific literature around 1999 and it "refers to the universal feeling of having too much to do but not enough time to deal with those demands."[195] You can have time famine outside of work of course, with that constant feeling of having too many errands that need to be completed but you feel you don't have enough time. But within the context of work (something we tend to bring home with us), we view our roles and actions within our organizations in such a way that even when we don't have a hard deadline and its business as usual, we still feel time famine. One study has shown that making time-saving purchases in our daily lives will promote happiness. Especially if we feel this time famine. This is important because we naturally feel that time is an essential commodity, yet our actions around hours-worked don't reflect that deep understanding of time.

So, if money is the- or one of the- reasons we go to work, and work is where we spend most of our waking hours, and we use the money earned to "buy" more of that time back, it's safe to say we're stuck in a time-wasting cycle. If we had a greater balance between work and time to do other activities, we wouldn't have as much of a need to buy our time back. Thus, if we wish to reduce the amount of time famine we experience, we must prioritize our time spent in and outside of work. Doing so will also open our schedules up to more time-consuming, yet enjoyable activities, like going through the effort of cooking at home. If we prioritize and respect our greatest asset we can live through time, not live to buy some of it back.[196]

The American work ethic favors outcomes over process. This mentality and the corresponding lifestyle it demands does not bode well for our best use of time. Our focus on success at all costs, success that's often not even real or true success, is a deeply ingrained facet of our culture and is responsible for keeping many of us in a time-wasting mindset.

Earlier I talked about the hedonic treadmill, where our feeling of satisfaction quickly dissipates after achieving a goal, yet we continuously run to the next reward to avoid the feeling of falling behind. This feeling is one we often find ourselves in. If this sounds like you today or at any point in your life, you're certainly not alone. Focusing only on our next reward, our next *outcome*, instead of living for the *process*, will constantly leave us leaving unfulfilled long term and more prone to wasting our time. It's sort of like living on cruise control, just going through the motions. Instead of working because we find the actual *act* purposeful and worth the time spent, we often work in a continuous state of moving *towards* something. As if our actions today and at this moment are only meant to get us to point B. The problem is that the goalpost keeps moving. There will always be another point B, or a point C, D, and so forth. Before we know it, we end up looking back at all of that time spent to get to point B and realize that much of it was squandered, so we then feel bad about the process- which only reduces the level of satisfaction received when we've completed the task.

An ideal work culture would be one where we value and respect time enough to make the most of it, instead of concerning ourselves only with our perception of *success* and satisfaction once we complete the work. The satisfaction felt is short-lived and quite frankly our time is never guaranteed. Other countries have a culture of work that is focused more on the process itself, such as Japan. Japan "holds in high esteem those who achieve "shokunin," which roughly translates to "mastery of one's profession." There, workers do their jobs well partly for the sake of doing them well and honing their craft, and "the process matters just as much as the outcome."[197] Workers want more from their work besides a paycheck to survive, they want to believe in something and belong to something meaningful. And when we take less pride in our jobs, we are also likely to feel less satisfied with them. Right now, the US ranks 36th in the world for workers' job satisfaction.[197] Shifting from an outcome mindset to a process mindset in our approach to work and time, will go a long way in increasing our job satisfaction.

On the flip side of success, there is also this idea of hard work. That hard work is more important than work in itself. I think one of the reasons we have no problem sacrificing so much of our time to ascertain short-lived goals and the accompanying feelings, is because we're living under the impression that *hard work* is simply what is required to make it in today's economy. Yet if time is our most valuable asset, why should how *hard* we work- whatever we may define that as- be our guiding light. I understand the importance of working hard but working smarter with a more balanced approach to work usually ends up being the most efficient use of time in the end anyways.

It's a false dichotomy between working harder and working smarter. Working harder is indeed ingrained in the American dream and our collective spirit. It is also true that our sense of individualism encouraged many Americans to work hard throughout our nation's history to achieve the great progress we see today. *But* we also ended up here through working smarter and prioritizing our time. Many people who have contributed to human progress in major ways, individuals we would consider *successful*, understand the importance of working smarter.

Former U.S. President Theodore Roosevelt was very careful to work smarter *and* harder. What this meant for him was mapping out a daily schedule, dedicating only specific time to each task at hand. Which for him was a lot, as he managed to write 4o published books, hundreds of articles, avidly played sports, read many books, and dedicated time to his naturalist endeavors. Roosevelt's work ethic was strong, and he accomplished so much because he understood the lessons from an idea like deep work. Instead of working eight continuous hours at the same task or doing the same work, he would schedule very short periods of time in which he had to accomplish smaller tasks. This meant working *only* on those specific tasks and with blistering intensity.[198] This style of work would be advantageous for most, but much of American work culture today does not value this type of schedule. Think about how much time would be saved if we worked in this way. Another example of someone who accomplished a lot and understood the importance of time management was Albert Einstein. Einstein would:

- *Sleep up to ten hours a night*
- *Eat breakfast and read the paper between 9 and 10*
- *Leave for work at 10:30 and work until 1*
- *Returned home at 1:30 for lunch, a nap, and a cup of tea*
- *The rest of his afternoon was spent at home, continuing work, seeing visitors, and dealing with other correspondence*
- *Supper at 6:30, followed by more work and more letters*[199]

You would think that someone who achieved so much would have barely slept, barely take time for daily walks- never mind naps- and dedicate most of his waking hours to his work. *"Keep in mind that besides the eight hours of work, each day also has eight hours for fooling around, and then there's also Sunday."*
– *Albert Einstein*

We can see that hard work isn't enough in and of itself. A strong work ethic doesn't mean working hard as much as it means working smart, with a balanced approach to work. Balanced work leads to better work. We must review the history of successful people and evaluate what it truly means to work within the context of our limited time each day. Our ethos of work should reflect the value that time has in our lives.

Mending the Intersection of Time and Work

Now that we understand some of the cultural characteristics of our relationship between work and time, we can look at solutions that address the underlying issues. One way to do this is to implement Flexible Working Arrangements (FWAs). "FWAs can include everything from weekend work to shift work, overtime, annual-hours contracts, part-time work, job sharing, flextime, temporary/casual work, fixed-term contracts, home-based work, teleworking and compressed working weeks." The crux behind FWAs is that "giving people more time to spend managing their personal responsibilities will energize them for their professional ones." "There is mounting evidence that these mutually beneficial agreements between employers and employees (providing alternate options as to when, where and how much a person works) have measurable psychological, social and economic impacts."[200]

These include reducing costs for employers such as working offsite, reducing workspace requirements, and overhead costs. It includes higher levels of worker satisfaction. There can also be an *increase* in effort from employees, the behaviors of which can be explained by social exchange theory. This theory "proposes that social behavior is the result of an exchange process" to maximize benefits and minimize costs. "According to this theory, developed by sociologist George Homans, people weigh the potential benefits and risks of social relationships. When the risks outweigh the rewards, people will terminate or abandon that relationship."[201]

If workers are given more flexibility in the way they work, they are likely to invest more in those social relationships. Another impact of an FWA is decreased turnover among employees, improved performance, and a reduction in absenteeism. These outcomes lead to greater long-term financial performance for the companies. There is also evidence of greater customer service and fewer customer complaints when employees have FWAs. "There is reduced psychological distress resulting from decreased work-family conflict", and relationships tend to be more invested in.[198] Lastly, they can aid employee outcomes like organizational commitment and job satisfaction- the latter being the dominant predictor of job performance. For these arrangements to work though, there must be trust between management and the employees. An increase in trust between managers and employees, or among coworkers is a win-win for all parties involved.[200]

We know how the five-day workweek came to be, but as history goes, the way we work today is much different than when the five-day, forty-hour workweek became the norm. We know we can't go over forty hours a week without getting paid overtime, but what about working less? Can we be just as productive or even more productive working only four days a week, for the same amount or reduced hours? The four-day workweek seems enticing, and it should. Working four days a week but being paid your normal pay (as if you were working five days) is not a new concept. Several countries and a few companies have already started this or at least implemented something similar. A four-day workweek would be approximately 208 working days a year, which equates to working roughly 57% days of the entire year, whereas we usually work roughly 72% days of the year.

To provide some context of how this would work or play out, we can look at Finland, which has been at the forefront of flexible work schedules since 1996 when they passed a law that gave "most employees the right to adjust their hours up to three hours earlier or later than what their employer typically requires." This would surely be a step in the right direction in the U.S. as many employees today are looking for flexibility in their work schedules. But Finland may not be done yet with changes to the workweek. Their new Prime Minister Sanna Marin proposed last year in 2019 "to put the entire country on a four-day workweek or six-hour workday."[202] So, either more time off in the late afternoon during weekdays or an extended three-day weekend, either of which would allow for a greater balance between working and other parts of life.

The six-hour workday has already been tested by Sweden, and the results were promising. For two years, 70 Swedish nurses tested this workweek out and the nurses ended up taking fewer sick days, "felt healthier and were more productive." Not to mention they were twenty percent happier (on average) and had more energy at work and in their spare time. Unfortunately, the only problem with this new schedule was the cost. Despite productivity gains, seventeen nurses had to be hired to make up for the lost hours. I'm willing to bet if you looked at costs for the employers of these nurses, much if not most of the costs required to hire new nurses would have been offset by long-term cost-savings resulting from the nurse's shorter work schedule. This is one example where we know fewer hours have mostly positive outcomes for both employees and employers.[203]

The cost problem illustrates that there may be a specific balance between working fewer hours and the associated labor costs- keeping in mind that there is potential for long-term cost savings from this new approach. There is more to this study, which is that certain industries require face-to-face time regardless of what hours employees work, meaning that someone will have to work the shifts that another worker gives up. Alternating employees based on Fridays or Mondays off is one approach to this problem.

The tech industry is an example where mandatory face-to-face hours aren't as necessary if at all, so could it benefit greatly from a four-day workweek? The short answer is yes, with some companies seeing a drop in sick leave, happier workers, fewer work conflicts, and a greater focus on the job. Greater focus meant less time playing on one's phone and idling during work hours because a short workday meant they could do all that extra stuff after hours. Sweden has seen mixed results for other organizations who tried the six-hour workday, with some keeping a shorter workweek, some going back to normal operations, and some finding a middle ground. In France, the standard workweek was reduced from 39 hours to 35 hours in 2000.[203]

What about outside of Europe or with larger operations? Microsoft Japan tested out a four-day workweek last summer, with workers receiving their usual five-day paycheck. According to the company, there was a productivity boost of 40%, while the company became more efficient in other areas too. Electricity costs fell by 23, and there were fewer costs for printing and other common materials. Due to the shooter work week, the company put its meetings on a diet. The normal duration of a meeting changed from 60 Minutes to 30 for nearly half of all meetings, and meeting attendance was capped at 5 employees. Microsoft Japan stated that there was often no reason for hour-long meetings or tying up multiple people from the same team.[204]

Outside of Japan, you also have the company Perpetual Guardian, a New Zealand trust management company, which saw "a 20% gain in employee productivity and a 45% increase in employee work-life balance after a trial of paying people their regular salary for working 4 days."[204] Other benefits included increased team engagement levels, job performance was maintained within four days, employees were able to work 30 hours for 37.5 hours of pay for the same output, and staff stress levels decreased from 45% to 38%. The company wasted no time in making the policy permanent. "Based on the outcomes, Perpetual Guardian initiated the Four-Day Week on a long-term, opt-in basis across its business from 1 November 2018."[205]

Andrew Barnes, the founder of Perpetual Guardian, took this novel idea of a 4-day work week and started an organization with his partner Charlotte Lockhart called *4 Day Week Global*. Their vision for the organization is to provide a community environment for companies, researchers/academics, and interested parties to be able to connect and advance this idea as part of the future of work.[206]

As mentioned earlier with burnout, one of the major reasons for having greater schedule flexibility is our technology. Our devices have made it easier than ever to do work at home, but it has also become difficult for employees to unplug from their work when they are not in the office. The US has cast nearly no legislation on flexible scheduling and laws related to a work-life balance. France on the other hand "has granted employees the right to disconnect from their jobs, limiting email and other communications after-hours."[204]

We sort of knew that expanding access and use of technology would lead to greater productivity throughout most industries, but we haven't quite addressed its impact on our lives in and out of work. Worker compensation has not grown alongside the increase in productivity over the past few decades. "From 1987 to 2015, productivity rose by as much as 5% annually in industry sectors from information to manufacturing and retail — but compensation never grew by more than 2% in each year of that same period."[204] Decades of stagnant wage growth have led to many employees seeking greater flexibility in hours worked, much of which had to be addressed due to the recent pandemic. Employers and employees alike have realized that much of the time spent at work, pre-pandemic, was time wasted. More people are realizing that much more work can be done at different times and in places other than the office.

So yes, we are starting to see a large increase in distributed work, but when it comes to permanent changes to the work schedule, the U.S. has made some progress. One example of this is the 9/80 work schedule. Some companies and organizations have started this schedule, where instead of a traditional 40-hour workweek five days a week, you have a compressed work schedule. The schedule consists of 8 nine-hour days, one eight-hour day, and one day off in a 2-week period. "Under a typical 9/80 arrangement, employees work four 9-hour days, followed by an 8-hour workday that is split into two 4-hour periods. The first 4-hour period ends the first workweek, and the next 4-hour period starts the following workweek. The employee then works four more 9-hour days in the second workweek and gets one day off."[207] By no means is this schedule robust or likely to make a major difference, but it's a good first step. A breakdown of the schedule below:

First Week	
Monday	9 hours
Tuesday	9 hours
Wednesday	9 hours
Thursday	9 hours
Friday	4 hours (first week ends) + 4 hours (second week begins)
Second Week	
Monday	9 hours
Tuesday	9 hours
Wednesday	9 hours
Thursday	9 hours
Friday	Off

Personally, I'm not a huge fan of this schedule. Between dealing with the payroll matters of making sure overtime doesn't occur and having to work 9-hour days, I mean at a certain point workers' productivity starts to cut off- usually before the end of an eight-hour day, never mind nine hours. I enjoy having a Friday off here and there but not if it means showing up to work half an hour earlier and leaving work half an hour later (i.e., 7:30 – 5:30), nor do I prefer adding an hour before or after the traditional work shift. As I said, this is my opinion, but it's key to remember that this schedule doesn't solve the productivity or time concerns. The problem with our current work schedule is that workers are not meant to work continuous eight-hour shifts, it's not the optimal, most productive. schedule, and it certainly doesn't respect workers' time and value in the workplace. The same points essentially apply here with the 9/80. I think fewer hours altogether would be more effective at providing a work-life balance and would truly address the concerns around wasting time.

Another problem that has come up with more people working from home or having to be flexible with work hours, is making sure employees are doing the work they are supposed to- now that supervisors can't oversee employees. Many companies and business leaders are hesitant to provide greater schedule flexibility or an increase in time spent working virtually because they are concerned with losing out on productivity and want to ensure employees are getting paid for actual work. I don't share this concern all that much, and I see it as a pessimistic view of our workers. Most workers want to do their work and feel valued for the work they do. Most people, including Americans, aren't trying to skip out on work, and a desire for a shorter workweek is not a sign that employees simply wish to avoid work altogether.

To illustrate this point, we can look at a 2018 survey conducted with Kronos, where author Dan Schawbel refers to what

he calls "the money question". The question was straightfor-
ward, as Schawbel recalls: "If your pay is constant, how many
days a week do you want to work?" One of the potential replies
was simply "none" but only 4% of workers selected that answer. Slightly more people chose one or two days, but the
biggest portion of workers- 34%- chose they wanted a four-day
workweek. "The current standard five-day week got 28% support, whereas 20% said they would prefer a three-day workweek."[204]

These numbers show that most people want to work, just
fewer days. Even with a shorter workweek, it doesn't appear
that people are inherently lazy. They feel the need to be productive and work most days. In our always-on and always-con-
nected world, it makes sense that people want flexibility. I
understand that there seem to be few incentives for companies
to make the switch to shorter workdays or workweeks and it
may be hard to imagine real, tangible benefits right off the bat-
especially when you think someone is getting paid for an extra
day they are not working. But if you think about the potential
productivity gains, and the countless benefits for both employers and employees mentioned throughout the book, you
can see that a greater "work-life balance" benefits everyone involved.

Here in the U.S., some companies are already interested in
this model of work. Some are moving to ten-hour shifts, four
days a week (so same number of hours, just compressed). The
burger chain Shake Shack shortened manager's work weeks
to four days at some stores. Recruitment spiked, especially
among women. Working four days meant being able to take
their kids to school one day a week, which is great in and of itself, but it also helps save money on daycare (one day per week
adds up). Other companies are scratching the forty hours and
simply moving to a 32-hour week without cutting pay. Com-
pressing the amount of time worked into a shorter number of

days is also known as a compressed workweek. A shorter work-week is even picking up some interest from politicians, with a Washington state senator recently introducing a bill to reduce the standard workweek to 32 hours.[208]

Progress has been slow here in the U.S. but hopefully, this pandemic has made everyone- both workers and organizations- think deeply about total hours worked and flexible scheduling. Workers are not just expendable task-accomplish-ers, they are real people who put in effort every day to make a living. The recent pandemic and spikes in unemployment should remind us how fragile our current system of work is.

The benefits of a reduced work schedule or four-day work-week are plentiful and could lead to a less vulnerable popula-tion of workers the next time we face a national crisis. Also, a more flexible work schedule does not have to be a one-size-fits-all solution for the entire country and every industry. The solution could be and should be tailored specifically for a spe-cific industry, business, or position. Finding the right balance in total hours worked is important to both employees and em-ployers, but for too long we've accepted the status quo. Just because we're used to working a certain way, doesn't mean it's the most optimal way or the right way.

You might think there's nothing more to do with time be-sides reducing or altering the hours and way in which we work, but there are more innovative ideas. There is one concept known as time banking. "Time banking is a bartering system for services, where people exchange services for labor-time based credits, rather than money."[209] "In joining a time bank, people agree to take part in a system that involves earning and spending "time credits." When they spend an hour on an activ-ity that helps others, they receive one-time credit. When they need help from others, they can use the time credits that they have accumulated."[210]

In theory, any type of service can be exchanged for another. An example of this in practice would be the following. Steve wants to start a garden but doesn't know how and Suzan wants to build a website for her new business but doesn't know how. Steven and Suzan could exchange time and complete each other's tasks. Let's say Suzan completes Steve's Garden in three hours and Steve completes Suzan's website in five. No money exchanges hands for the services rendered, the only costs that are absorbed by each party are the materials used. In this instance, Steve emerges from the arrangement with two extra labor-time credits on account in the time bank to use in the future.

"Time banking originates from the ideas of various 19th-century socialist thinkers, including Pierre-Joseph Proudhon and Karl Marx, who advocated various versions of labor-time based chartal currencies. Rather than issuing paper notes, modern time banking utilizes electronic recordkeeping of credits and debits for registered members. The term "Time Banking" was coined and trademarked by American law professor and social justice advocate Edgar Cahn. Cahn promoted Time Banking as a means for community self-help and to fill the gap in public social services during a period when the Reagan administration was pushing cuts to spend on social programs."[209] In his book *No More Throw-Away People*, Cahn outlined five core principles of time-banking which are:

- *We Are All Assets: Everyone has something to contribute*
- *Redefining Work: Rewards all work, including unpaid and care work*
- *Reciprocity: Helping each other build strong relationships and community trust*
- *Social Networks: Belonging to a social network gives our lives more meaning*

> *· Respect: Respect is the basis for a healthy and loving community and lies at the heart of democracy*[209]

You can see the similarities between these core principles and the messages of this book around workers and their relationship to our communities and time itself. I agree with all five principles, and I think they are foundational to living a good life, as well as being a respected and essential member of society. Much of what is wrong with our system and culture of work today is that it is missing these core principles. Working in the U.S. is set up so that workers are not all viewed as assets, only those who work hard and have the right talent and skills have something to contribute.

We don't include unpaid and care work as "real work" when we really should because it's the foundation of our communities. We don't have a healthy amount of reciprocity and community trust is often neglected- otherwise, we wouldn't have homeless people living outside massive corporate buildings and elite universities with billions in endowment surrounded by communities that experience extreme poverty and a lack of investment. We understand the importance of social networks in providing meaning to our lives, but our culture doesn't take advantage of this to its full extent.

Lastly, we don't show respect for every worker in this country. We demonstrate respect for grocery clerks when we have a pandemic and then we take away their new and necessary living wages. We look up at athletes and CEOs but neglect the importance of truck drivers and stay-at-home parents. Every one of us is essential to a healthy and loving community, and respect for everyone leads to a stronger democracy, not a weaker one.

But back to the idea of time-banking. Time banking has been adopted by a few communities over the years, but for the most part, has not been implemented and successful long-term. Cahn states that "The money-based market system fails to reward many types of critical work—the work of raising healthy children, building strong families, caring for the elderly, revitalizing neighborhoods, preserving the environment, advancing social justice, and sustaining democracy—and we believed that there should be a way to honor and reward that kind of work."[210] "It functions as a hybrid system between a true monetary economy of indirect exchange and a reciprocal gift economy characteristic of informal, pre-capitalist, and primitive economies. As such, it can have some of the advantages and disadvantages of both types of economic systems."[209]

> *The advocates of time banking, from the early socialist writers to present-day proponents, emphasize its advantages in building (or restoring) community, inclusion, volunteerism, and social assistance. It is promoted as helping to foster community ties and encourage people who would not normally get involved in traditional volunteering. It seeks to overcome the problems of the social and economic alienation between producers and consumers that is widely believed to characterize industrial capitalist economies and has often formed the rationale for social unrest and revolutionary communism. It formally and tangibly recognizes the economic value of labor services that are not traditionally traded in the formal monetary economy (or would be diminished by doing so) but that often form the basis of valuable social capital. Above all, it has been championed for enabling people with low incomes to access services that would be unaffordable to them in the traditional market economy.*
>
> *However, the overhead costs, problems with managing the relative prices of different services, and difficulty of maintaining participation in effective competition with*

the larger money economy often spell problems for time banking systems. The operations of the time bank itself must somehow be financed, particularly those that require goods and services which cannot be purchased with time bank-issued labor-time credits. This means both an initial and ongoing requirement for some source of external funding in outside money, which can become prohibitive. Pricing of labor-time units for various services and types of labor is a persistent problem for time banking. If the value of the credits is allowed to float according to voluntary, mutual terms of exchange between participants (or priced proportionate to market wages in the local currency) the time bank becomes nothing more than a competing (inferior) form of currency, one handicapped by its own self-imposed limits of acceptability. If the prices in labor-time credits are set by the time bank, then the system will eventually run up against the same knowledge, calculation, and incentive problems faced by any centrally planned economy, which will sharply limit its scale and viability.

Lastly, if the value of labor-time credits is locked in at parity for all types of services and labor, then the system will face an enormous adverse selection problem. Those with the least valued labor-time (such as babysitters) will enthusiastically participate and those with the most highly valued labor-time (such as physicians) will opt out and sell their services for money instead. Because the inherent limits of the nature of time banking impose these overhead and pricing issues, the time banking system gives up much of the economic advantage that a system of indirect monetary exchange makes possible. Its acceptance will be limited, and it will always depend on the existence of a broader money-based economy using some other currency, within which it has to function. Un-

less imposed by law on the population (as advocated by early socialist proponents), time banking will tend to be confined to relatively small communities or social networks, trading in a limited selection of labor services.[209]

There is certainly feasibility in using time banking among specific communities or social networks. One could imagine time banking for the arts, such as consumers exchanging time with artists like performers, singers, musicians, and so forth. There are plenty of other low-cost forms of labor that could benefit from such a system, which is especially useful to low-income people and services that don't usually offer a lot of monetary benefits. More on Time Banks:

In 1995, Cahn founded an organization called Time-Banks USA. For two decades, TimeBanks USA has served as an incubator for new time banking initiatives. Over that period, time banking has evolved from a set of experimental programs into a movement that has spread globally. The movement has spawned conferences, regional associations, training materials, scholarly papers, and multiple software systems. Today organized time banking takes place in more than 30 countries—including China, Russia, and various countries in Africa, Europe, North America, and South America.

In the United States, there are about 500 registered time banks, and together they have enrolled more than 37,000 members. The smallest of them has 15 members; the largest has about 3,200. In the United Kingdom, time banks have enrolled about 32,000 members, and more than 3,000 organizations have registered to use one of the major time banking software platforms. Worldwide, time bank databases document more than 4 million hours of service. (And that figure understates the true

scope of time bank participation: Survey data indicate
that at least 50 percent of time bank members do not
record their hours of service regularly.)[210]

The way TimeBanks USA and other time banks operate is mostly through specially created software that operates somewhat like craigslist where people can list services, track time spent or time debt (time banking), and so forth. Several real-life examples of time banks currently being used include The Arroyo SECO Network of TimeBanks (ASNTB), which covers 13 neighborhoods in Los Angeles and in Rhode Island, where a group of parents who have children with bipolar disorder, schizophrenia, or autism use time banking to create a kind of extended family. The parents use time-banking time banking to prevent the institutionalization of their children, which has saved the state government millions of dollars that would otherwise be spent on support services.[210]

Time banks can provide an innovative solution to some of the challenges we are faced with today. These include building a sense of community, in response to the idea that our sense of community has only thinned over the past few decades. Another solution is to fill the widening care gap we are faced with in our aging population. Then there are environmental challenges- everything from natural disasters to pollution- would be greatly served through quick, responsive, and flexible volunteer networks.

A time bank can serve those needs. Time banks aren't just fixed into the physical world, either. You could start a time bank for digital work and digital time. This could impact things such as local news organizations operating online where they can be paid to be advertised to, for a specific amount of time (i.e., I browsed the internet or Facebook for one hour today, and one hour of being shown ads gives me one hour of time in exchange for something else).

All in all, I think time banking can act as a complementary currency to our current system of exchanging time for money. Exchanging time for time can allow our country, or society at large, to fill in the gaps that our current economic system does not. This certainly isn't an excuse for our current system to continue neglecting workers and our communities, but time banking can prove useful under the right conditions. It can be a "medium of exchange that advances goals that money does not and cannot. It fosters community-building efforts that have the potential to prevent or neutralize the negative externalities created by the relentless pursuit of profit."[210] It also has the potential to measure the parts in our society that are not measured by GDP, as mentioned earlier.

Chapter 17

A New Definition

We have investigated the state of American work-life and what it means to experience work in this country today. We have analyzed the various structures which guide our work and American culture writ large. And in recent chapters, we have redesigned work to better serve our 21st century needs and the needs of every American worker. To finish this conversation about work, it is important that I leave you with a better definition of what work should be in an ideal United States of America. Most of us agree on the basic tenets of living a purposeful and meaningful life. We understand the importance of and shared value of having a healthy family, safety for ourselves and our community, economic security, and we want a better future for our kids, to name a few. The way we talk about work needs to be tied directly to the other aspects of our lives that we rely on- health, economic security, safety, strong communities, education, and so forth.

Furthermore, we need to take our greater understanding of what work is *not supposed to be*, and what work *is supposed to be* when creating this definition and perspective around work. Pulling from previous chapters of the book and from major themes about what is wrong with work in America, sheds light on what work shouldn't be.

Work should not be a nine-to-five schedule just because that's the status quo. The status quo has brought us to this unsustainable point in how we work today, and it's always been exclusionary.

Work shouldn't be eight continuous hours a day unless you're being paid wages by the hour and are being paid a living wage. Contrastingly, work within the knowledge economy is best suited for deep work where you will likely reach a point before eight hours- maybe four to six- where productivity and focus start to fade.

Work shouldn't be time spent making much less than your time is truly worth. Everyone's time and contribution should be respected enough to at least be provided a living wage. It shouldn't be compensated with starvation wages, that barely pay rent, full-time.

Work shouldn't be done at a workplace designed for our cave-living ancestors, where our physical and social well-being are not priorities. We spend most of our waking hours at our workplace, so our workplace design should be important.

Work shouldn't be disconnected from the realities of American education today.

Work shouldn't be based on shareholder value and limited liability on the part of corporate America.

Work shouldn't be conducted with the framework that we have unlimited and expendable resources and capital on this planet- whether it's workers or goods. We don't. There is no argument to that, we simply do not have unlimited resources, which means that our consumption-based economy is not sustainable in its current state.

Lastly, work isn't just about working hard and "making a living". Work shouldn't treat our time as an expendable commodity. Work shouldn't be completely manual work, completely leisurely, or completely idle.

Now that we know what work shouldn't be, we can determine what work should be.

Work should consist of the best work schedule for specific workers doing specific work, appropriately considering how time is best utilized for the type of work involved. This means instead of the traditional 9-5 schedule, you could schedule a 9-3, five days a week, a 9-5, four days a week, or some sort of schedule designed for optimal productivity *and* wellbeing.

Work should be realistic in that productivity is not always achieved according to the status quo. Just because the forty-hour workweek is the most common number of hours worked, doesn't mean it's the most optimal for you as an employer or employee.

Work should be one of respecting the time and effort of all workers and paying them enough to make a living wage. The cost of living is not cheap and has only gone up, as wages have stagnated. Less than the bare minimum is unsustainable and costly to society.

Work should be done within a workspace designed ideally for optimal human performance, but at least with enough comfort that workers aren't burned out by long-term physical and mental exhaustion, pain, and health issues.

Work should respect and work with employees on issues related to education and school. It is in the best interest of employers, the government, and educational institutions to come together around solutions to childcare, knowledge and skill development, and preparation for the workforce. All these issues are related and if our education system reflects how we view our work and our collective value to this country, then we have a lot of work to do.

Work should be based on the value individual workers provide as well as the compensation they receive for their time and work.

Work should be conducted within the framework that global resources and capital are limited and finite. Work should shift away from the consumption-based model of an economy, and towards sustainability.

Lastly, work should be about purpose and opportunity. Work should treat time less as a commodity for exploitation and more as an investment. Work should embrace more leisure and idleness. Without balancing work with leisure and idleness, work is only a means to an end, when we know that work should be the end.

The Oxford definition of work is an "activity involving mental or physical effort done in order to achieve a purpose or result."[110] That definition is clearly not sufficient, but at the same time, there really is no one way to define work. The true meaning of work in its entirety is subjective, and that is why I will not define work in its entirety here in this book. *But*, if we know the difference between what work should and shouldn't be, we are in the right place. From there, we can each define work according to what it means to us. Personally, I think the point of work is to spend *time* in service to our purpose, while simultaneously providing value to those around us- our friends, family, community, and more.

The one part of defining work should be that we *live through our work*. That's it. The co-founder of both Quest Nutrition and Impact Theory, Tom Bilyeu, summed this idea up in talking about the formula for fulfillment and work, and I find that this outlook truly sticks. He said, "Work your ass off to do very good at something that you care deeply about that allows you to serve not only yourself but other people." That to me is a good summation of what work should be, but it very well may change person to person. Work might mean something entirely different to you and that's okay.

Epilogue

If you do what you love, you never work a day in your life

I used to think many Americans were just apathetic about reforming our structure of work, about political and economic reform. But I've come to see that that is not actually the case. Most Americans do care about their work and these deep issues about their place in the world. But the problem is that so many people are just exhausted and worn out by the broken political and economic systems which are supposed to be working in their best interest. It's not so much apathy as it is not knowing where to start. Heck, sometimes there really isn't anywhere *to* start.

Addressing how our lives are valued in the context of work and living a purposeful life is no easy task. Doing so involves being *vulnerable* and taking *ownership* of the failed systems which guide us- states of being that not everyone is willing to embrace. Only when more Americans have this buy-in, this ownership over the solutions, will we start to redesign and trust these overarching systems.

What I hope this book has done is instill a sense of buy-in within you and convince you that there are better ways to think about work and live each day with purpose. How we spend our time working and how we treat our workers is a direct reflection of how and who we value in society. We spend too much of our time working for us not to consider *how* we work in today's constantly changing political, economic, and social environment.

For too long in this country, we have looked at work from the wrong perspective, with the wrong lens. Work is so much more than just a paycheck. It is a large part of who we are, a part of our identity. Our purpose in life, whatever it is and however different it may be from everyone else, provides value to our communities. There is almost a niche for everything today, not to mention a new job is created just about every single day. There is no reason we can't dedicate our entire lives to something we deeply care about and that is rewarding. Redefining work requires us to contemplate what *work-life* balance truly is and who really achieves it. We all deserve balance.

I'm a quarter way through life, and I have already spent much of it working for nothing more than a paycheck. I've even used work as an escape because it's all too easy to get lost going through the motions. It's not easy, however, to break this mindset and truly change our culture of work. Yet the systems we have set up for ourselves make it very difficult for us to truly embrace a life filled with purposeful work. The cracks in these systems have never been more illuminated than they are now, and we are paying the price. More of us are starting to look at the political, economic, and social structures that were supposed to prepare us for and support us during a crisis, in a different light. Many of us are even speaking up about these concerns. Now is the time to take a step back and look at what is driving all of this chaos and inequality. Let's take the time we have now, discuss what is of true value to us, and come together around a renewed vision of work and life with a sense of purpose and urgency.

This dialogue must include individual workers, but to create rapid, necessary change, we must ask our leaders in business and government to step up and take the initiative. Imagine if CEOs and large corporations decided to move to a four-day workweek or raised the minimum wage to a living wage, and what the second and third-order effects would be. Imagine if that change was met in reciprocity by the federal government deciding a part of the solution will be more worker rights and a form of guaranteed income.

Now is the time for action. Placing old bandages on new wounds will not suffice with the level of inequality and exploitation of workers in this country. Now is the time to redefine what we value in life, and redesign our work to revolve around our lives, not the other way around.

To bring this book to a close, I will tell one last story. We are in a new age of work- work in the 21st century. This change in how we work and how we view our role in society comes with it some important decisions. Our decision is not unlike that of the demigod Heracles:

> When he was reaching man's estate, he went off alone to decide what manner of life he should pursue. As he sat reflecting, he saw two women of great stature coming towards him. The first, Eudaimonia (Happiness), but also called Kakia (vice), promised him the easiest and pleasantest road: 'You shall taste all pleasure and hardships you will never know.' The other, Arete (Virtue), says that she will tell him the truth without deception: 'Of all that is good and noble the gods give nothing to man without toil and diligence.' She ends her account of the goods which come from following her path by saying: 'After completing such labors, Heracles, child of noble parents, you can win the most blessed happiness.' Heracles had no need to work, but all know what he chose - a life of ceaseless labor in the service of mankind.[21]

Most of us can relate to Heracles and his hard work. But most of us can't relate to his sense of purpose. Nor do most of us 'win the most blessed happiness' from our labor. The American ethic is one of a Heracles spirit, strong and true. And we have been told that we can live a Heracles-like life if we work hard enough. But we're not gods. And until we reform work in

America, 'all that is good and noble' will be out of reach. Let's work together and build the future we know we deserve.

Let us not simply exist, let us live. Let us live.

Notes

[1] https://www.reuters.com/article/us-health-life-expectancy/us-life-expectancy-declining-due-to-more-deaths-in-middle-age idUSKBN1Y02C7#:~:text=U.S.%20life %20expectancy%20declining%20due%20to%20more%20deaths%20in%20middle%20age,-Linda%20Carroll&text= (Reuters%20Health)%20%2D%20After%20rising, Americans%2C%20a%20new%20study%20suggests.

[2] https://www.apa.org/news/press/releases/2017/11/lowest-point

[3] https://www.inc.com/jeff-haden/scientists-just-discovered-mid-life-crisis-peaks-at-age-47-heres-how-to-minimize-effect-of-happiness-curve.html

[4] https://globalwellnessinstitute.org/industry-research/the-future-of-wellness-at-work/

[5] https://news.gallup.com/poll/165269/worldwide-employees-engaged-work. aspx

[6] https://www.gallup.com/workplace/311561/employee-engagement-continues-historic-rise-amid-coronavirus.aspx

[7] https://www.gallup.com/workplace/316064/employee-engagement-hits-new-high-historic-drop.aspx

[8] https://news.gallup.com/poll/310250/worry-stress-fuel-record-drop-life-satisfaction.aspx

[9] https://qz.com/work/1561830/why-the-eight-hour-workday-doesnt-work/

[10] https://www.calnewport.com/books/deep-work/

[11] https://www.vouchercloud.com/resources/office-worker-productivity

[12] https://www.lifehack.org/articles/featured/how-to-use-parkinsons-law-to-your-advantage.html

[13] https://www.wired.com/story/eight-hour-workday-is-a-lie/

[14] https://www.politifact.com/factchecks/2015/sep/09/viral-image/does-8-hour -day-and-40-hour-come-henry-ford-or-lab/

[15] https://www.history.com/this-day-in-history/ford-factory-workers-get-40-hour-week

[16] https://www.bls.gov/news.release/union2.nr0.htm

[17] https://www.cnbc.com/2017/05/03/how-the-8-hour-workday-changed-how-americans-work.html

[18] https://www.craigstorti.com/

[19] https://www.theguardian.com/news/datablog/2015/jun/05/french-more-holidays-work-less-productivity

[20] https://qz.com/1316428/one-of-historys-greatest-philosophers-thought-work-makes-you-a-worse-person/

[21] https://www.jstor.org/stable/642580

[22] http://www.gutenberg.org/ebooks/26159

[23] https://www.pewresearch.org/fact-tank/2019/08/29/facts-about-american-workers/

[24] https://www.investopedia.com/terms/p/purchasingpower.asp

[25] https://www.acorns.com/money-basics/the-economy/what-is-pur-chasing-power-and-how-does-inflation-affect-it-/#:~:text=Purchas-ing%20power%20
doesn't%20just,to%20more%20cash%2Dstrapped%20consumers.

[26] https://www.businessinsider.com/how-americans-spend-most-of-their-money-2017-1

[27] https://www.curbed.com/2018/4/10/17219786/buying-a-house-mortgage-government-gi-bill

[28] https://www.nbcnews.com/business/consumer/rents-have-risen-nationwide-making-it-tough-potential-homeowners-save-n863386

[29] https://www.urban.org/urban-wire/mapping-black-homeowner-ship-gap

[30] National Low-Income Housing Coalition: Out of Reach, *The High Cost of Housing*. (2020)

[31] https://www.itdp.org/2019/05/23/high-cost-transportation-united-states/

[32] https://www.valuepenguin.com/how-much-we-spend-food#:~:text=Back%20 in%201900%2C%20fami-lies%20spent,its%20total%20budget%20on%20food.

[33] https://www.bls.gov/opub/reports/consumer-expenditures/2017/home.htm

[34] https://www.ncbi.nlm.nih.gov/pmc/articles/PMC4783380/

[35] https://www.newsweek.com/town-called-malnourished-248087

[36] https://www.pewresearch.org/fact-tank/2018/08/07/for-most-us-workers-real-wages-have-barely-budged-for-decades/

[37] https://www.theatlantic.com/ideas/archive/2020/08/middle-class/615238/

[38] https://livingwage.mit.edu/

[39] Saunders, E. G. 2015. *Do you really need to hold that meeting?* https://hbr.org /2015/03/do-you-really-need-to-hold-that-meeting

[40] https://www.onelegal.com/blog/10-alternatives-to-meetings-your-firm-should-try/

[41] Courtney, E. 2021. *Benefits of remote work.* https://www.flexjobs.com/blog/ post/benefits-of-remote-work/

[42] https://www.wired.co.uk/article/work-from-home-surveillance-software

[43] https://news.gallup.com/poll/306695/workers-discovering-affin-ity-remote-work.aspx

[44] https://www.gigeconomydata.org/basics/what-gig-worker

[45] https://www.theverge.com/2019/5/14/18623467/uber-driver-free-lancers-employees-federal-labor-lawyer-contractor

[46] Mommy Burnout: How to Reclaim Your Life and Raise Healthier Children in the Process. 2018. Dr. Sheryl Ziegler

[47] https://www.who.int/mental_health/evidence/burn-out/en/

[48] Burnout: The Secret to Unlocking the Stress Cycle. 2019. Emily Nagoski and Amelia Nagoski

[49] Nesse R. & Young, E. 2000. Evolutionary Origins and Functions of the Stress Response. Retrieved from http://www-per-sonal.umich.edu/~nesse/Articles/Stress& Evolution-2000.PDF

[50] Beauregard, et al. 2018. "Gendered Pathways to Burnout: Results from the SALVEO study". Retrieved from https://academic.oup.com/an-nweh/article/62/4/426 /4870017

[51] Houkes et al. 2011. "Development of burnout over time and the causal order of the three dimensions of burnout among male and female GPs. A three-wave panel study". Retrieved from: https://bmcpub-lichealth.biomedcentral.com/articles /10.1186/1471-2458-11-240

[52] Laskowski, E. "What are the risks of sitting too much?". Retrieved from https://www.mayoclinic.org/healthy-lifestyle/adult-health/expert-answers/sitting/ faq-20058005

[53] https://www.weightwatchers.com/us/wwhs

[54] https://www.cdc.gov/workplacehealthpromotion/health-strate-gies/index. html

[55] https://www.who.int/occupational_health/healthy_work-place_framework.pdf

[56] Desilver, D. 2018. "For most U.S. workers, real wages have barely budged in decades". Retrieved from https://www.pewresearch.org/fact-tank/2018/08/07/for-most-us-workers-real-wages-have-barely-budged-for-decades/

[57] https://www.dol.gov/agencies/whd/flsa

[58] https://usafacts.org/articles/how-most-americans-get-their-health-insurance -medicare-employ-ers/#:~:text=More%20than%20two%2Dthirds%20of,insurance%

20coverage%20is%20employer%2Dprovided.&text=Such%20poli-
cies%20would%20mean%20shifts,to%20US%20Census%20Bu-
reau%20data.

[59] https://www.bls.gov/opub/ted/2020/94-percent-of-man-
agers-56-percent-of-construction-and-extraction-workers-had-paid-sick-
leave.htm?view_full

[60] Hart, Fernandez, & Treene. 2020. Retrieved from https://www.ax-
ios.com/ coronavirus-paid-sick-
leave-0a8fda7f-5bdd-44b8-81d5-304651f29b51.html

[61] https://www.dol.gov/general/topic/benefits-leave/fmla

[62] Rose, J. 2012. Retrieved from https://www.theatlantic.com/busi-
ness/archive/ 2012/05/how-to-break-free-of-our-19th-century-factory-
model-education-system/ 256881/

[63]https://www.ted.com/talks/ken_robinson_says_schools_kill_cre-
ativity/transcript?language=en#t-357987

[64] https://nces.ed.gov/pubs2017/2017098/index.asp

[65] https://www.pewresearch.org/internet/fact-sheet/internet-broad-
band/

[66] Miller, Campbell, Cohen, & Hancock. 2019. "Addressing the $1.5
Trillion in Federal Student Loan Debt. Retrieved from https://www.amer-
icanprogress.org/ issues/education-postsecondary/reports/2019/ 06/12/
470893/addressing-1-5-trillion-federal-student-loan-
debt/#:~:text=About% 2043%20million%20adult%20 Americans,not%20backed%20by%20the%20government.

[67] Issa, N. 2019. "U.S. Average Student Loan Debt Statistics in 2019".
Retrieved from https://www.credit.com/personal-finance/average-stu-
dent-loan-debt/

[68] Nitro College. 2018. "Student Loan Debt: A Current Picture of Student Loan Borrowing and Repayment in the United States." Retrieved
from https://www. nitrocollege.com/research/average-student-loan-debt

[69] Seraphin, C. 2019. "General Education Requirements: What's the
Point?". Retrieved from https://www.collegexpress.com/articles-and-ad-
vice/majors-and-academics/articles/college-academics/general-educa-
tion-requirements-whats-point/

[70] Flanagin, J. 2015. "The traditional US college model forces students to pay for class they don't need". Retrieved from https://qz.com/
477052/the-4-year-us-college-degree-is-an-expensive-time-waster/

[71] Horton, A. P. 2020. "The skills gap means companies are increasingly considering candidates from non-traditional paths. Could targeted,
bite-sized chunks of education help you get a job?"

[72] Schochet, L. 2019. "The Child Care Crisis Is Keeping Women Out
of the Workforce". Retrieved from https://www.americanprogress.org/is-

sues/early-childhood/reports/2019/03/28/467488/child-care-crisis-keep-ing-women-workforce/

[73] McCarthy, N. 2019. "The Evolution of U.S. Teacher Salaries In The 21st Century". Retrieved from https://www.forbes.com/sites/niallmc-carthy/2019/04/02 /the-evolution-of-u-s-teacher-salaries-in-the-21st-century-infographic/#6959d1b2 77f0

[74] Weir, M. 2019. "10 alarming facts about teacher pay in the United States". Retrieved from https://www.businessinsider.com/10-alarming-facts-about-teacher-pay-in-the-united-states-2019-10#teacher-salaries-have-decreased-by-45-over-the-last-10-years-8

[75] Brooks, A. 2020. "'Success Addicts' Choose Being Special Over Be-ing Happy". Retrieved from https://www.theatlantic.com/family/archive/2020/07/why-success-wont-make-you-happy/614731/

[76] History. 2019. Retrieved from https://www.history.com/topics/re-formation/ reformation#:~:text=The%20Protestant%20Reforma-tion%20was%20the,continent%20in%20the%20modern%20era.

[77] Covert, B. 2019. "The American Work Ethic". Retrieved from https://long reads.com/2019/04/08/the-american-worth-ethic/

[78] Hoover, H. 2017. "The Future of American Individualism". Re-trieved from https://www.hoover.org/research/future-american-individu-alism

[79] https://www.history.com/topics/us-presidents/herbert-hoover

[80] Bui, Q. & Miller, C. 2015. "The Typical American Lives Only 18 Miles From Mom". Retrieved from https://www.nytimes.com/interactive/2015/12/24/upshot/24 up-family.html

[81] https://www.northamerican.com/infographics/where-they-grew-up

[82] https://www.reuters.com/article/us-usa-families/extended-family-household-on-the-rise-in-u-s-idUSTRE62H0E020100318

[83] Future Learn. 2021. https://www.futurelearn.com/courses/de-velop-cultural-intelligence/0/steps/49772#:~:text=Individual-ism%20stresses%20individual%20goals%20and,by%20personal%20re-wards%20and%20benefits

[84] Davis, W. 2020. "The Unraveling of America". Retrieved from https://www. rollingstone.com/politics/political-commentary/covid-19-end-of-american-era-wade-davis-1038206/

[85] Easterlin, R. 2003. "Explaining Happiness". Retrieved from https://www.ncbi. nlm.nih.gov/pmc/articles/PMC196947/

[86] Scott, E. & Gans, S. 2020. "How to Deal With FOMO in Your Life". Retrieved from https://www.verywellmind.com/how-to-cope-with-fomo-4174664

[87] Futterman, M. 2020. "Michael Phelps: 'I Can't See Any More Suicides'". Retrieved from https://www.nytimes.com/2020/07/29/sports/olympics/michael-phelps-documentary-weight-of-gold.html#:~:text=Phelps%20distills%20that%20dynamic%20near,its%20premiere%20on%20Wednesday%20night.

[88] Weir, K. 2013. "Feel like a fraud?". Retrieved from https://www.apa.org/grad psych/2013/11/fraud

[89] Ninivaggi, F. 2019. "Loneliness: A New Epidemic in the USA". Retrived from https://www.psychologytoday.com/us/blog/envy/201902/loneliness-new-epidemic-in-the-usa

[90] Renken, E. 2020. "Most Americans Are Lonely, And Our Workplace Culture May Not Be Helping". Retrieved from https://www.npr.org/sections/health-shots/ 2020/01/23/798676465/most-americans-are-lonely-and-our-workplace-culture-may-not-be-helping#:~:text=More%20than%20three%20in%20five,may%20be%20on%20the%20rise.

[91] https://www.cdc.gov/workplacehealthpromotion/tools-resources/workplace-health/mental-health/index.html

[92] Luna, T. 2016. "10 Signs That You're in a Rut". Retrieved from https://www. psychologytoday.com/nz/blog/surprise/201605/10-signs-youre-in-rut?amp

[93] Merriam-webster.com

[94] Appiah, A. 2018. "The myth of meritocracy: who really gets what they deserve?". Retrieved from https://www.theguardian.com/news/2018/oct/19/the-myth-of-meritocracy-who-really-gets-what-they-deserve

[95] Menand, L. 2019. "Is Meritocracy Making Everyone Miserable". Retrieved from https://www.newyorker.com/magazine/2019/09/30/is-meritocracy-making-everyone-miserable

[96] https://www.youngfoundation.org/promote_home/promote_home_middle/ the-red-baron/

[97] https://www.capenet.org/facts.html#:~:text=There%20are%2034%2C576 %20private%20schools,2%20of%20the%20PSS%20Report).

[98] Cooper, M. 2015. "The False Promise of Meritocracy". Retrieved from https:// www.theatlantic.com/business/archive/2015/12/meritocracy/418074/

[99] Adams, B. 2018. "Viewpoint: The Myth of Meritocracy". Retrieved from https://www.shrm.org/hr-today/news/hr-magazine/0918/pages/the-myth-of-meritocracy.aspx

[100] Castilla, Emilio J., and Stephen Benard. "The Paradox of Meritocracy in Organizations." *Administrative Science Quarterly* 55, no. 4 (2010): 543-676.

[101] Dijk, H., Kooij, D., Karanika-Murray, M., De Vos, A., and Bertolt Meyer. 2020. "Meritocracy a myth? A multilevel perspective of how social inequality accumulates through work". Retrieved from https://journals.sagepub.com/doi/full/10.1177/2041 386620930063

[102] Reeves, Richard V. and Katherine Guyot. 2018. "Fewer Americans are making more than their parents did- especially if they grew up in the middle class". Retrieved from https://www.brookings.edu/blog/up-front/2018/07/25/fewer-americans-are-making-more-than-their-parents-did-especially-if-they-grew-up-in-the-middle-class/

[103] Wahba, Phil. 2020. "The number of black CEOs in the Fortune 500 remains very low". Retrieved from https://fortune.com/2020/06/01/black-ceos-fortune-500-2020-african-american-business-leaders/

[104] Robert Costanza, Maureen Hart, Ida Kubiszewski, John Talberth, A Short History of GDP: Moving Towards Better Measures of Human Well-being, The Solutions Journal, Volume 5, Issue 1, January 2014, Pages 91-97 (https://www.the solutionsjournal.com/article/a-short-history-of-gdp-moving-towards-better-measures-of-human-well-being/)

[105] Dickinson, Elizabeth. 2011. "GDP: a brief history". Retrieved from https:// foreignpolicy.com/2011/01/03/gdp-a-brief-history/

[106] https://www.bea.gov/news/2020/gross-domestic-product-2nd-quarter-2020 -advance-estimate-and-annual-update

[107] Grochala, Sara. 2013. "Timeline of Industrial Capitalism". Retrieved from https://headlong.co.uk/ideas/industrial-capitalism/

[108] Weinberg, Meyer. 2002. "A Short History of American Capitalism". Retrieved from https://newhistory.org/CH01.htm

[109] Oxford Dictionaries. 2020.

[110] https://www.investopedia.com/ask/answers/010915/what-are-most-famous -cases-oligopolies.asp#:~:text=An%20oligopoly%20is%20when%20a,type%20of% 20product%20or%20service.

[111] https://en.wikipedia.org/wiki/United_States_antitrust_law

[112] https://www.theodorerooseveltcenter.org/Learn-About-TR/TR-Encyclopedia/Capitalism-and-Labor/The-Sherman-Act.aspx

[113] Newton, Casey. 2020. "Antitrust investigations aren't the biggest threat to Facebook's future". Retrieved from https://www.theverge.com/interface/2020/7/21/ 21331226/facebook-antitrust-investigation-ftc-india-tiktok-splinternet

[114] Lecher, Colin. 2019. "How low prices could make for an antitrust case against Amazon". Retrieved from https://www.theverge.com/2019/5/13/18563379/ amazon-predatory-pricing-antitrust-law

[115] https://en.wikipedia.org/wiki/Consumerism

[116] https://en.wikipedia.org/wiki/Conspicuous_consumption#cite_note-2

[117] https://tradingeconomics.com/united-states/consumer-spending

[118] Bhattarai, Abha. 2019. "'Retail apocalypse' now: Analysts say 75,000 more U.S. stores could be doomed". Retrieved from https://www.washingtonpost.com/ business/2019/04/10/retail-apocalypse-now-analysts-say-more-us-stores-could-be-doomed/

[119] https://www.womply.com/blog/is-online-shopping-killing-main-street-these -3-facts-prove-brick-and-mortar-retail-isnt-going-anywhere/

[120] John, Steven. 2019. "11 incredible facts about the $700 billion US trucking industry". Retrieved from https://markets.businessinsider.com/news/stocks/ trucking-industry-facts-us-truckers-2019-5-1028248577#

[121] Day, Jennifer and Andrew Hait. 2019. "Number of Truckers at All-Time High". Retrieved from https://www.census.gov/library/stories/2019/06/america-keeps-on-trucking.html#:~:text=More%20than%203.5%20million%20people, occupations%20in%20the%20United%20States.

[122] Premack, Rachel. 2019. "None of the people who oversee the federal laws that govern truck drivers were ever truck drivers themselves". Retrieved from https://www.businessinsider.com/no-fmcsa-administrator-was-truck-driver-2019-1?utm_source=msn.com&utm_medium=referral&utm_content=msn-slideshow&utm_campaign=bodyurl

[123] https://sentientmedia.org/how-many-animals-are-killed-for-food-every-day/#:~:text=More%20than%20200%20million%20animals,around%20the%20world%20every%20year.

[124] https://www.who.int/influenza/human_animal_interface/avian_influenza/ h5n1_research/faqs/en/#:~:text=Human%20cases%20of%20H5N1%20avian,mortality%20rate%20is%20about%2060%25.

[125] https://www.cdc.gov/onehealth/basics/zoonotic-diseases.html

[126] https://www.history.com/topics/united-states-constitution/citizens-united

[127] https://www.investopedia.com/articles/07/stock-exchange-history.asp

[128] https://www.investopedia.com/terms/b/broker.asp

[129] Domhoff, William. "Wealth, Income, and Power". Retrieved from https://who rulesamerica.ucsc.edu/power/wealth.html

[130] Ingraham, Christopher. 2017. Retrieved from https://www.washingtonpost .com/news/wonk/wp/2017/12/06/the-richest-1-percent-

now-owns-more-of-the-countrys-wealth-than-at-any-time-in-the-past-50-years/

[131] https://www.investopedia.com/terms/e/earningsreport.asp

[132] https://www.investopedia.com/terms/s/share-holder.asp#:~:text=A%20 shareholder%2C%20also%20re-ferred%20to,benefits%20of%20a%20business'%20success.

[133] https://www.investopedia.com/terms/s/shareholder-value.asp

[134] Denning, Steve. 2019. "Why Maximizing Shareholder Value is Finally Dying". Retrieved from https://www.forbes.com/sites/stevedenning/2019/08/19/why-maximizing-shareholder-value-is-finally-dy-ing/#4cf84da96746

[135] Friedman, Milton. 1970. "A Friedman Doctrine-- The Social Responsibility Of Business Is to increase its profits". Retrieved from https://www.nytimes.com/ 1970/09/13/archives/a-friedman-doctrine-the-social-responsibility-of-business-is-to.html

[136] Denning, Steven. 2013. "The Origin of 'The World's Dumbest Idea': Milton Friedman". Retrieved from https://www.forbes.com/sites/stevedenning/2013/06/26 /the-origin-of-the-worlds-dumbest-idea-milton-friedman/#d629c2d870e8

[137] Makower, Joel. "Milton Friedman and the social responsibility of business". Retrieved from https://www.greenbiz.com/article/milton-fried-man-and-social-responsibility-business

[138] Schwab, Klaus. 2016. "The Fourth Industrial Revolution: what it means, how to respond". Retrieved from https://www.weforum.org/agenda/2016/01/the-fourth-industrial-revolution-what-it-means-and-how-to-respond/

[139] https://www.investopedia.com/terms/p/privatizing-profits-and-socializing-losses.asp

[140] Adam Smith, *Theory of Moral Sentiments*, p. 352.

[141] https://www.britannica.com/topic/lobbying

[142] https://www.investopedia.com/articles/investing/043015/why-lobbying-legal-and-important-us.asp

[143] https://www.senate.gov/CRSpubs/9c14ec69-c4e4-4bd8-8953-f73daa1640 e4.pdf

[144] Drutman, Lee. 2015. "How Corporate Lobbyists Conquered American Democracy". Retrieved from https://www.theatlantic.com/business/archive/2015/04 /how-corporate-lobbyists-conquered-ameri-can-democracy/390822/

[145] https://www.investopedia.com/articles/02/041702.asp#:~:text=A%20stock %20buyback%20oc-curs%20when,its%20shares%20from%20the%20market-

place.&text=A%20company%20might%20buyback%20shares,to%20im-prove%20its%20financial%20ratios.

[146] Useem, Jerry. 2019. "The Stock-Buyback Swindle". Retrieved from https:// www.theatlantic.com/magazine/archive/2019/08/the-stock-buyback-swindle/ 592774/

[147] Stansbury, Anna and Lawrence H. Summers. "Declining worker power and American economic performance". Retrieved from https://www.brookings.edu/bpea-articles/declining-worker-power-and-american-economic-performance/#:~:text= The%20authors'%20esti-mates%20suggest%20that,share%20of%20income%20going%20to

[148] https://www.goldmanandehrlich.com/common-issues-with-em-ployment-contracts/

[149] Campbell, Alexia and Alvin Chang. 2018. "There's a good chance you've waived the right to sue your boss". Retrieved from https://www.vox.com/2018/8/1/ 16992362/sexual-harassment-manda-tory-arbitration

[150] https://www.history.com/topics/19th-century/labor

[151] https://www.bls.gov/news.release/union2.nr0.htm

[152] McGaughey, Ewan. 2018. "Corporate Law Should Embrace Putting Workers On Boards: The Evidence Is Behind Them". Retrieved from https://corpgov.law. harvard.edu/2018/09/17/corporate-law-should-embrace-putting-workers-on-boards-the-evidence-is-behind-them/

[153] Palladino, Lenore. 2019. "Worker Representation on U.S. Corpo-rate Boards". Retrieved from https://corpgov.law.harvard.edu/2019/12/ 30/worker-representation-on-u-s-corporate-boards/

[154] Semuels, Alana. 2015. "Getting Rid of Bosses". Retrieved from https://www. theatlantic.com/business/archive/2015/07/no-bosses-worker-owned-cooperatives/397007/

[155] https://www.usworker.coop/home/

[156] https://www.ted.com/talks/lorna_davis_a_guide_to_collabora-tive_leadership

[157] https://www.ted.com/talks/hamdi_ulukaya_the_anti_ceo_play-book?language=en

[158] https://bcorporation.net/about-b-corps#:~:text=Certi-fied%20B%20 Corporations%20are%20businesses,to%20bal-ance%20profit%20and%20pur-pose.&text=B%20Corps%20form%20a%20commu-nity,as%20a%20force%20for%20good.

[159] https://ltse.com/

[160] SEC Form 1. Retrieved from https://www.sec.gov/files/form1.pdf

[161] https://www.npr.org/transcripts/848313604

[162] https://www.ted.com/talks/ ai_jen_poo_the_work_that_makes_all_other_ work_ possible/transcript?language=en#t-135987

[163] https://www.ted.com/talks/kate_raworth_a_healthy_economy_should_be_ designed_to_thrive_not_grow#t-940984

[164] Raworth, Kate. 2017. "A Doughnut for the Anthropocene: humanity's compass in the 21st century". Retrieved from https://www.the-lancet.com/journals/ lanplh/article/PIIS2542-5196(17)30028-1/fulltext

[165] Andester, Nikita. 2019. "GDP Alternatives: 7 Ways to Measure a Country's Wealth". Retrieved from https://ethical.net/politics/gdp-alternatives-7-ways-to-measure-countries-wealth/

[166] https://wellbeingeconomy.org/wego

[167] TED. 2019. "Why governments should prioritize well-being | Nicola Sturgeon." *YouTube*, https://www.youtube.com/ watch?v=gJzSWacrkKo

[168] https://wellbeingeconomy.org/women-in-power-countries-with-female-leaders-suffer-six-times-fewer-covid-deaths-and-will-recover-sooner-from-recession

[169] Brueck, Hilary. 2019. "An economist has a wild proposal to give all kids in the US up to $60,000 at birth". Retrieved from https://www.businessinsider.com/ inequality-baby-trust-fund-plan-kids-up-to-60000-at-birth-2018-10

[170] Langlois, Shawn. 2020. "Bill Ackmen on saving capitalism: Every child in the U.S. could be given enough money at birth to become millionaires by retirement". Retrieved from https://www.marketwatch.com/ story/bill-ackman-on-saving-capitalism-every-child-in-the-u-s-could-be-given-enough-money-at-birth-to-become-millionaires-by-retirement-11598893294

[171] http://www.businessdictionary.com/definition/demand-side-economics .html

[172] https://www.scottsantens.com/martin-luther-king-jr-basic-income-mlk

[173] Kesslen, Ben. 2020. "'Powerful in its simplicity': As the pandemic endures, mayors call for guaranteed income". Retrieved from https://www.nbcnews.com/ news/us-news/powerful-its-simplicity-pandemic-endures-mayors-across-country-call-guaranteed-n1236783

[174] Emison, Linnea Feldman. 2020. "The Promising Results Of A Citywide Basic -Income Experiment". Retrieved from https://www.newyorker.com/news/news-desk /the-promising-results-of-a-citywide-basic-income-experiment

[175] https://www.whitehouse.gov/presidential-actions/executive-or-der-reducing-poverty-america-promoting-opportunity-economic-mobil-ity/

[176] https://www.pewsocialtrends.org/2020/01/09/trends-in-income-and-wealth -inequality/

[177] Rosalsky, Greg. 2019. "If a Wealth Tax is Such a Good Idea, Why Did Europe Kill Theirs?". Retrieved from https://www.npr.org/sections/money/2019/02/26/ 698057356/if-a-wealth-tax-is-such-a-good-idea-why-did-europe-kill-theirs

[178] https://www.taxpolicycenter.org/briefing-book/how-does-corpo-rate-income -tax-work

[179] Zarroli, Jim. 2016. "How Bernie Sanders' Wall Street Tax Would Work". Retrieved from https://www.npr.org/2016/02/12/466465333/sanders-favors-a-speculation-tax-on-big-wall-street-firms-what-is-that

[180] https://www.investopedia.com/terms/v/valueaddedtax.asp

[181] Rogan, Joe. 2017. "Jordan Peterson on Universal Basic Income – Joe Rogan." *YouTube*, https://www.youtube.com/watch?v=v7gKGq_MYpU

[182] Malesic, Jonathan. 2017. "America Must Divorce Dignity From Work". Retrieved from https://newrepublic.com/article/141664/america-must-divorce-dignity-work

[183] Thompson, Derek. 2018. "Busting the Myth of 'Welfare Makes People Lazy'". Retrieved from https://www.theatlantic.com/business/archive/2018/03/welfare-childhood/555119/

[184] Kennedy, Brian and Cary Funk. 2015. "Personality and interest in science, health topics". Retrieved from https://www.pewresearch.org/sci-ence/2015/12/11/ personality-and-interest-in-science-health-topics/

[185] https://www.washingtonpost.com/nation/2021/03/03/stockton-universal-basic-income/

[186] Musulin, Kristin. 2020. "Mayors form UBI advocacy coalition". Retrieved from https://www.smartcitiesdive.com/news/mayors-universal-basic-income-coronavirus-cities/580743/

[187] Blitzer, Ronn. 2020. "Pittsburgh launches 'guaranteed income' program with Jack Dorsey money". Retrieved from https://www-foxbusi-ness-com.cdn.ampproject .org/v/s/www.foxbusiness.com/money/pitts-burgh-guaranteed-income-program-jack -dorsey.amp usqp=mq331AQFKAGwASA%3D&amp_js_v=0.1#referrer=https%3A %2F %2Fwww.google.com&amp_tf=From%20%251%24s&amp-share=https%3A %2F%2Fwww.foxbusiness.com%2Fmoney%2Fpitts-burgh-guaranteed-income-program-jack-dorsey

[188] https://www.nlc.org/article/national-league-of-cities-and-stan-ford-basic-income-lab-release-first-ever-guide-for

[189] Payne, Adam. 2020. "Germany is beginning a universal-basic-income trial with people getting $1,400 a month for 3 years". Retrieved from https://www-businessinsider-com.cdn.ampproject.org/v/s/www.businessinsider.com/germany-begins-universal-basic-income-trial-three-years-2020-8?amp=&usqp=mq331 AQFKAG-wASA%3D&amp_js_v=0.1#refer-rer=https%3A%2F%2Fwww.google.com&amp_tf=From%20%251%24s&ampshare=https%3A%2F%2Fwww.businessinsider.com%2Fgermany-begins-universal-basic-income-trial-three-years-2020 8%3Famp%23referrer%3Dhttps%253A%252F%252Fwww.google.com%26amp_tf%3DFrom% 2520%25251%2524s

[190] https://www.whitehouse.gov/wp-content/uploads/2019/09/The-State-of-Homelessness-in-America.pdf

[191] https://www.cbsnews.com/news/andrew-yang-on-creating-a-trickle-up-economy/

[192] https://en.wikipedia.org/wiki/The_Theory_of_the_Leisure_Class

[193] https://www.thephilosophyofeverything.com/blog/2016/4/13/the-philosophy-of-work

[194] Phil Hammond (15 September 2010). *Sex, Sleep or Scrabble: Seriously Funny Answers to Life's Quirkiest Queries*. Black & White Publishing. p. 18. *ISBN 978-1-84502-526-7.*

[195] Howard, Jacqueline. 2018. "How to fight 'time famine' and boost your happiness". Retrieved from https://www.cnn.com/2017/07/24/health/time-famine-stress-happiness-study/index.html

[196] Ashley V. Whillans, Elizabeth W. Dunn, Paul Smeets, Rene Bekkers, Michael I. Norton. *Buying time promotes happiness*. Proceedings of the National Academy of Sciences Jul 2017, 201706541; DOI: 10.1073/pnas.1706541114

[197] Abadi, Mark. "11 American work habits other countries avoid at all costs". Retrieved from https://www.businessinsider.com/unhealthy-american-work-habits-2017-11

[198] Feloni, Richard. 2016. "Theodore Roosevelt used this productivity trick to get more done in a couple hours than most people do in a day". Retrieved from https://www.businessinsider.com/theodore-roosevelt-productivity-trick-2016-1

[199] https://jrbenjamin.com/2013/08/08/the-old-elephants-tricks/#:~:text= He%20worked%20until%201%3A00,more%20work%20and%20more%20letters.

[200] https://4dayweek.com/flexible-working-arrangements

[201] Cherry, Kendra. 2020. "How the Social Exchange Theory is Used". Retrieved from https://www.verywellmind.com/what-is-social-exchange-theory-2795882

[202] Cheng, Michelle. 2020. "Finland's new prime minister wants her country on a four-day workweek". Retrieved from https://qz.com/work/1780373/finlands-prime-minister-wants-her-country-on-a-four-day-workweek/

[203] Chapman, Ben. 2017. "What happened when Sweden tried six-hour working days". Retrieved from https://www.independent.co.uk/news/business/news/sweden-six-hour-working-day-what-happened-trial-a7574126.html

[204] Chappell, Bill. 2019. "4-Day Workweek Boosted Workers' Productivity By 40%, Microsoft Japan Says". Retrieved from https://www.npr.org/2019/11/04/ 776163853/microsoft-japan-says-4-day-workweek-boosted-workers-productivity-by-40

[205] https://4dayweek.com/four-day-week-trial/

[206] https://4dayweek.com/about

[207] https://toggl.com/track/9-80-work-schedule/#:~:text=Under%20a%20typical%209%2F80,into%20two%204%2Dhour%20periods.&text=The%20key%20to%20successfully%20adhering,after%20midday%20the%20same%20day.

[208] Noguchi, Yuki. 2020. "Enjoy The Extra Day Off! More Bosses Give 4-Day Workweek A Try". Retrieved from https://www.npr.org/2020/02/21/807133509/ enjoy-the-extra-day-off-more-bosses-give-4-day-workweek-a-try

[209] https://www.investopedia.com/terms/t/time-banking.asp#:~:text=Time%20 banking%20is%20a%20bartering,to%20supplement%20government%20social%20services

[210] Cahn, Edgar S. and Christine Gray. 2015. "The Time Bank Solution". Retrieved from https://ssir.org/articles/entry/the_time_bank_solution

[211] Roll, Rich. "Why Mindset Is Everything: Tom Bilyeu | Rich Roll Podcast." *YouTube*, 26 Feb. 2019, https://www.youtube.com/watch?v=prIqWU54NME.

CPSIA information can be obtained
at www.ICGtesting.com
Printed in the USA
LVHW051931240122
709212LV00007B/478

9 780578 999661